A FEW OF THE PEOPLE—AND PATHOLOGIES—
YOU'LL ENCOUNTER IN . . .

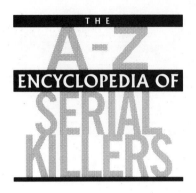

THE
A-Z
ENCYCLOPEDIA OF
SERIAL
KILLERS

JEFFREY DAHMER [see *Necrophilia*]: His idea of a perfect relationship was having sex with his victims' corpses . . . and their various body parts.

H. H. HOLMES [see *Lady Killers*]: The smooth-talking ladies' man coaxed scores of young women into his infamous "Castle of Horrors," financing his enterprise in part by selling their skeletons to medical schools.

EDMUND KEMPER [See *Animal Torture*]: When authorities finally brought him in, the so-called "Co-Ed" killer was asked what a fitting punishment would be. "Death by torture," he replied.

TED BUNDY [See *Pornography*]: On Florida's death row Bundy blamed prolonged exposure to pornography as the cause of his blood lust. Antiporn groups trumpeted the confession, but Bundy was probably doing what he did best: lying.

THE
A-Z
ENCYCLOPEDIA OF
SERIAL KILLERS

Harold Schechter
and David Everitt

POCKET BOOKS

New York   London   Toronto   Sydney   Tokyo   Singapore

An *Original* Publication of POCKET BOOKS

 POCKET BOOKS, a division of Simon & Schuster Inc.
1230 Avenue of the Americas, New York, NY 10020

Copyright © 1996 by Harold Schechter and David Everitt

ISBN: 0-671-53791-1

First Pocket Books trade paperback printing October 1996

10 9 8 7 6 5 4 3 2

POCKET and colophon are registered trademarks of Simon & Schuster Inc.

Cover design by Brigid Pearson
Cover art by Chris Pelletiere
Text design by Stanley S. Drate/Folio Graphics Co. Inc.

Printed in the U.S.A.

THE

A-Z

ENCYCLOPEDIA OF

SERIAL KILLERS

FOREWORD

We are writing this foreword in the fall of 1995, when the number one film at the box office is *Seven,* a dark, intensely creepy thriller about a serial murderer who contrives to kill his victims in accordance with the seven deadly sins (lust, greed, gluttony, sloth, pride, anger, and envy). The American public's long-standing interest in psychopathic butchers—the same morbid fascination that, back in 1991, made Jeffrey Dahmer a *People* magazine cover boy and Jonathan Demme's *The Silence of the Lambs* an Oscar-winning blockbuster—is still going strong.

Indeed, what was initially a fringe phenomenon—an obsession with blood-crazed psychokillers that was more or less limited to diehard splatter-movie fans—has become so mainstream that publications as traditionally staid (if not stuffy) as *The New York Review of Books* and *The New Yorker* have jumped on the bandwagon of late. The former ran a major essay on serial killers by novelist Joyce Carol Oates, while the latter did an extended, preexecution profile of John Wayne Gacy that included exclusive excerpts from the unpublished writings of "America's most notorious killer."

Moralizing critics have been quick to condemn this phenomenon (labeled "serial chic") as still another nasty symptom of societal rot, along with gangsta rap and ads for Calvin Klein underwear. We would point out that in considering the significance of pop phenomena it is always useful to put things in a broader cultural context. For better or worse, human beings have always been intrigued by anything that is monstrous, aberrant, or criminal. And grisly murder has been the subject of story and song, of art high and low, for centuries. True-crime books have been around since at least the 1600s, when John Reynolds's *God's Revenge Against Murder and Adultery* was one of the most popular works in England. During the late eighteenth century, the British public devoured the true-crime accounts in *The Newgate Calendar*, while Victorian readers thrilled to the gory details of murders, mutilations, and torture dished out by *The Illustrated Police News*, the most popular periodical of its day.

In our own country, the media frenzy set off by the atrocities of Dr. H. H. Holmes, "America's first serial killer," was akin to the hysteria generated by the O.J. trial a century later. In 1895, Chicagoans lined up around the block when an enterprising showman opened an H. H. Holmes "Murder Museum," complete with gruesome mock-ups of the "arch-fiend's" crimes. And the exploitation of mayhem and murder has not been restricted to schlockmeisters. Serious artists from Cézanne to Francis Bacon—as well as novelists from Dostoevsky to Dreiser—have made violent crime the subject of their work.

In short, we don't see America's fascination with serial killers as an aberration but rather as a contemporary manifestation of an age-old human reality. Moreover—insofar as telling stories or swapping jokes or watching movies about fearful things represents a method of coping—this fascination is not at all unhealthy. In late twentieth-century America, the serial killer has come to embody a host of gnawing anxieties: anxieties about runaway crime and sexual violence and the breakdown of civil conduct. If we are haunted to the point of obsession by the figure of the psychopathic killer, it is not because we revel in the sadistic and ghastly (though there is some of that, too, built into the archaic depths of the psyche) but rather because, like children who love to hear spooky stories at bedtime, reading or hearing about serial killers is a way of gaining a sense of control over our fears.

Though there have been plenty of books about serial murder in the past few years, *The A to Z Encyclopedia of Serial Killers* is the first to deal with the phenomenon in all its aspects: historical, biographical, criminological, psychological, and cultural. The entries cover every topic we could conceive of, from **Advertisements and Animal Torture to Zines and Zombies**. Readers will notice that some words within each entry are boldfaced; these are key names and concepts that are treated in separate entries of their own.

For all the genuine horror and revulsion they inspire in us, there's no point in denying that serial killers exert a dark attraction. They appeal not just to our morbid interest but also to our need to comprehend an ultimate human mystery: how people who seem so ordinary, so much like the rest of us, can possess the hearts and minds of monsters.

In recognition of the need to confront and explore that "mystery of iniquity" (as Herman Melville describes it), we offer the following pages.

ADS

Back in the old days, desperate singles in search of a mate might turn to a professional matchmaker. Nowadays, they are more likely to look under the Personals section of the classified ads. Of course, when it comes to getting anything through the classifieds—whether it's a used car, aluminum siding, or a blind date—it pays to take heed of the old warning Buyer Beware! That Handsome SWM or Sensual DWF who sounds so appealing in print might turn out to be very different in person. Occasionally, in fact, he or she might turn out to be a serial killer.

Using classifieds as a way of snaring potential victims is a ploy that dates back at least as far as the early 1900s. That's when the infamous American **Black Widow**, Belle Gunness, lured a string of unwary bachelors into her clutches by placing matrimonial ads in newspapers across the country: "Rich, good-looking widow, young, owner of a large farm, wishes to get in touch with a gentleman of wealth with cultured tastes." There was a certain amount of misrepresentation in this classified, since Gunness was actually fat, fiftyish, and bulldog ugly. She wasn't lying about being a rich widow, though, since she had murdered at least fourteen husbands after separating them from their life savings.

In France, Gunness's near-contemporary Henri Landru, known as the "Bluebeard of Paris," also found his lover-victims through the newspapers. Some of the classifieds were matrimonial ads in which Landru presented himself as a wealthy widower searching for a mate. In others, he pretended to be a used furniture dealer looking for merchandise. In either case, if the person who responded was a lonely woman of means, Landru would turn on the charm. The results were always the same. The woman's possessions would end up in his Parisian apartment. The woman herself would end up as a pile of ashes in the stove of his country villa.

In the late 1950s, a sexual psychopath and bondage nut named Harvey Murray Glatman (see **Photographs**) was able to procure victims by posing as a professional photographer and placing ads for female models. After luring an unwary woman to his "studio," Glatman would rape her, truss her up, take pictures of her while she screamed in terror, then strangle her. (Glatman's case served as the real-life basis for Mary Higgins Clark's best-selling novel *Loves Music, Loves to Dance*.)

More recently, an Alaskan baker named Robert Hanson—who was ultimately convicted of four savage sex killings, though he was allegedly responsible for seventeen—used the Personals page of his local newspaper to attract several of his victims. Hanson, who was married with children, would send his family off on a vacation then take out a classified, seeking women to "join me in finding what's around the next bend." After snaring a victim, he would fly her out to the wilderness in his private plane. Then, after raping her at knifepoint, he would strip off her clothing, give her a head start, and (in a sick, real-life duplication of the famous short story "The Most Dangerous Game") stalk her like an animal.

Scariest of all, perhaps, was the wizened cannibal and child killer Albert **Fish,** who regularly scoured the classifieds in his endless search for victims. In 1928, Fish came across a Situation Wanted ad placed by a young man named Edward Budd, who

Albert Fish

Albert Fish; from *52 Famous Murderers* trading cards *(Courtesy of Roger Worsham)*

was looking for a summer job in the country. Masquerading as the owner of a big Long Island farm, the monstrous old man visited the Budd household, intending to lure the Budd boy to an abandoned house and torture him to death. Fish altered his plans when he laid eyes on Edward's little sister, a beautiful twelve-year-old girl named Grace. It was the little girl who ended up dead, dismembered, and cannibalized—and all because her brother's innocent ad brought a monster to their door.

ADVERTISING FOR VICTIMS

In the 1989 film *Sea of Love,* a serial killer with a seductive line goes trolling for male victims in the classifieds. When a sucker bites, the killer reels him in, then leaves him facedown on the mattress, a bullet in the back of his skull.

As he did nine years earlier in *Cruising,* Al Pacino plays a homicide detective who goes undercover to catch the killer. By placing his own ad in the papers, he turns himself into live bait. In the process he plunges into a turbulent affair with Ellen Barkin—who may or may not be the killer.

A riveting thriller, *Sea of Love* is especially good at conveying the dangerous undercurrents that run beneath the surface of big city singles life, where lonely people looking for a good catch sometimes end up with a barracuda.

ALLIGATORS

W hen it comes to getting rid of human remains, most serial killers prefer to keep things simple, relying on such standbys as shallow graves, basement crawl spaces, river bottoms, and remote, densely wooded areas (see **Disposal**). Occasionally, however, a serial killer may resort to more exotic expedients.

Back in the 1930s, for example, a hard-drinking reprobate named Joe Ball ran a seedy roadhouse named (ironically enough) the Sociable Inn on Highway 181 outside Elmsdorf,

Texas. Behind this rowdy dive, Ball installed a cement pond and stocked it with a brood of five, full-grown alligators. To keep his pets fat and happy, Ball fed them a diet of horse meat, live dogs, and human body parts—the remains of various female employees he murdered and dismembered. The exact number of his victims remains unknown, since Ball went to his death without confessing. When two sheriffs who were investigating the disappearance of a pretty young waitress named Hazel Brown showed up to question the brutish barkeep, he whipped out a pistol from the drawer beneath his cash register and fired a bullet into his heart.

The alligator's first cousin—the West African crocodile—has also been exploited for this nefarious purpose. In the 1920s, Carl Panzram—arguably the most unregenerate murderer in the annals of American crime—journeyed to Portuguese West Africa as a merchant seaman. Making his way down the coast, he hired a canoe and the services of a half-dozen locals to help him hunt crocodiles. Panzram ended up by shooting all six of the Africans in the back and feeding their corpses to the ravenous reptiles.

Crocodilians haven't been the only creatures whose indiscriminate eating habits have come in handy to homicidal maniacs.

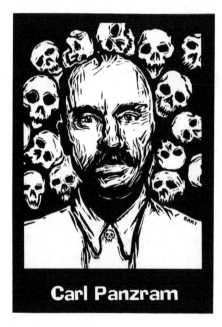

Carl Panzram; from *52 Famous Murderers* trading cards *(Courtesy of Roger Worsham)*

In turn-of-the-century California, a farmer named Joseph Briggen fed his prize hogs the body parts of butchered farm hands. Briggen's porkers invariably fetched top dollar at local auctions. When people asked for the secret of his success, he would just smile and reply: "It's all in the feeding."

> *"I have no desire whatever to reform myself. My only desire is to reform people who try to reform me, and I believe the only way to reform people is to kill 'em. My motto is: Rob 'em all, rape 'em all, and kill 'em all."*
>
> CARL PANZRAM

ANIMAL TORTURE

Childhood cruelty toward small, living creatures isn't necessarily a sign of psychopathology. Lots of little boys who enjoy pulling the wings off of flies grow up to be lawyers or dentists. The sadistic behavior of budding serial killers is something else entirely. After all, it's one thing to chop an earthworm in two because you want to watch the separate halves squirm; it's quite another to eviscerate your neighbor's pet kitten because you enjoy listening to its agonized howls.

The case histories of serial killers are rife with instances of juvenile animal torture. As a boy, for example, Henry Lee **Lucas** enjoyed trapping small animals, torturing them to death, then having sex with the remains. The earliest sexual activity of the appalling Peter **Kürten**—the "Monster of Düsseldorf"—also combined sadism with bestiality. At thirteen, Kürten discovered the pleasures of stabbing sheep to death while having intercourse with them.

Instead of more conventional items, like baseball cards and comic books, little Jeffrey **Dahmer** collected roadkill. According to neighbors, he also liked to nail bullfrogs to trees and cut open live fish to see how their innards worked. One of the favorite childhood pastimes of **Moors Murderer** Ian Brady (see **Killer Couples**) was tossing alley cats out of tenement windows and watching them splat on the pavement. Cats, in fact, are a favor-ite target of youthful sociopaths. Edmund **Kemper** was only ten when he buried the family cat alive, then dug up the corpse and decapitated it. And former FBI Special Agent Robert K. Res-sler—the man credited with coining the term "serial killer"—mentions one sadistic murderer who was nicknamed "Doc" as a child because he liked to slit open the stomachs of cats and see how far they could run before they died.

Animal torture is, in fact, such a common denominator in the childhoods of serial killers that it is considered one of the three major warning signals of future psychopathic behavior, along with unnaturally prolonged bed-wetting and juvenile pyromania (see **Triad**).

The vast majority of little boys who get their kicks from dis-membering daddy longlegs or dropping firecrackers into anthills lose their stomach for sadism at an early age. The case is very different with incipient serial killers. Fixated at a shockingly primitive stage of emotional development, they never lose their craving for cruelty and domination. Quite the contrary: it con-tinues to grow in them like a cancer. Eventually—when dogs, cats, and other small, four-legged creatures can no longer satisfy it—they turn their terrifying attentions to a larger, two-legged breed: human beings.

ARISTOCRATS

For the most part, the only truly remarkable thing about mod-ern-day serial killers is their grotesque psychopathology. Otherwise, they tend to be absolute nobodies. It is precisely for this reason that they are able to get away with murder for so long. No one looking at, say, Joel Rifkin—the Long Island land-scape gardener who slaughtered a string of prostitutes and stored their bodies in the suburban home he shared with his adoptive parents—would ever suspect that this utterly nonde-script individual was capable of such atrocities.

For many serial killers, in fact, the notoriety they achieve through their crimes is, if not their main motivation, then cer-tainly an important fringe benefit. Murder becomes their single claim to fame—the only way they have of getting their names in the paper, of proving to the world (and to themselves) that they are "important" people.

In centuries past, the situation was frequently different. Far from being nonentities, the most notorious serial killers of medieval times were people of great prominence and power. The most infamous of these was the fifteenth-century nobleman Gilles de Rais. Heir to one of the great fortunes of France, Gilles fought alongside Joan of Arc during the Hundred Years War. For his courage in battle, he was named marshal of France, his country's highest military honor.

Following Joan's execution in 1431, however, Gilles returned to his ancestral estate in Brittany and plunged into a life of unspeakable depravity. During a nine-year reign of terror, he preyed on the children of local peasants. Unlike today's low-born serial killers, the aristocratic Gilles didn't have to exert himself to snare his victims; his servants did it for him. Whisked back to his horror castle, the children (most of them boys) were tortured and dismembered for the delectation of the "Bestial Baron," who liked to cap off his pleasure by violating their corpses. Executed in 1440, he is widely regarded as the model for the fairy tale monster Bluebeard.

A female counterpart of Gilles was the Transylvanian noblewoman Elizabeth Bathory, a vampiric beauty who believed she could preserve her youth by bathing in the blood of virgins. According to conservative estimates, Bathory butchered and drained the blood of at least forty young women before her arrest in 1610.

Her tally was topped by her near contemporary, the French noblewoman Marie Margueritte de Brinvilliers. Having run through a fortune, this profligate beauty decided to knock off her father in order to get her hands on his estate. In her efforts to concoct an indetectable poison, she volunteered her services at the Hôtel Dieu—Paris's public hospital—and began trying out different formulas on her patients, ultimately dispatching at least fifty of them. In 1676, she was beheaded for her crimes.

Closer to our own time, some **Jack the Ripper** buffs (or "Ripperologists," as they prefer to be called) speculate that the legendary "Butcher of Whitechapel" was actually Edward, Duke of Clarence, Queen Victoria's grandson and heir to the throne of England. As tantalizing as this theory sounds, it is almost certainly a complete fantasy, akin to the wilder Kennedy assassination scenarios. The unglamorous truth is that Jack was probably nothing more than a knife-wielding nobody—just like the scores of hideously sick nonentities who have followed in his bloody footsteps.

ART

S erial killer art can be divided into two major categories: 1. works of art *about* serial killers, and 2. works of art *by* serial killers.

To start with the latter: the best known of all serial killer artists was John Wayne **Gacy**, who began dabbling in oil painting while in prison. Though Gacy painted everything from Disney characters to Michelangelo's *Pietà*, his trademark subject was Pogo the Clown—the persona he adopted during his prearrest years, when he would occasionally don circus makeup and entertain the kids at the local hospital. Gacy's amateurish oils could be had for a pittance a decade ago, but their value increased as they became trendy collectibles among certain celebrities, like film director John Waters and actor Johnny Depp. Since Gacy's execution, the cost of his paintings has shot even

Pogo the Clown; **painting by John Wayne Gacy** *(Courtesy of Mike Ferris)*

higher. While some of his oils are explicitly creepy (like his so-called Skull Clown paintings), even his most "innocent"—like his depictions of Disney's Seven Dwarves—have an ineffable malevolence to them.

For a while, Gacy's exclusive art dealer was the Louisana funeral director and serial killer enthusiast, Rick Staton (see **The Collector**). Under Staton's encouragement, a number of other notorious murderers have taken up prison arts and crafts. Staton—who started a company called Grindhouse Graphics to market this work and has staged a number of Death Row Art Shows in New Orleans—has represented a wide range of quasi-creative killers, including Richard "Night Stalker" **Ramirez** (who does crude but intensely spooky ballpoint doodles); Charles **Manson** (who specializes in animals sculpted from his old socks); and Elmer Wayne Henley. Henley—who, along with his buddy Dean Corll, was responsible for the torture-murder of as many as thirty-two young men—likes to paint koala bears.

As devoted as he is to promoting the work of these people, even Staton concedes that they possess no artistic talent. There are a couple of exceptions, however. Lawrence Bittaker—who mutilated and murdered five teenage girls—produces some truly original pop-up greeting cards. The most gifted of the bunch, however, is William Heirens, the notorious "Lipstick Killer," who has been in prison since 1946 and who paints exquisitely detailed watercolors.

As far as serious art goes, (i.e., art about, not by, serial killers) probably the greatest serial murder paintings ever created were the work of Otto Dix, the famous German expressionist who was obsessed with images of sadistic sexual mutilation and produced a series of extraordinary canvases on the subject. His contemporary George Grosz (who posed as **Jack the Ripper** in a famous photographic self-portrait) also created a number of works about sex-related killings, including the harrowing *Murder on Acker Street*, which depicts a cretinous killer scrubbing his hands after decapitating a woman, whose horribly mangled corpse occupies the center of the picture. (If you're interested in a brilliant study of sexual murder in Weimar Germany—which reproduces several dozen works by Dix and Grosz—check out the 1995 book *Lustmord* by Harvard professor Maria Tartar.)

The spiritual heir of Dix and Grosz is the astonishing Joe Coleman, America's preeminent painter of serial killers (see **The**

Apocalyptic Art of Joe Coleman). Coleman's work has inspired a number of younger artists, including the young Brooklyn painter Michael Rose, whose subjects range from religious martyrdoms to grisly accidents to the atrocities of Albert **Fish**. Another Brooklyn artist, Chris Pelletiere, has done a series of stunning portraits of some of America's most notorious killers, including Charles Starkweather, Henry Lee **Lucas**, and Ed **Gein**.

Finally, there is the well-known Pop surrealist Peter Saul. Now in his sixties, Saul has been offending sensibilities for the past three decades with canvases like *Donald Duck Descending a Staircase*, *Puppy in an Electric Chair*, and *Bathroom Sex Murder*. Rendered in a garish, cartoony style, Saul's recent paintings of serial killers—which include grotesque depictions of John Wayne **Gacy's** execution and Jeffrey **Dahmer's** eating habits—are among his most electrifying works.

THE APOCALYPTIC ART OF JOE COLEMAN

Joe Coleman in his "odditorium" *(Photo by Steve Bonge)*

America's premier painter of serial killers, Joe Coleman is also the only significant artist ever to perform as a geek. Indeed, one of his most powerful self-portraits—*Portrait of Professor Momboozoo*—shows the crucified

Coleman with a bitten-off rat's head jutting from his mouth. Like so much of Coleman's work, it's an astounding image, one that sums up three of the major themes of his art: horror, sideshow sensationalism, and (insofar as devouring the body and blood of a rodent represents a grotesque parody of the Lord's Supper) religious obsession.

Coleman was born on 11/22/55—a date (as he likes to point out) full of doubles, prefiguring his own fascination with linked dualities: sinner and saint, heaven and hell, corruption and purity, killer and victim. Growing up across from a cemetery and steeped in Catholicism, he developed an early fascination with death and disease, suffering and sacrifice. His childhood imagination was also shaped by two books: the Bible (particularly its juicier stories of sex and violence) and a volume on Hieronymous Bosch, whose teeming, demonic dreamscapes made a profound impression on Coleman's budding artistic sensibility.

Indeed, though Coleman is often classified under the ever-so-slightly disparaging category of "naive" or "outsider" artist, his work falls into a mainstream tradition that extends from such medieval painters as Bosch and Breughel to modern German expressionists like Dix and Grosz. It's also true, however, that—as accomplished and sophisticated as Coleman's paintings are—there is, in his densely textured, meticulously detailed style, a distinctly folk-art quality. He is, in short, a complete original, an all-American delineator of the darkest recesses of the soul. If Bosch had coupled with Grandma Moses, their unholy offspring would have been Joe Coleman.

In the festering landscape of Coleman's art, legendary serial killers like Carl **Panzram** and Charles **Manson** become mad visionaries, driven by a savage need to rip away the comforting illusions of conventional society and expose the terrible realities of existence: random horror, inexorable death. Coleman is quick to point out that his paintings are self-portraits, and the same ferocious drive is evident everywhere in his work. He uses his paintbrush like a vivisectionist's scalpel, to penetrate to the bloody innards, the guts of existence. Beneath our skins, his art seems to say, we are nothing but blood, shit, and phlegm, with a latent tumor undoubtedly lurking somewhere in our cells. But there is another element, too, one that redeems his work from sheer morbidity: the belief, or at least the hope, that if he penetrates far enough, he will discover something much deeper—the soul.

As one critic has commented, Joe Coleman has put the *pain* back in painting. But his work blazes with power and meaning. For those unfamiliar with it, we strongly recommend his book *Cosmic Retribution* (Fantagraphic Books, 1992)—the only art volume (so far as we know) with an enthusiastic jacket blurb by Charles Manson.

> *"My earliest drawings were of the crucifixion of Christ. That's one thing that's going to turn little boys on—that your religion has to do with a guy getting nailed to a fucking cross and all this blood spurting out and all these saints being set on fire. That's the kind of religion I like."*
>
> JOE COLEMAN

AXE MURDERERS

Though the figure of the axe-wielding maniac is a staple of horror movies and campfire tales, he is largely a figment of the popular imagination. In reality, serial killers rarely rely on axes.

The most famous axe in American criminal history, of course, was the one that belonged to Miss Lizzie Borden, who, according to folklore, used it to give her sleeping stepmother "forty whacks" in the face (and when she saw what she had done, she gave her father forty-one). Lizzie, however, was no serial killer but a chubby, thirty-two-year-old spinster with long-simmering resentments who apparently went berserk one sweltering day in August 1892. In short, her crimes (assuming she committed them, which seems fairly certain, in spite of her acquittal) were a one-shot deal—a lifetime's worth of stifled emotions exploding in a single savage deed.

Another fatal female who was handy with an axe was the notorious Belle Gunness (see **Black Widows**), who murdered at least fourteen of her husbands and suitors. Some apparently were poisoned, others were dispatched in their sleep with a hatchet. Though the fat, ferocious Gunness cut a more frightful figure than the ladylike Miss Lizzie, she was no wild-eyed thrill killer. Rather, she was a cold-blooded mercenary, killing to collect on her spouses' life-insurance policies or inherit their savings.

Closer than either of these lethal ladies to the popular stereotype of the axe-wielding psycho was a hard-bitten drifter named Jake Bird. Roaming around Tacoma in 1947, Bird hacked a mother and daughter to pieces with an axe he found in their

Lizzie Borden; from *52 Famous Murderers* trading cards *(Courtesy of Roger Worsham)*

woodshed. Alerted by the victims' dying shrieks, neighbors summoned the police, who managed to subdue Bird after a violent struggle. Bird pled innocent until forensic analysis established that the stains on his trousers were human blood and brain tissue. Before his execution in 1949, he confessed to no fewer than forty-four murders throughout the United States, a number of them committed with his weapon of choice—the axe.

The most fear-provoking axe killer in the annals of American crime, however—one who kept a whole city in a state of panic for over two years—was a maniac whose identity remains unknown. This is the shadowy figure known as the "Axeman of New Orleans."

On the night of May 23, 1918, a New Orleans couple named Maggio was butchered in bed by an intruder who smashed their skulls with an axe blade, then slit their throats with a razor, nearly severing the woman's head. Thus began the reign of terror of the so-called "Axeman," a real-life boogeyman who haunted the city for two and half years. His MO was always the same. Prowling through the darkness, he would target a house, chisel out a back-door panel, slip inside, and find his way to the bedroom. There, he would creep toward his slumbering victims, raise his weapon, and attack with demoniacal fury. Altogether, he murdered seven people and savagely wounded another eight.

Panic gripped the city, particularly since the police were helpless to locate the killer. Hysterical citizens pointed fingers at various suspects, including a supposed German spy named Louis Besumer and a father and son named Jordano, who were actually convicted on "eyewitness testimony" that later proved to be fabricated. Since many of the victims were Italian grocers, there was also a theory (wholly unsubstantiated) that the killer was a Mafia enforcer. To cope with their fears, citizens resorted to morbid humor, throwing raucous New Orleans-style "Axeman parties" and singing along to a popular tune called "The Mysterious Axeman's Jazz."

Though the killer was never identified, some people believe that he was an ex-con named Joseph Mumfre, who was shot down by a woman named Pepitone, the widow of the Axeman's last victim. Mrs. Pepitone claimed that she had seen Mumfre flee the murder scene. Whether Mumfre was really the Axeman remains a matter of dispute, but one fact is certain: the killings stopped with his death.

BATHTUBS

Exploring the spooky labyrinth of Buffalo Bill's basement at the climax of Thomas Harris's *The Silence of the Lambs*, Clarice Starling happens on a ghastly sight: a "big bathtub ... almost filled with hard red-purple plaster. A hand and wrist stuck up from the plaster, the hand turned dark and shrivelled, the fingernails painted pink." Clarice has stumbled onto one of the monster's former victims, who has been turned into some sort of grotesque tableau.

Like the rest of us, of course, real-life serial killers require an occasional bath and so can't clog up their tubs with decomposed corpses encased in red-purple plaster of Paris. Some, however, have put their tubs to specialized uses.

For obvious reasons, bathtubs made a handy place to dismember corpses. After picking up a female hitchhiker in January 1973, for example, Edmund **Kemper** shot her in the head, then drove the body back home, hid it in his bedroom closet, and went to sleep. The next morning, after his mother left for work, he removed the corpse, had sex with it, then placed it in his bathtub and dismembered it with a Buck knife and an axe.

Dennis **Nilsen**'s tub, on the other hand, was used for a more traditional purpose. He liked to bathe his lovers in it. Of course, they were dead at the time. Like Jeffrey **Dahmer**, this British serial killer murdered his homosexual pickups partly because he was desperate for companionship. Turning them into corpses was his way of ensuring that they wouldn't leave in the morning. After strangling a victim, Nilsen would engage in a regular ritual, tenderly cleaning the corpse in his tub, then lovingly arranging it in front of the TV or stereo or perhaps at the dining room table, so he could enjoy its company until it became too decomposed to bear.

And then there is the occasional serial killer who turns his tub into a killing device, like the British **Bluebeard**, George Joseph Smith, the notorious "Brides in the Bath" murderer, who drowned three of his seven wives for their insurance money.

Of course, the most famous of these bathroom fixtures is the shower-tub combo where Janet Leigh meets her brutal end at the hands of Norman Bates. Thanks to Hitchcock's *Psycho,* countless unclad starlets have been butchered by maniacs while soaping up in the shower or relaxing in a bubble bath. Every now and then, a knife-wielding psycho will even pop out of a tub as in *Fatal Attraction.* But on the whole, these are perils that hardly ever occur outside the movies. For the most part, bathtubs are perfectly safe—as long as you don't slip on the soap.

BED-WETTING

See **Triad.**

DAVID BERKOWITZ

5. DAVID BERKOWITZ: "Son of Sam"

David Berkowitz; from *Bloody Visions* trading cards *(© & ™ 1995 M. H. Price and Shel-Tone Publications. All rights reserved.)*

It was the era of New York disco fever—of platform shoes, leisure suits, dancing to the Bee Gees while a mirrored globe spun and flashed overhead. But for a little more than a year, between 1976 and 1977, the disco beat turned into a pulse of fear as a gun-wielding madman prowled the city streets at night. His weapon was a .44 revolver—and at first the tabloids tagged him the ".44-Caliber Killer."

The terror began on July 29, 1976, when two young women were shot in a parked car in the Bronx. Young people in cars—often dating couples—would continue to be the killer's targets of choice. On one occasion, however, he gunned down a pair of young women sitting on a stoop. On another, he shot a woman as she walked home from school. Frantically she tried protecting her face with a book—but to no avail. The killer simply raised the muzzle of his weapon to the makeshift shield and blasted her in the head. Before his rampage was over, a total of six young New Yorkers were dead, seven more severely wounded.

At the scene of one double murder, police found a long, ranting note from the killer. "I am the 'Son of Sam.' I am a little brat," he wrote. From that point on, the killer would be known by his bizarre new nickname.

For months, while the city was gripped by panic, police made no headway. When a break finally came, it happened as a result of a thirty-five-dollar parking ticket. On July 31, 1977, when a couple was shot along the Brooklyn shore, a witness noticed someone driving away from the scene in a car that had just been ticketed. Tracing the summons through their computer, the police came up with the name and address of David Berkowitz, a pudgy-faced postal worker living in Yonkers.

When police picked him up, they found an arsenal in the trunk of Berkowitz's car. Son of Sam had been planning an apocalyptic act of carnage—a kamikaze assault on a Long Island disco.

Under arrest, Berkowitz explained the meaning of his bizarre moniker. "Sam" turned out to be the name of a neighbor, Sam Carr, who—in Berkowitz's profoundly warped mind—was actually a "high demon" who transmitted his orders to kill through his pet dog, a black Labrador retriever. Insane as this story was, Berkowitz was found mentally fit to stand trial. He was eventually sentenced to three hundred years in the pen, where he has recently undergone a religious conversion and become a jailhouse televangelist, preaching the gospel on public-access TV.

"*I didn't want to hurt them, I only wanted to kill them.*"
DAVID BERKOWITZ

BLACK WIDOWS

Classic serial sex-murder—in which a sadistic sociopath is driven to stalk, slay, and commit unspeakable acts on a succession of strangers—is an outrage perpetrated almost exclusively by men. As two-fisted culture critic Camille Paglia puts it, "There are no female Jack the Rippers" (see **Women**). On the other hand, women who murder a whole string of their mates, often for mercenary reasons, are relatively common in the annals of crime. These female counterparts of the male **Bluebeard**-type killer are known (in homage to the deadly arachnid that devours its mates after sex) as "Black Widows."

The most infamous of this breed was the legendary Belle Gunness, née Brynhild Storset, who came to this country from a small fishing village in Norway in 1881. Like other nineteenth-century immigrants, the enterprising young woman found America to be a land of plenty, where she could put her God-given talents to the most profitable use. As it happened, Belle's particular talent was serial murder. After a fire destroyed her Indiana farm in 1908, searchers found the decomposed remains of at least a dozen people on her property, some interred in the basement of the gutted house, others buried in the muck of the hog pen or planted in her garden. Most of her victims were either prospective husbands or hired hands who doubled as lovers. Their deaths allowed Gunness to cash in on their insurance policies and loot their bank accounts. Like the sow that devours its farrow, she also murdered two of her own infant children after insuring their lives. Gunness has gained legendary status not only because of the enormity of her crimes but also because she disappeared without a trace, slipping (like **Jack the Ripper**) into the realm of folklore and myth.

Other notorious Black Widows followed Gunness's avaricious pattern. In the mid-nineteenth century, America's "Queen Poisoner," Lydia Sherman, bumped off one husband after another in order to inherit their savings. Reluctant to split her new bounty with anyone else, she also poisoned her children, dispatching more than one of her victims with arsenic-spiked hot chocolate. In a strikingly similar fashion, her British contemporary Mary Ann Cotton liquidated a whole string of spouses and

children. Their deaths were attributed to "gastric fever"—until a postmortem on her final victim, her seven-year-old stepson, turned up traces of arsenic in his stomach.

Not all Black Widows, however, are motivated by greed. The matronly multicide Nannie Doss—dubbed the "Giggling Granny" by the press because she chuckled with amusement while confessing her crimes—became incensed when police accused her of killing four husbands for their insurance policies (which were, in fact, pretty paltry). An avid reader of true-romance fiction, Nanny insisted that she had murdered for love, not money. "I was searching for the perfect mate, the real romance of life." When a husband didn't measure up, she simply dispatched him (slipping liquid rat poison into his corn whiskey or stewed prunes), then went in search of another Prince Charming. Of course, her explanation was not entirely convincing, since her victims also included her mother, two sisters, two children, one grandson, and her nephew. Nannie Doss was sentenced to life in prison, where she died of leukemia in 1965 after

Mary Ann Cotton; from *Bloody Visions* trading cards *(© & ™ 1995 M. H. Price and Shel-Tone Publications. All rights reserved.)*

writing her memoirs for *Life* magazine. She murdered neither for love nor money. She killed because she enjoyed it.

BLASPHEMY

For the most part, this is an outrage perpetrated by devil-worshipping cultists who delight in blaspheming the orthodox rituals of Christianity (see **Satanism**). The central ceremony of Satanic worship, for example, is the so-called Black Mass, an obscene travesty of the Catholic mass involving baby sacrifice, orgiastic sex, and other abominations.

There is, however, at least one serial killer who added blasphemy to his staggering list of outrages. After murdering his final victim—an eighty-eight-year-old grandmother named Kate Rich—Henry Lee **Lucas** carved an upside-down cross between the old woman's breasts. Then he raped her corpse.

ROBERT BLOCH

Say the word *Psycho* to most people and they will immediately visualize scenes from the classic horror film: Janet Leigh getting slashed to pieces in a shower, Martin Balsam being set upon by an old biddy with a butcher knife, Anthony Perkins smiling insanely while a fly buzzes around his padded cell. But while it was Alfred Hitchcock's genius that made *Psycho* into a masterpiece, it was another imagination that first dreamed up Norman Bates and his motel from hell. It belonged to Robert Bloch, one of the most prolific and influential horror writers of the century.

Born in Chicago in 1917, Bloch began publishing stories in the pulps while still a teenager. He received encouragement from his pen pal and muse, horrormeister H. P. Lovecraft (who named a character after Bloch in his story "The Haunter of the Dark"). After working as an advertising copywriter in Milwaukee, Bloch quit to become a full-time writer in the early 1950s. He specialized in tales whose macabre twisted endings make them read like extended sick jokes. Psychopathic killers figure prominently in his fiction. One of his best-known stories is titled, "Yours Truly, Jack the Ripper."

In 1957, Bloch—who had relocated to Los Angeles to write screenplays—moved back to Wisconsin so that his ailing wife could be close to her parents. He was living in the town of Weyauwega, less than thirty miles from Plainfield, where police broke into the tumbledown farmhouse of a middle-aged bachelor named Edward **Gein** and discovered a collection of horrors that sent shock waves around the nation. Fascinated by the incredible circumstances of the Gein affair—particularly by the fact (as he later put it) "that a killer with perverted appetites could flourish almost openly in a small rural community where everybody prides himself on knowing everybody else's business"—Bloch hit on the idea for a horror novel. The result was his 1960 thriller, *Psycho*, about the schizophrenic mama's boy, Norman Bates—a monster who (like Dracula and King Kong) has become a permanent icon of our pop mythology.

Bloch wrote hundreds of short stories and more than twenty novels, in addition to dozens of screenplays and television scripts. However, when he died, on September 23, 1994, the headlines of his obituaries invariably identifed him (as he predicted they would) as the "Author of *Psycho*." As interpreted by Hitchcock, this pioneering piece of serial-killer literature set the pattern for all cinematic slasher fantasies of the past thirty-five years. In spite of his lifelong obsession with psychopathic killers, Bloch himself was the gentlest of men, who had little use for the kind of graphically gory horror movies his own work had inspired. When asked his opinion of films like *The Texas Chainsaw Massacre*, the man who gave birth to Norman Bates admitted, "I'm quite squeamish about them."

BLUEBEARDS

Reputedly modeled on the fifteenth-century monster Gilles de Rais (see **Aristocrats**), the folktale character Bluebeard is a sinister nobleman who murders a succession of wives and stores their corpses in a locked room in his castle. In real life, the term is used to describe a specific type of serial killer who, like his fictional couterpart, knocks off one wife after another.

There are two major differences between a "Bluebeard" killer and a psycho like Ted **Bundy**. The latter preys on strangers, whereas the Bluebeard type restricts himself to the women who are unlucky (or foolish) enough to wed him. Their motivations differ, too. Bundy and his ilk are driven by sexual sadism; they are lust murderers. By contrast, the cardinal sin that motivates the Bluebeard isn't lust but greed. For the most part, this kind of serial killer dispatches his victims for profit.

The most infamous Bluebeard of the twentieth century was a short, balding, red-bearded Frenchman named Henri Landru (the real-life inspiration for Charlie Chaplin's black comedy *Monsieur Verdoux*). In spite of his unsightly appearance, Landru possessed an urbane charm that made him appealing to women. It didn't hurt, of course, that there were so many vulnerable women around—lonely widows of the millions of young soldiers who had perished on the battlefields of World War I. An accomplished swindler who had already been convicted seven times for fraud, Landru found his victims by running matrimonial ads in the newspapers. When a suitable (i.e., wealthy, gullible) prospect responded, Landru would woo her, wed her, assume control of her assets, then kill her and incinerate the corpse in a small outdoor oven on his country estate outside Paris. He was guillotined in 1922, convicted of eleven murders—ten women, plus one victim's teenaged son.

Even more prolific was a German named Johann Hoch, who emigrated to America in the late 1800s. In sheer numerical terms, Hoch holds some sort of connubial record among Bluebeards, having married no fewer than fifty-five women, at least fifteen of whom he dispatched. Like Landru, he never confessed, insisting on his innocence even as the hangman's noose tightened around his neck.

Another notorious Bluebeard from across the sea was the Englishman George Joseph Smith, who became known as the "Brides in the Bath" murderer for his habit of drowning his wives in the tub in order to collect on their life insurance. Like Landru and Hoch, Smith vehemently proclaimed his innocence, leaping up during his trial and shouting, "I am not a murderer, though I may be a bit peculiar!" The jury didn't buy it, at least the first part. He was hanged on Friday, August 13, 1915.

Though the killer who snares his female victims with his suave, attentive manners seems quintessentially European, our own country has produced its share of Bluebeards. Born and bred in Kansas, Alfred Cline looked like a Presbyterian minister—one of the reasons, no doubt, that he was able to win the trust of so many well-to-do widows, eight of whom he married and murdered between 1930 and 1945. Even Cline's favorite killing device—a poisoned glass of buttermilk—was as American as could be.

Then there was Herman Drenth, who dispatched an indeterminate number of victims in his homemade gas chamber outside Clarksburg, West Virginia. He was hanged for five murders in 1932. Unlike most Bluebeards, Drenth was an admitted sadist, deriving not only financial profit but also sexual pleasure from his crimes. Watching his victims die, he told police, "Beat any cathouse I was ever in."

> ### "I may be a bit peculiar."
> **GEORGE JOSEPH SMITH,**
> the "Brides in the Bath" murderer

BOARD GAMES

Though it seemed unlikely to become the next Trivial Pursuit, a board game called Serial Killer set off a firestorm of outrage when it was put on the market a few years ago. The brainchild of a Seattle child care worker named Tobias Allen, Serial Killer consisted of a game board printed with a map of the United States, four serial killer playing pieces, "crime cards," "outcome cards," and two dozen plastic "victims" (in the possibly ill-advised form of dead babies).

With the roll of a die, each player would move along the map and draw a "crime" card. Each card would involve either a "high-risk" or a "low-risk" crime, and the player would collect victims accordingly. As Allen explained, "A high-risk crime

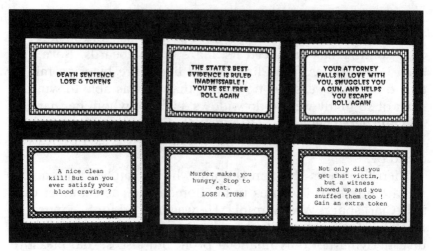

Game cards from *Serial Killer* board game *(Courtesy of Tobias Allen)*

might be breaking into the house of a prominent citizen and killing him. A low-risk crime would be murdering a prostitute or a street person. Whoever has the highest body count at the end of the game wins."

Though Allen intended the game as "a bit of a spoof on the way we glorify mass destruction," many people failed to see the humor. A number of Canadian politicians mobilized to ban the game's sale in their country. The fact that it came packaged in a plastic body bag apparently didn't help.

> *"A quiet dorm could turn into a house of horrors when you visit! This campus is crawling with cops, though—so beware!"*
>
> "Crime card" from Serial Killer board game

BODY PARTS

See **Trophies**.

TED BUNDY

Ted Bundy; from
Bloody Visions **trading**
cards *(© & ™ 1995 M. H.*
Price and Shel-Tone
Publications. All rights
reserved.)

He was a genuine Jekyll and Hyde—a clean-cut Joe College type, so attractive and charming that young women, meeting him for the first time, would climb into his car without hesitation. Once there, however, they found themselves face-to-face with a monster: an implacable lust murderer who tortured and killed with maniacal glee.

Ted Bundy's bestial alter ego first came roaring to the surface during his student days at the University of Washington. In 1974, he killed seven women in as many months and inflicted permanent brain damage on another, using a metal rod to fracture her skull, than ramming it into her vagina. From Seattle, he moved to Salt Lake City, enrolling in the University of Utah school of law. Before long, he had established himself as an up-and-coming young Republican with bright political prospects. At the same time, however, the creature that lurked beneath this brilliant facade continued to lust after blood. Young women began disappearing from the Salt Lake area—including a police chief's teenage daughter, whose nude and mutilated remains were eventually found in a canyon.

Bundy also made occasional forays into Colorado, where at least five other young women vanished and died. In 1976, he was finally arrested but managed to escape twice, once by climbing through a courthouse window, the second time by sawing a hole in the ceiling of his cell.

In January 1978 he turned up in Tallahassee, Florida. By now, the monster inside him—his evil Mr. Hyde—was taking control. No longer did Bundy bother to coax young women into his car. Instead, he simply slipped into their rooms at night and pounced with demoniacal fury. In once case, he nearly chewed off the nipple of a victim, then bit her buttocks so savagely that he left teeth marks in her flesh. Those marks were his undoing. After Florida police arrested him in February—for driving a stolen vehicle—they were able to match photographs of the bite marks with impressions of Bundy's teeth.

At his trial, the erstwhile law student acted as his own attorney. He failed to impress either the judge or the jury—though he *was* able to delay his execution for ten years following his conviction. In a desperate effort to fend off death, he also began cooperating with authorities. Interviewed by agents of the FBI's Behavioral Science Unit, he offered invaluable insights into the psychology of serial killers. He also confessed to twenty-eight murders (though he is suspected of more, perhaps as many as one hundred).

Ultimately, the legal process caught up with him. He was electrocuted in February 1989. Outside the prison walls, hundreds of people toasted his death with champagne.

"We serial killers are your sons, we are your husbands, we are everywhere. And there will be more of your children dead tomorrow."

TED BUNDY

CALENDARS

As everyone knows, there's a "theme" calendar available for enthusiasts of every stripe, from cat fanciers to Tolkien fanatics to connoisseurs of fine art. To satisfy the demand of hardcore horror fans (or "gorehounds" as they fondly refer to themselves), John Marr—publisher of the popular **Zine** *Murder Can Be Fun*—offers a handsome yearly datebook, the perfect gift for those discriminating people who like to keep track of such important anniversaries as the date of David **Berkowitz**'s second

Murder Can Be Fun Datebook (Courtesy of John Marr)

Film Threat magazine's 1990 "Mass Murderer" calendar; art by Glenn L. **Barr** *(Courtesy of Chris Gore, © 1989 Film Threat, Inc.)*

CALENDAR OF AN ORGANIZED PSYCHOTIC

Several years ago, a sick but amusing item concocted by some cleverly macabre wit made the rounds—one of those anonymous laugh getters that gets passed from hand to hand (or faxed from machine to machine). It pretended to be the monthly calendar of the world's most anally retentive psychokiller. As an example of hilariously black humor, it remains, in our opinion, unsurpassed. We don't know the name of the demented genius who produced it, but here it is:

CALENDAR OF AN ORGANIZED PSYCHOTIC — August

Sunday	Monday	Tuesday	Wednesday	Thursday	Friday	Saturday
				1 SET FIRE TO CATHOLIC SCHOOL	2 BUY S+M MAGAZINES AND CUT OUT ALL THE FACES IN THE PICTURES.	3 GO FLASHING IN PARK
4 CALL MOM AND MAKE HER CRY. THREATEN TO KILL DAD.	5 MASTURBATE ALL DAY	6 GRAPPLE WITH SELF-HATRED AND ATTEMPT SUICIDE	7 STARE AT WALL AND ATTEMPT TO STOP BREATHING	8 ROCK BACK AND FORTH ALL DAY	9 DROOL AND HYPERVENTILATE	10 3 P.M. MEETING WITH PAROLE OFFICER— KILL HIM
			C A T A T O N I A			
11 STEAL CAR. DESTRUCTIVE RAMPAGE? RAPE WEEK>	12 RAPE 2 PROSTITUTES	13 RAPE RAPE TEENAGE GIRL + GET CAUGHT	14 GET RAPED IN JAIL BY SADIST GUARDS	15 ESCAPE RAPE JAIL AND RAPE EX-WIFE	16 PARTICIPATE IN RAPE GANG RAPE OF BAGLADY	17 RAPE YOUNG FILIPINO BOY
18 RAPE AND ON THE SEVENTH DAY HE RESTED.	19 GO TO CLINIC FOR AIDS TEST. WRITE TO PRESI-DENT + PREDICT HIS DEATH.	20 TERRORIZE LAUNDROMATS SCRATCH BUTT IN PUBLIC	21 PANHANDLE ALL DAY, THEN ROB 7-11 WITH TOY GUN.	22 AIDS TEST RESULT— CROSS FINGERS. KILL ANIMAL FOR GOOD LUCK	23 IF HAVE AIDS, COMMIT SUICIDE. IF NOT, CELEBRATE AT GAY BAR	24 SLASH THROATS OF 3 DRUNKS IN ALLEY
25 ATTEMPT SUICIDE AGAIN— GO TO HOSPITAL	26 IN HOSPITAL STEAL DRUGS + TAKE THEM ALL. VOMIT ON NURSE	27 BUY HIGH-POWERED RIFLE. MUTILATE LEFT ARM WITH POCKET KNIFE	28 TAKE POT SHOTS AT CARS ON FREEWAY	29 SPEND ALL DAY TYPING HYSTERICAL TRACT ABOUT REVELATIONS, SPERM + GRAVITY.	30 TORTURE NEIGHBOR-HOOD CATS WITH CATTLE PROD	31 DRINK VIRGIN'S BLOOD TO PURIFY BODY. HIJACK PLANE TO GALAPAGOS ISLANDS

"Son of Sam" killing (October 23) and Gary Gilmore's execution (December 4). A tour de force of research, Marr's macabre desk calendar manages to come up with a different depressing event for every single day of the year. For information, contact: John Marr, P.O. Box 640111, San Francisco, CA 94109.

Several years ago, the cult magazine *Film Threat* put out a slick Mass Murderer calendar, featuring witty caricatures of America's most infamous psychos (Ed **Gein**, Albert **Fish**, Ted **Bundy**, John Wayne **Gacy**, and eight more) by artist Glenn L. Barr. Unfortunately, the magazine no longer produces this item, and original copies of the rare, out-of-print 1990 edition have become coveted **Collectibles** among serial killer buffs.

CANNIBALISM

E ver since the Stone Age, human beings have indulged in cannibalism, either for dietary or ritual reasons. The prehistoric hominids known as *Homo erectus* enjoyed supping on the brains of their fellow cavemen. Aborigines throughout the world, from New Zealand to North America, routinely devoured the hearts of enemy warriors as a way of absorbing their courage. Ceremonial cannibalism was a central feature of the Aztec religion. And Fijians consumed human flesh (which they called *puaka balava* or "long pig") just because they liked its taste.

In the Judeo-Christian tradition, however, cannibalism is regarded with such intense abhorrence that—when faced with a choice between eating other humans or starving to death—some people have opted for the latter. (This was the case, for example, with several survivors of the famous 1972 plane crash that stranded a party of young Uruguayans in the high Andes.) As a result, of all the horrors associated with serial killers, cannibalism strikes many people as the worst. When Thomas Harris, author of *The Silence of the Lambs*, set out to create the most monstrous serial killer imaginable, the result was Dr. Lecter, aka "Hannibal the Cannibal," whose idea of a gourmet meal is human liver with fava beans and a nice Chianti on the side.

In point of fact, however, real-life cannibal killers are relatively few and far between. For reasons that can only be surmised, Germany has produced a disproportionately high percentage of twentieth-century people eaters. During the social chaos of the 1920s, the hideously depraved Fritz **Haarmann** slaughtered as many as fifty young boys, dined on their flesh, then sold the leftovers as black market beef. His equally degenerate countryman Georg Grossmann also supplemented his income by peddling human flesh, though his preferred victims were plump young females, whose meat he made into sausages. Yet another postwar German cannibal was Karl Denke, an innkeeper who killed and consumed at least thirty of his lodgers.

At about the same time in America, the sadomasochistic madman Albert **Fish** was roaming the country, preying on small boys and girls. He was finally executed for the abduction-murder of a pretty twelve-year-old named Grace Budd, parts of whose body he made into a stew. In recent years, the "Milwaukee Monster," Jeffrey **Dahmer**, has served as a grotesque reminder that the forbidden urge to consume human flesh may still lurk beneath the surface of supposedly civilized life.

Albert Fish murdering Grace Budd; painting by Michael Rose

Appalling as they were, Dahmer's crimes were outstripped by the Russian "Mad Beast," Andrei **Chikatilo**, who—with a confirmed body count of fifty-two victims—holds the record as the worst serial killer of modern times. Among his countless atrocities, Chikatilo devoured the genitals of some of his victims—a practice that left him (according to his captors) with a telltale case of bizarre halitosis.

In the realm of serial-killer cinema, cannibalism features prominently in Tobe Hooper's splatter classic *The Texas Chainsaw Massacre*, about a family of deranged good ol' boys who turn unwary teens into barbeque. Like *Psycho* and *The Silence of the Lambs*, Hooper's movie was inspired by the crimes of Edward **Gein**. Ostensibly, investigators found unmistakable signs of cannibalism in Gein's horror house—a human heart in a frying pan, a refrigerator stocked with paper-wrapped body parts. This allegation, however, was just one of many hysterical rumors that floated around in the wake of his crimes. Though Ghoulish Gein committed all sorts of unspeakable acts, cannibalism was apparently not one of them. He did, however, enjoy eating baked beans from a bowl made out of a human cranium.

CARDS, COMICS, AND COLLECTIBLES

A few years ago, a company called Eclipse Enterprises started marketing a set of true-crime trading cards, featuring full-color portraits of America's most infamous serial killers (among other notable lawbreakers). Predictably enough, a coast-to-coast chorus of outraged voices immediately denounced these collectibles as dangerously immoral, and at least one locality—Nassau County in Long Island, New York—passed a law forbidding their sale to minors.

Of course, what these right-minded folk failed to realize is that American children have always gotten a charge out of all that is violent, gross, and offensive to adult sensibilities. At least as far back as the 1940s, there were trading cards depicting famous gangsters. Members of the boomer generation can fondly recollect the famous Civil War series of bubble gum cards, which depicted such educational scenes as soldiers getting impaled on one another's bayonets and young men having their limbs blown off by cannon fire. Another kiddie classic, the legendary Mars Attacks trading cards, featured explicit images of humans having their bodies destroyed by the flesh-dissolving rays of alien invaders.

By contrast, Eclipse's true-crime series was positively tasteful, consisting of nothing but rather handsomely painted, full-face portraits. Take our word for it—in terms of sheer repulsiveness, the Garbage Pail Kids were infinitely more objectionable.

Why kids (particularly little boys) should get such a kick out of all kinds of gross-out merchandise, from rubber vomit to Gummi worms, is a question we'll leave to the child psychologists (though we suspect that managing anxieties by creating games around them has something to do with it). But the notion that a three-by-five-inch illustration of Jeffrey **Dahmer**'s face might cause "juvenile crime and impair ethical development" seems highly dubious, to say the least.

As it happened, a federal magistrate concurred with that opinion and ruled that Nassau County's ban on these trading cards was unconstitutional. By that time, however, the point was somewhat moot, since Eclipse Enterprises had already gone out of business.

Luckily for collectors of serial-killer trading cards, two other companies continue to market their own sets. Shel-Tone Publications (P.O. Box 45, Irvington, NJ 07111) has produced three different series of murder cards, Bloody Visions I, II, and III, all of them researched, written, and illustrated by Michael H. Price, horror maven and film critic for the *Fort Worth Star-Telegram*.

Another company, Mother Productions (P.O. Box 325, Atwood, CA 92601), offers two collector sets of its own, 52 Famous Murderers and Cold-blooded Killer Cards. Like the Eclipse and Shel-Tone series, these cards avoid any graphic visual depictions of bloodshed and murder. Each card consists of an artful, often highly expressionistic portrait of the subject, with a brief biography on the back.

Trading cards haven't been the only controversial collectibles.

Jeffrey Dahmer comic book from Boneyard Press (*Courtesy of Hart D. Fisher*)

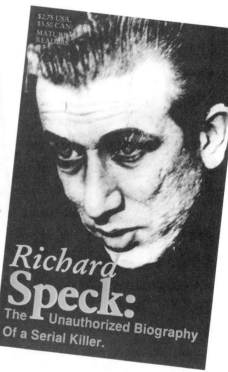

Cover of Richard Speck comic book from Boneyard Press (*Courtesy of Hart D. Fisher*)

Ed Gein comic cover by Pat Gabriele (*Courtesy of Hart D. Fisher*)

Charles Manson T-shirt collection *(Courtesy Damon Fox)*

Serial-killer fashions *(Courtesy of Damon Fox)*

THE COLLECTOR

Rick Staton *(Photo by Arbie Goings, Jr.)*

In the realm of coveted collectibles, serial-killer memorabilia doesn't quite rank with early American coins, rare commemorative stamps, and Golden Age superhero comics. Still, there are some serious collectors out there—people who would regard an original Ed **Gein** autograph as more valuable than a Mickey Mantle rookie card.

One of the most prominent of these is Rick Staton, an affable Louisiana funeral director, who—like so many members of the baby boom generation—developed an early taste for the macabre from his childhood exposure to creature-feature television shows, Roger Corman horror movies, and *Famous Monsters of Filmland* magazine.

In 1990, Staton—who until that time had collected nothing more controversial than grade-B movie posters—heard that John Wayne **Gacy** had taken up oil painting in prison. Staton struck up a correspondence with Gacy and eventually became his art dealer, selling original Gacy paintings (mostly of clowns) to a roster of clients that included celebrity collectors like Johnny Depp, John Waters, and Iggy Pop.

Before long, Staton had also contacted other infamous killers—including Charles **Manson**, Richard **Speck**, Richard **Ramirez**, and Henry Lee **Lucas**—who were soon turning out everything from crude ballpoint doodles to oil-painted seascapes, which Staton sold through a mail-order business called "Grindhouse Graphics" (see **Art**).

In the meantime, Staton assembled his own personal collection of serial-killer artifacts and memorabilia, which currently includes such unique items as a bird painting on canvas by Richard **Speck**; Polaroid photos of Henry Lee **Lucas** and David **Berkowitz**; Ted **Bundy**'s autograph; the high school diploma of **Hillside Strangler** Kenneth Bianchi; cards and letters from Jeffrey **Dahmer**, Edmund **Kemper**, and a host of other notorious killers; charcoal rubbings of Ed **Gein**'s grave marker; soil from Gary **Heidnik**'s front yard; and many works by John Wayne **Gacy**, including a unique painting of Michelangelo's *Pietà*.

Though Staton understands that his interests are bound to raise eyebrows, he makes no bones about his hobby (so to speak). Straightforward and self-aware, he knows that monsters have always exerted a fascination for people—partly because, in confronting them, we are facing and coping with our own deepest fears and forbidden desires.

A few years ago, relatives of some of Jeffrey **Dahmer**'s victims sued a company called Boneyard Press of Champaign, Illinois, for publishing a Dahmer comic book. The same company has also put out comics about Richard **Speck** and Ed **Gein**. Gein's story was also told in an earlier "underground" comic *Weird Trips* No. 2, which featured a memorable cover illustration of ol' Ed in his kitchen by artist William Stout.

Perhaps the most powerful serial-killer comic around is *From Hell*, illustrated by Eddie Campbell and written by Alan Moore, one of the most highly regarded creators in the field. This eight-part saga about **Jack the Ripper** is published by the Kitchen Sink Press of Northampton, Massachusetts, and is available in most comic book specialty shops.

The ultimate sourcebook for serial-killer collectibles is *The Catalogue of Carnage*, put out by Foxx Entertainment Enterprises (327 West Laguna, Tempe, Arizona 85282). This is a veritable Spiegel home-shopping catalogue for the "gorehound" set. The Cryptkeeper himself couldn't ask for a wider selection of ghoulish *objets* to decorate his vault. Whether you're looking for a candy dish cast from a genuine human skull, a hyper realistic severed arm made of lifelike, hand-painted latex, or a handsome Charles **Manson** T-shirt to wear to your next dinner party, this is where you'll find it.

CAUSES

What turns a person into a serial killer? There's no shortage of theories. Unfortunately none of them is completely convincing.

One of the most intriguing (if controversial) comes from the little-known field of paleopsychology. According to this view, our civilized brains are built on a primitive, animalistic core known as the R-complex. Deep inside every one of us are the savage instincts of our apelike ancestors. For the vast majority of people, this basic, brute nature is kept in check by our more highly evolved faculties—reason, intelligence, and logic. But for various reasons, a small fraction of people are controlled by their primitive brains. In esssence, advocates of this view see serial killers as throwbacks—bloodthirsty, Stone Age savages living in the modern world.

Freudian theorists take a similar view, though they talk about the id instead of the R-complex and see serial killers not as latter-day apemen but as profoundly stunted personalities, fixated at an infantile stage of psychosexual development. Because of their traumatic upbringings, compulsive killers never progress beyond the emotional development of a two-year-old. Put a porcelain vase in a toddler's hands and it will end up in little pieces. Serial killers act the same way. They love to destroy things. To them, a human being is just a breakable object—something to be taken apart for pleasure.

Other explanations run the gamut from the physiological (head injuries, hormonal imbalances, genetic deficiencies) to the sociological (class resentment, overpopulation, too much exposure to media violence). There are even environmental theories. One expert has proposed that serial murderers are suffering from a disease caused, among other factors, by toxic pollutants.

Whatever other factors may or may not be involved, one common denominator seems to be that they all have an atrocious family background. The appalling **Upbringing** of most, if not all, serial killers clearly contributes to their pathology, turning them into people so full of hate and self-loathing that sadistic murder becomes their substitute for intimacy (see **Sadism**). Still even a truly dreadful upbringing doesn't seem to be a sufficient explanation. After all, countless human beings suffer traumatic childhoods without growing up to be serial lust killers.

Ultimately, the root causes of serial murder are unknowable—as mysterious in their way as the sources of Mozart's musicianship or Einstein's mathematical genius. Perhaps the only possible answer is the one provided by the great American novelist Herman Melville in his masterpiece *Billy Budd*. Pondering on the depravity of the villainous John Claggart, who sets out to destroy the innocent hero for no discernible reason, Melville concludes that Claggart's "evil nature" was "not engendered by vicious training or corrupting books or licentious living" but was "born with him and innate."

Sometimes, in short, "elemental evil" simply takes a human form.

> *"Toward the accomplishment of an aim which in wantonness of atrocity would seem to partake of the insane, he will direct a cool judgment sagacious and sound. These men are madmen, and of the most dangerous sort."*
>
> **HERMAN MELVILLE**, *Billy Budd*

CESARE LOMBROSO AND "CRIMINAL MAN"

A hundred years ago, an Italian physician named Cesare Lombroso invented the field of "criminal anthropology," a forerunner of the current theory of "paleopsychology." Lombroso believed that criminals were "atavisms"—savage, apelike beings born, by some unexplained evolutionary quirk, into the modern world. Because they were throwbacks to a prehistoric past, criminals could be identified by certain physical characteristics. They actually possessed the anatomical traits of apes—thick skulls, big jaws, high cheekbones, jutting brows, long arms, thick necks, etc.

A serial killer named Vincenz Verzeni helped convince Lombroso that his theory was valid. After strangling two women outside Rome, Verzeni disembowelled the corpses and, in one case, drank the victim's blood. Examining the vampire killer after his arrest, Lombroso discovered that the young man—with his large jaw, bull neck, malformed ears, and low forehead—was a perfect specimen of "primitive humanity." Before long, Lombroso was claiming that you could identify a "born criminal" purely by his physical features. Called to testify at the trial of one young suspect, Lombroso argued that the man must certainly be guilty because he had big ears, a crooked nose, a sinister look, and a tattoo.

Needless to say, Lombroso's theory of "criminal man" has been thoroughly discredited by now—especially his notion that you can identify a murderer just by looking at him.

At least thirty young women—who once met a handsome, clean-cut young fellow named Ted **Bundy**, who looked nothing in the world like an ape—could have told the famous criminologist just how wrong he was.

CHARACTERISTICS

B esides the obvious ones—sick minds, sociopathic personalities, unspeakable desires, etc.—serial killers tend to share a number of characteristics. In a paper presented to the International Association of Forensic Sciences in 1984, FBI Special Agent Robert K. Ressler and several of his colleagues listed the following "general characteristics" of serial sex-murderers:

1. Over 90 percent of them are white males.
2. They tend to be intelligent, with IQs in the "bright normal" range.
3. In spite of their high IQs, they do poorly in school, have a hard time holding down jobs, and often work as unskilled laborers.
4. They tend to come from markedly unstable families. Typically, they are abandoned as children by their fathers and raised by domineering mothers.
5. Their families often have criminal, psychiatric, and alcoholic histories.
6. They hate their fathers. They hate their mothers.
7. They are commonly abused as children—psychologically, physically, and sexually. Sometimes, the abuser is a stranger. Sometimes, it is a friend. Often, it is a family member.
8. Many of them end up spending time in institutions as children and have records of early psychiatric problems.
9. They have a high rate of suicide attempts.
10. They are intensely interested from an early age in voyeurism, fetishism, and sadomasochistic pornography.

For other characteristics of serial killers, see the following entries: **Causes**, **Triad**, and **Upbringing**.

ANDREI CHIKATILO

According to the party line, serial killers didn't exist in the Soviet state. There was only one problem with this assertion. Even while Communist officials were declaring that serial murder was strictly "a decadent Western phenomenon," one of the most monstrous psychopaths in the annals of crime was at large in the Russian port-city of Rostov.

He was Andrei Chikatilo—a mousy-looking forty-two-year-old factory clerk, married, with children. Possessed by a monstrous blood lust, he targeted easy prey—boys, girls, defenseless young women. Usually, he would lure them away from bus stops with the promise of a ride or a meal. Leading them into a lonely stretch of woods, he would pounce like a werewolf, committing unspeakable atrocities on his victims, often while they were still alive. (Cutting out their tongues, biting off their nipples, slicing off their noses, gouging out their eyes, devouring their genitals—these were just a few of the horrors he perpetrated.) So fierce was his appetite for human blood that, during one four-week span in 1984, he butchered no less than six young victims.

Chikatilo's unwitting accomplice in these hideous crimes was the Soviet totalitarian system. According to Communist dogma, crime could not exist in a classless people's republic like the USSR. Rather than admit that they were wrong, Soviet authorities covered up Chikatilo's monstrous spree. As a result, during the "Mad Beast's" twelve-year reign of terror, Soviet citizens didn't even know that a serial killer was on the loose. Instead of being on their guard, they were left vulnerable to his advances.

The police finally nabbed Chikatilo in 1990. He was charged with a staggering fifty-three murders, though the true total may have been even higher. At his trial, he was kept locked inside a steel cage to protect him from his victims' relatives. He was executed in 1994.

For a compelling dramatization of the case, we highly recommend *Citizen X*, a 1995 made-for-cable movie (available on video) starring Stephen Rea, Donald Sutherland, Max von Sydow, and—in a thoroughly chilling portrayal—Jeffrey DeMunn as Chikatilo.

> *"What I did was not for sexual pleasure.*
> *Rather it brought me some peace of mind."*
> ANDREI CHIKATILO

CHILDHOOD

See **Upbringing.**

CIVIL SERVANTS

S ay the phrase "disgruntled postal worker" these days and people immediately picture a wild-eyed madman mowing down his co-workers with an AK-47. For whatever reason, sorting and delivering mail seems to be an appealing line of work for potential mass murderers. Either that or there is something about the job that turns people into human time bombs.

To be fair to postal workers, theirs are not the only governmental ranks from which homicidal maniacs have sprung. In the late 1950s, a Scottish sociopath named Peter Manuel was holding down a civil service job with the City of Glasgow Gas Board. During his off-hours, however, Manuel was leading a sinister secret life. A lifetime criminal with a long record of convictions for offenses ranging from burglary to rape, Manuel murdered his first victim—a seventeen-year-old girl whose body he dumped on a golf course—in January 1956. Before long, he had slaughtered a total of eight people, including two entire families who were shot in their skulls as they slept in their beds at night.

Manuel's countryman, the notorious Dennis **Nilsen**—whose crimes bore a sickening resemblance to those of Jeffrey **Dahmer**—also worked as a civil servant. Employed by the British Manpower Services Commission, Nilsen was a dedicated professional who helped downtrodden young men find gainful work. By night, however, he was not assisting young men but preying on them. After having sex with one of his gay pickups, Nilsen would kill the young victim, then keep the rotting corpse around his flat for "companionship." When the decay became unbearable, Nilsen would finally dismember and dispose of the body.

Nilsen's monstrous career—which left fifteen victims dead— began in late 1978. Just one year earlier, the crimes of another notorious serial killer came to an end. In August 1977, the gun-crazy madman known as "Son of Sam" was apprehended after the biggest manhunt in New York City history. The public responded to his arrest with two equally intense emotions—relief at his capture and amazement at his identity. Instead of a slavering monster, the great boogeyman of the disco age turned out to be a pudgy-face nonentity named David **Berkowitz**, regarded by his fellow employees as a quiet, courteous nebbish.

Berkowitz's job?

He worked as a letter sorter for a post office branch in the Bronx.

CLANS

In our age of splintered homes, broken marriages, and latchkey children, it's heartwarming to read about the large, close-knit families of yesteryear, bound together by common interests and shared activities. Unless, of course, those interests and activities included serial murder, gang rape, and even cannibalism—as was the case with two notorious killer clans of the past, the Beanes and the Benders.

According to legend, Sawney Beane was a fifteenth-century Scottish peasant who grew fed up with farming and turned to highway robbery. With his hard-bitten common-law wife, he holed up in a seaside cavern on the Galloway coast and sired a large brood of children. Eventually, through incestuous mating, the family swelled to forty-eight members, who subsisted by preying on unwary travelers, devouring their flesh, and pickling the leftover meat in seawater.

No one knows how many people fell victim to this feral clan— estimates run as high as one thousand. To the local inhabitants, the cause of these disappearances was a mystery. Was it a pack of man-eating wolves? Or some supernatural creature? The truth finally came to light when a husband and wife, returning from a village fair, were attacked by the barbarous Beanes, who fell upon the woman, slit her throat, and began feasting on her flesh. A second party, coming upon this appalling scene, informed the authorities. Before long, King James led a party of four hundred troops to the Galloway coast, where the Beanes' unspeakable hideout—its walls hung with human body parts— was uncovered. The entire family was captured and executed, the men put to slow torture, the women burned alive at the stake.

In our own country, a fiendish family known as the "Bloody Benders" perpetrated a string of atrocities during the 1870s. Headed by a brutish patriarch, John, and his equally savage wife (known only as "Ma"), the Benders were German immigrants who settled on the rugged Kansas frontier, where they ran a crude ramshackle "hotel." More than a dozen weary travelers who stopped there for a meal or a good night's rest never made it any farther. While daughter Kate served the stranger his dinner, Papa Bender and his son, John Jr., would sneak up from behind and smash the unwary victim on the skull with a sledgehammer. Then the body would be stripped, robbed, and buried. When a posse finally searched the place, they found the remains of a dozen victims, including a little girl who had been brutally raped before being buried alive beneath her father's corpse. By the time these atrocities were uncovered, however, the Benders had already fled. To this day no one knows what became of them.

The old-fashioned tradition represented by the Benders and Beanes ("the family that slays together, stays together") has been perpetuated in our own era by a family named the McCrarys. A nomadic band of small-time robbers, the McCrarys committed a string of holdups from coast to coast during a yearlong spree in the early 1970s. Along the way, the three McCrary males (father Sherman, son Danny, and son-in-law Raymond Carl Taylor) abducted twenty-two young women—waitresses, salesclerks, customers—from the crime scenes, then raped them, shot them in the head, and ditched the bodies. Through it all, the two McCrary women—Mama Carolyn and daughter Ginger McCrary-Taylor—stood by their men. "I love my husband very much," declared Ginger after the vicious killer clan was apprehended. "And it never occurred to me to do anything other than to stay with him."

SAWNEY BEANE ON FILM

Actually, there *are* no films about Sawney Beane. Two commendable horror movies, however, have been loosely inspired by the man-eating exploits of the legendary Scottish clan of cannibals.

The scarier of the pair is Wes Craven's low-budget shocker, *The Hills Have Eyes* (1977), about a family of vacationing midwesterners whose station wagon breaks down in the California desert, where they are set upon by a clan of mutant cannibals whose members include a truly alarming character named Pluto (played by a truly alarming-looking actor, Michael Berryman).

Less intense—though still well worth seeing—is the 1972 British horror movie *Raw Meat* (also known as *Death Line*). During the 1800s (according to the film) a gang of laborers, digging a tunnel for the London subway, were trapped underground by a cave-in. Since saving them was too expensive, they were simply abandoned down there. The movie concerns their modern-day descendents, a clan of inbred cannibals who still dwell in the subterranean reaches of the London subway system, preying on unlucky commuters. In spite of its lurid title and premise, the movie—starring Donald Pleasence, with a cameo by Christopher Lee—is surprisingly restrained and even (pardon the expression) tasteful.

COLLEGE COURSES

N o, you can't go to school to learn how to become a serial killer. On the other hand, if you're a student at prestigious Amherst College, you can take Professor Austin Sarat's course entitled Murder. That is, if you can find a seat in the lecture hall.

Professor Sarat's course, which he first offered in the spring of 1995, has proved to be the most popular in Amherst history, surpassing even Human Sexuality. In its first semester, more than three hundred students—fully a fifth of the entire student body—enrolled in it.

Not that it's a Mickey Mouse course. On the contrary. The reading list consists of such heavyweight titles as Dostoyevsky's *Crime and Punishment*, Camus's *The Stranger*, and Shakespeare's *Macbeth*. As Professor Sarat points out, violence is not only an inescapable feature of life but a central theme of world literature. "You can't read your favorite Greek play or Shakespeare or Russian novel without confronting murder," he says. "This is a way to teach [students] the great books and moral reasoning."

Of course, not all of the class requirements are literary masterpieces. Among their other assignments, students are also required to watch segments of *Geraldo*, listen to Snoop Doggy Dogg's "Murder Was the Case," and attend screenings of *The Silence of the Lambs*, *Psycho*, and *Pulp Fiction*.

> *"We are a killing society, awash with violence. I told the students the first day that murder is a window into American culture."*
>
> PROFESSOR AUSTIN SARAT

COOLING-OFF PERIOD

See **Definition**.

COURTROOM THEATRICS

Given their bizarre psychological makeup, it's no wonder that when serial killers are brought to trial, they sometimes create outrageous scenes. After spending their lives in the shadows, like bugs under a rock, they suddenly find themselves thrust onto center stage, with an audience that (in the media age) can number in the millions. With the whole world watching, some of these psychos proceed to put on quite a show.

During his 1924 trial, Fritz **Haarmann**—the infamous "Vampire of Hanover," who murdered at least twenty-eight young boys by chewing through their throats—carried on like a talk show host. Puffing on a fat cigar, he heckled the witnesses and made frequent quips about his appalling crimes.

Haarmann's countryman, the German sex-murderer Rudolph Pleil, used his trial as a platform for establishing his lethal preeminence. Pleil was charged with the rape-murder of nine women. Possessed of a perverse vanity, Pleil was indignant at these accusations, insisting that he was actually responsible for twenty-eight homicides. At his trial, he demanded that the official transcript refer to him as *"der beste Totmacher"*—"the best death-maker."

At roughly the same time in America, the "Lonely Hearts Killers," Martha Beck and Raymond Fernandez, were on trial for a trio of killings, including the murder of a two-year-old child (see **Killer Couples**). At one point, the mountainous Beck—determined to demonstrate her undying love—detoured on her way to the witness stand to hurl herself into the arms of her skinny Latin lover (a scene not unlike the one in Walt Disney's *Fantasia* when the hippo ballerina dives into the arms of her reptilian dance partner).

Few trials, however, have been as outrageous as that of Charles **Manson** and his "family" of drug-crazed hippie assassins. Manson began the proceedings by marching into the courtroom with a big *X* carved into his forehead. "I have X-ed myself out of your world," was his lucid explanation for this bizarre self-mutilation. At the height of the trial's madness, Manson lunged at the judge and tried to assault him.

Since the psychology of serial killers is such an unholy blend of derangement and cunning, it's hard to know when their weird courtroom behavior is genuine and when they are just putting on an act. The latter may well have been the case in the trial of Andrei **Chikatilo**, the Russian "Mad Beast" who murdered, raped, and cannibalized over fifty young women and children. Chained inside an iron-barred cage—which was installed in the courtroom to protect him from the vengeful relatives of his victims—Chikatilo spent his time swaying autistically, spewing obscenities, baying at the judge, and shouting out insane remarks (at one point, he began yelling about his one-man battle against the Assyrian Mafia; at another, he claimed he was pregnant and lactating). If Chikatilo's behavior was a calculated act, designed to persuade observers of his legal insanity, it did not meet with success. He received the ultimate pan for his performance—a bullet to the back of the skull from a Russian executioner.

CULTS

In essence, a cult is a surrogate family, headed by a strong, charismatic leader who functions as a father substitute. Cult members are required to behave like obedient children and do whatever Daddy says—whether that involves committing mass suicide by swallowing poison-spiked Kool-Aid or committing serial murder.

Undoubtedly the most notorious crimes of the Aquarian Age were the Tate-LaBianca murders, carried out by Charles **Manson**'s renegade "family" of psycho-hippies. The crimes became a worldwide sensation, partly because of their appalling savagery—seven people butchered over two nights, including the pregnant actress, Sharon Tate. But equally unsettling were the killers themselves. Beginning as more-or-less typical "flower children"—part of the mass migration of drugged-out adolescents who drifted to California during the Summer of Love—they had been transformed into the pawns of a malevolent spellbinder willing to commit random slaughter at his whim.

According to some reports, Manson and his tribe dabbled in satanism. Ever since the 1960s, America has been terrified (and titillated) by reports of rampant devil worship, involving everything from ritual animal mutilation to the use of human "breed-

Charles Manson; from *52 Famous Murderers* trading cards (*Courtesy of Roger Worsham*)

ers"—fertile young women who are impregnated for the express purpose of producing sacrifical infants. If TV tabloid shows like *Geraldo* are to be believed, our country is full of satanic cults, generally made up of diabolical suburbanites or wild-eyed teens who receive their instructions from Lucifer by playing Black Sabbath records in reverse. Fortunately, most of these reports are nothing more than the quasi-pornographic fantasies of religious nuts or people who have watched one too many viewings of *Rosemary's Baby*. Devil cults that perform human sacrifice are blessedly rare. But they do exist—as a young man named Mark Kilroy was unlucky enough to discover in March 1987.

Kilroy, a twenty-one-year-old student at the University of Texas, was on spring vacation with some friends in Matamoros, Mexico, when he disappeared during an evening of bar hopping. His whereabouts remained a mystery until investigators were led to a remote ranch that served as the headquarters for a local drug-smuggling gang. The leader of this bloodthirsty crew was a self-styled sorcerer named Adolfo de Jesus Constanzo—aka *El Padrino* ("The Godfather")—who preached a hodgepodge of Cuban Santeria, Haitian Voodoo, Aztec Santismo, and an obscure African-derived religion called Palo Mayombe. Whenever a big drug deal was about to go down, Constanzo's cult would seek supernatural protection by sacrificing a human victim, whose heart and brain would be cooked in a cauldron and devoured in a cannibal feast. When the *federales* finally rounded up the gang, they found the mutilated remains of fifteen victims (including Kilroy) who had been sacrificed to the cult's crazy-quilt religion.

CULT OF DOOM

Your average modern-day thug tends to be a relatively scary character, particularly when he's armed with a 9mm handgun. Still, compared to the original Thugs—a notorious cult of killers that existed in India for at least six centuries—even a Mafia hitman seems like a wimp.

A secret society of robbers and murderers, the Thugs were devotees of the cannibal goddess Kali, in whose name they committed their innumerable crimes. The word *thug* itself is a bastardization of the Hindu word *thag*, meaning a rogue or deceiver. Deception was crucial to their murderous technique. Posing as innocent travelers, a group of Thugs would join up with a party of pilgrims or traders (their favorite targets). Then—after luring the party to a suitable spot—the Thugs would sneak up on their victims and strangle all of them at once while chanting prayers to the goddess. After mutilating and gutting the corpses, the killers would bury the bodies and hold a ritual feast on the graves.

Generation after generation of Thugs strangled countless victims throughout India. (Children of cult members were inducted into the society and taught the prescribed method of murder on clay dummies.) Finally, beginning in 1830, the British launched a virtual war on the Thugs, wiping out the death cult by 1860.

For sheer exotic evil, the Thugs are hard to beat; it's no surprise that two of the most colorful adventure films of all time have used these Kali-worshipping cultists as villains—-George Stevens's *Gunga Din* and Steven Spielberg's *Indiana Jones and the Temple of Doom*.

JEFFREY DAHMER

Jeffrey Dahmer; from *True Crime Trading Cards Series Two: Serial Killers and Mass Murderers;* art by Jon Bright. *(Courtesy of Jon Bright and Valarie Jones)*

Folklorists sometimes refer to "Forbidden Chamber" stories—tales about young men or women who, while exploring an ogre's castle, open a secret door and discover a roomful of butchered bodies. In 1991, this nightmare really happened—not in a decaying castle somewhere deep in the Black Forest but in a rundown apartment house in a seedy neighborhood of Milwaukee.

On the night of July 22, a dazed and terrified young man, with a pair of handcuffs dangling from one wrist, flagged down an MPD squad car. A "weird dude" had just tried to kill him, he told the police. His story led the officers to apartment no. 213 of a nearby building. Inside, they discovered a virtual warehouse of human remains. The sickening inventory included a human head sitting on a refrigerator shelf, skulls stashed in a closet, body parts packed in a blue plastic barrel, decomposed hands lying in a lobster pot, an assortment of bones stored in cardboard boxes, and a freezer full of viscera—lungs, livers, intestines, kidneys. There was also a collection of sickening Polaroids, including one of a male torso eaten away by acid from the nipples down. The occupant of this charnel house, a meek, soft-spoken young man named Jeffrey Dahmer, made no effort to conceal the stomach-churning evidence of his unspeakable crimes.

Dahmer had killed seventeen men in all, most of them young African Americans he had picked up in gay bars. He drugged them, strangled them, and dismembered their bodies with an electric saw. He ultimately confessed to the most unimaginable depravities, including cannibalism and necrophiliac rape (disembowelling a corpse and having sex with the viscera was one of his particular pleasures). On several occasions, he also performed makeshift lobotomies on his still-living victims, drilling holes in their skulls and injecting their brains with muriatic acid in an effort to turn them into **Zombies**.

Dahmer's deranged appetites went all the way back to his childhood. As a boy, he loved to collect and dissect roadkill and to butcher small creatures. Former acquaintances would recall finding cats and frogs nailed to trees in the woods behind the Dahmer home. On one occasion, some neighborhood boys came upon a dog's head impaled on a stick.

Dahmer progressed from **Animal Torture** to homicide at the age of eighteen, when—after picking up a young male hitchhiker and bringing him home for sex—he bludgeoned the young man to death, then dismembered the body and buried the parts in the woods. Two years later, Dahmer exhumed the decomposed remains, pulverized the bones with a sledgehammer, and scattered the pieces around the woods.

The "Milwaukee Monster" was ultimately sentenced to fifteen consecutive life sentences, amounting to a total of 936 years. But his prison term—and his life—came to an abrupt end in 1994, when he was beaten to death by a fellow inmate.

> *"I really screwed up this time."*
> **JEFFREY DAHMER,** to his father

DEATH WISH

It's obvious that, in one sense, *all* serial killers have a death wish—they wish to inflict death on as many people as possible. But many of them also have a death wish in the strict, Freudian sense of the term: a desire to bring about their own destruction. The long list of serial killers who have either committed or attempted suicide includes such notorious figures as Karl Denke, Georg Grossmann, Gary **Heidnik**, Joseph Kallinger, and Henry Lee **Lucas.**

Some of these psychopaths have killed themselves as a way of escaping the law. Joe Ball, the Florida hardcase who disposed of his unwanted lovers by feeding them to his pet alligators, put a bullet through his heart rather than submit to arrest (see **Alligators**). Leonard Lake—who built a torture bunker on his California ranch where he and his partner, Charles Ng, murdered an indeterminate number of victims—swallowed a cyanide capsule immediately after his arrest (see **Partners**).

By contrast, other serial killers fulfill their death wish by engineering their own capture and eventual execution. Six years after murdering and then cannibalizing a twelve-year-old girl, Albert **Fish** sent a note to her mother describing the crime. Though Fish scratched out the return address embossed on the envelope, he did such a halfhearted job that police had no trouble deciphering the address and tracking him down. The criminal career of serial sex-killer Bobby Joe Long came to an abrupt end when he simply let one of his kidnapped victims go. The young woman instantly went to the police and provided them with a detailed description of her abductor, his apartment, and his car. That some serial killers desperately want to be captured was made clear by the famous lipstick-scrawled plea that sex-killer William Heirens left on a bedroom wall—"For heaven's sake catch me before I kill more. I cannot control myself."

It's not very surprising that serial killers are often suicidal. Brought up by dreadfully abusive parents who fill them with the sense that all human beings—beginning with themselves—are just so much worthless garbage, serial killers are consumed with despair and self-loathing. After his conviction for first-degree murder, Harvey Murray Glatman—a sadistic creep who shot photos of his bound-and-gagged victims before strangling them to death—suggested that execution would be the most appropriate punishment. When the judge obliged by sentencing him to the gas chamber, Glatman remarked, "It's better this way. I knew this is the way it would be." Other serial killers—like Mormon-missionary-turned-child-killer Arthur Gary Bishop—have expedited their own deaths by refusing to appeal their death sentences. For killers like these, life becomes a growing nightmare. Eventually, they yearn for escape.

It is possible that the most famous of all serial killers, Jack the Ripper, fell into this category. Though his identity remains a mystery, the fact that his crimes ceased abruptly after his fifth and final atrocity suggests that—overwhelmed by revulsion at the growing horror of his deeds—the "Whitechapel Monster" took his own life.

Of course, given the bizarre psychology of serial killers, it's no surprise that some of them have welcomed death for other infinitely weirder reasons. According to certain accounts, Peter Kürten—the "Monster of Düsseldorf"—couldn't wait to be executed. Aroused since childhood by the sight and sound of spurting blood, Kürten claimed he would die a happy man if he could hear the blood gushing from his own neck stump at the moment of beheading.

DEFINITION

L ike certain other terms—*obscenity*, for example—*serial killing* is surprisingly tricky to define. Part of the problem is that police definitions tend to differ from popular conceptions. According to some experts, a serial killer is any murderer who commits more than one random slaying with a break between the crimes. There is certainly some validity to this viewpoint. If (for example) Ted **Bundy** had been caught after committing only a couple of atrocities, he wouldn't have gained worldwide notoriety—but he still would have been what he was: a demented personality capable of the most depraved acts of violence. Still, it's hard to think of someone as a serial killer unless he's killed a whole string of victims.

How many victims constitute a "string"? Again, it's hard to be precise. The most infamous serial killers—**Bundy**, **Gacy**, **Dahmer**, etc.—are the ones responsible for double-digit murders. Most experts seem to agree, however, that to qualify as a serial killer, an individual has to slay a minimum of *three* unrelated victims.

The notion of a *string* implies something else besides sheer number. A serial killer must perpetrate a number of random killings with an emotional "cooling-off" period between each crime. This hiatus—which can last anywhere from hours to years—is what distinguishes the serial killer from the **Mass Murderer**, the homicidal nut who erupts in an explosion of insane violence, killing a whole group of people all at once. Thus, the official FBI definition of serial homicide is "three or more separate events with an emotional cooling-off period between homicides, each murder taking place at a different location."

According to other definitions, however, there is another key element that must be present if a crime is to be considered the work of a true serial killer. One of the hotly debated issues among criminologists is whether there is such a thing as a *female* serial killer. Without doubt, there are many women who fit the loosest definition—people who commit more than one random killing over a period of time. For example, there are the so-called **Black Widows**, who bump off one hubby after another. There are lethal **Nurses** who quietly dispose of troublesome patients, often over the course of many years. There are homicidal **Housekeepers**, who go from job to job, sometimes wiping out entire families. What the crimes of such fatal females lack, however, is an element that makes the deeds of **Jack the Ripper**, Jeffrey **Dahmer**, John Wayne **Gacy**, etc., so profoundly nightmarish: an element of unspeakable sexual **Sadism**. According to many experts, true serial homicide always involves the savage violation and mutilation of the victim's body. In this view *serial killing* is essentially synonymous with **Lust Murder**.

In short, the definitions of serial murder run from the very broad ("any offender, male or female, who kills over time") to the highly specific ("three or more unrelated killings separated by a cooling-off period and involving sadistic, sexual violence"). But it's the latter defintion that most people (including us) have in mind when they use the phrase "serial killer."

COINING A PHRASE

In earlier times, psychopathic killers who butchered a succession of random victims were generally described in supernatural terms—demons, fiends, monsters. In the late 1800s, one ingenious journalist, searching for a way to describe the infamous Dr. H. H. **Holmes**, invented the term "multi-murderer"—a snappily alliterative coinage that never caught on. Other common terms used to describe these creatures include lust murderers, recreational killers, homicidal maniacs, and stranger-killers. But none of these seemed to capture the frightening new phenomenon that began plaguing America in the late 1960s.

Credit for the phrase "serial killer" goes to Special Agent Robert K. Ressler, one of the pioneers of the FBI's Behaviorial Science Unit (and an acknowledged model for the character Jack Crawford of Thomas Harris's *The Silence of the Lambs*). According to Ressler's account (published in his book, *Whoever Fights Monsters*), he was lecturing at the British Police Academy when one of the participants referred to "crimes in series." Impressed with the phrase, Ressler began using a variation—"serial killers"—in his classes at Quantico.

Ressler acknowledges another source, too: the old-time serial adventures (like *Flash Gordon* and *The Phantom*) that used to be part of kiddie movie matinees. Like a child left in a state of tense excitement after one of these weekly cliff-hangers, the serial killer can't wait to commit his next atrocity.

And his next. And his next . . .

ALBERT DeSALVO

In his short, deranged life, Albert DeSalvo acquired several nicknames. In his late twenties, he became known as the "Measuring Man," a serial sex-molester who went from door to door, posing as a scout for a modeling agency. If a woman fell for this line and invited him in, he would produce a tape measure and proceed to check out her assets—a ploy that allowed him to indulge his taste for crude sexual fondling.

A few years later, after serving a brief prison sentence, he progressed from molestation to rape, assaulting hundreds of women throughout New England during a two-year span in the early 1960s. During this period, he was known as the "Green Man," so-called because of the green work clothes he favored while committing his crimes.

It was his third nickname, however, that ensured him enduring infamy. In 1962, DeSalvo became known as the "Boston Strangler," a smooth-talking sadist who savagely murdered thirteen women during an eighteen-month reign of terror.

The product of an insanely brutal **Upbringing**, DeSalvo acquired an early taste for sadism. One of his favorite childhood pastimes was placing a starving cat in an orange crate with a puppy and watching the cat scratch the dog's eyes out. He got married while in the army and maintained a more-or-less normal facade as a husband and father, even while committing some of the most shocking crimes in American history. (Of course there were strains in the marriage. Among other things, DeSalvo was possessed of a demonic libido and demanded sex as often as six times a day.)

His earliest murder victims were elderly women. Each of them had willingly let her killer into her apartment. Posing as a building repairman, the glib, smooth-talking DeSalvo had no trouble gaining entrance. Besides raping and strangling the women, he enjoyed desecrating their corpses, sometimes by shoving bottles or broomsticks into their vaginas. After finishing with his victim, he would leave a grotesque signature, knotting his makeshift garrote (often a nylon stocking) into a big, ornamental bow beneath the dead woman's chin.

Toward the end of 1962, DeSalvo's MO suddenly changed. He began preying on much younger women. And his murders became even more vicious—and bizarre. In one instance, he stabbed his victim nearly two dozen times. He left another corpse propped against the headboard of her bed, a pink bow tied around her neck, a broomstick handle jutting from her vagina, and a Happy New Year's card resting against her left foot.

Eventually, DeSalvo was arrested not for the "Boston Strangler" murders but for one of the "Green Man" rapes. During a stint at a state mental hospital, however, he began boasting of his strangling career to a fellow inmate. Only then did authorities discover that they had unwittingly nabbed the infamous killer.

In the end, DeSalvo, was never punished for the "Boston Strangler" crimes. Through a deal struck by his lawyer—F. Lee Bailey—DeSalvo was spared the chair and given a life sentence for the "Green Man" rapes instead. Not that Bailey's efforts did DeSalvo much good in the end. He was stabbed to death by a fellow inmate in November 1973.

> *"Me? I wouldn't hurt no broads. I love broads."*
> ALBERT ''BOSTON STRANGLER'' DeSALVO

DISPOSAL

To get away with gruesome murder again and again, a serial killer has to possess a fairly high degree of fiendish cunning. Snaring a victim is the first challenge he has to meet. Once he has perpetrated his atrocities, he is faced with another, even more pressing problem—what to do with the remains. The solutions to this grisly dilemma range from the straightforward to the diabolically elaborate.

Some serial killers simply leave their victims where they lay, occasionally taking the time to wreak some grotesque indignity on the remains. For example, Albert **DeSalvo**, the "Boston Strangler," liked to tie big ornamental bows around the throats of his female victims, as though he were leaving a gift-wrapped present for the police.

DeSalvo's bizarre bow-tying practice made for an unmistakable "signature." Understandably enough, many other homicidal maniacs prefer to leave no trace of their identities at all. For some sociopaths, the simplest approach to corpse disposal is the best. Ted **Bundy**, the **Hillside Stranglers**, and the Green River Killer, for example, simply dumped the bodies of their victims out in the open—in forests, along riverbanks, on the slopes bordering freeways. Others made perfunctory attempts at concealment, burying the bodies in shallow graves, or shovelling dead leaves over the remains. John Wayne **Gacy** didn't even bother to leave home. He simply stuck the dead bodies of his young male victims under the crawl space of his house—at least until he ran out of room, at which point he began tossing them into a nearby river.

By contrast, there are some serial killers who go to great lengths to obliterate every trace of their victims, often by immersing the bodies in acid, covering them with **Quicklime**, or incinerating them in **Ovens**.

Then there are those serial killers whose disposal methods can best be described as wildly (if not insanely) unorthodox. Joe Ball, for example, got rid of his murdered mistresses by feeding their flesh to his pet **Alligators**, while the monstrous Fritz **Haarmann** chopped up his victims and sold their flesh to his neighbors, passing it off as black-market beef.

The longer a serial killer remains on the loose, of course, the more proficient he tends to become. With corpse disposal, as with most human skills, practice makes perfect. Special agents of the FBI's Behavioral Science Unit describe one serial killer who was thrown into a state of almost panicky confusion when faced with the ravaged remains of his first victim. By the time he committed his second homicide, he had already worked out a sophisticated disposal method, taking four painstaking hours to dismember the body in his bathroom before bagging up the parts and depositing them in supermarket Dumpsters.

Of course, there are some serial killers who prefer not to dispose of their victims at all. Both Dennis **Nilsen** and his American counterpart, Jeffrey **Dahmer**, were so desperate for companionship that they went to great, highly deranged lengths to keep the corpses close by. Of course, since both men occupied cramped apartments, even they had to face up to the fetid reality after a while and get rid of their rotting house guests. Nilsen's solution was sublime in its simplicity, if not entirely practical—he chopped up the bodies and flushed the chunks down the toilet, a method that eventually led to his arrest when the plumbing in his apartment building became clogged with gobs of decomposing human flesh.

> *"I got a dead body on my hands. People saw me come in here. How am I going to pack this one out? Am I gonna put it in a double bag or a sheet and carry it out of here? I figured the smaller the better. I chopped the body up, stuffed some in the refrigerator, dumped the guts in a vacant lot, throwing pieces here and there, whatever came out of the bag first. I was scared."*
>
> Anonymous serial killer,
> describing his first experience with body disposal

DOCTORS

From Dr. Jekyll to Dr. Lecter, the fiendish physician has long been a staple of horror fantasy. Unfortunately, this nightmarish figure is not just a figment of the pop imagination. The annals of crime contain notable examples of psychopathic M.D.'s who stand the Hippocratic Oath on its head by using their skills to do harm.

Given his dexterity at dissection, there has always been speculation that **Jack the Ripper**—the first and most famous of modern serial killers—was someone with surgical training. "Ripperologists" have come up with several candidates: a Russian doctor and homicidal maniac named Michael Ostrog, who ended up in a mental asylum; another Russian, Dr. Alexandr Pedachenko, described as a "criminal lunatic" exiled to London by the tsar's secret police; and an English surgeon named Stanley who allegedly confessed to the Whitechapel murders on his deathbed.

Jack's contemporary, H. H. **Holmes**, was America's original M.D.—i.e., Medical Deviate. After receiving his degree from the University of Michigan at Ann Arbor, Holmes made his way to Chicago, where he constructed his notorious "Murder Castle," complete with a basement dissection lab. Though Holmes worked as a pharmacist, not a physician, he was able to put

Herman Mudgett, aka Dr. H. H. Holmes; from *True Crime Trading Cards Series Two: Serial Killers and Mass Murderers;* art by **Jon Bright** *(Courtesy of Jon Bright and Valarie Jones)*

HERMAN MUDGETT

his surgical training to profitable use by selling the stripped and mounted skeletons of his victims to local anatomy schools.

At roughly the same time, a British psychopath named Thomas Neill Cream—who received his medical degree from Montreal's McGill University and did postgraduate work at the prestigious Royal College of Physicians and Surgeons at Edinburgh—was busily dispatching victims on both sides of the Atlantic. After killing several women through botched, illegal abortions, Dr. Cream—who was residing in Chicago at the time—poisoned his mistress's husband by lacing the man's epilepsy medicine with strychnine. Released after a ten-year stint in Joliet, he sailed for England, where he embarked on a career as a serial killer of prostitutes—poisoning five London streetwalkers before he was caught, tried, and hanged in 1892. Dr. Cream is regarded as another Ripper candidate, since he is reputed to have cried, "I am Jack the—" just as he plunged through the trapdoor of the gallows.

Fifty years later and across the English Channel, residents of the Rue Le Sueur in Paris were assaulted by an overpowering stench issuing from a neighborhood building. When firemen broke in, they were horrified to discover a stack of dismembered bodies decomposing in the basement. The building, it turned out, belonged to Dr. Marcel **Petiot**, who claimed that the corpses were those of Nazi collaborators killed by the Resistance. It wasn't until the war ended that the appalling truth emerged: the victims were actually wealthy French Jews, desperate to flee Nazi-occupied France. Posing as a Resistance member who would smuggle them to freedom—for a fee—Petiot arranged to have the unsuspecting victims arrive at his house with all their valuables. Then he would administer an "immunization shot"— actually a lethal injection of strychnine—lock them in a chamber (where, through a peephole, he could watch them die in agony), appropriate their belongings, and dispose of their remains in his furnace. Unrepentant to the end, Dr. Petiot went to the guillotine with a smile in 1946.

One of the most remarkable of medical monsters is the Swedish physician Dr. Teet Haerm, who killed and dismembered at least nine women in the mid-1980s. In a horrifically ironic twist, Dr. Haerm—who served as the medical examiner for the Stockholm police—actually performed autopsies on several of his own victims.

ESCAPE

With their diabolical cunning, serial killers are often able to elude the law for long periods of time—months, years, sometimes forever (see **Whereabouts Unknown**). There have also been a number of notorious serial killers who have been captured after massive manhunts, only to pull off successful escapes.

Back in the 1920s, when Harry Houdini was wowing audiences by miraculously extricating himself from submerged steamer trunks, buried coffins, and other apparently escape-proof receptacles, Earle Leonard **Nelson**, the so-called "Gorilla Murderer," contrived some impressive feats of his own. Sentenced to a state mental asylum, he managed to break out so often that the authorities finally gave up trying to recapture him. In 1926, Nelson embarked on his lethal career as a serial rapist and strangler, a terrifying figure who came to be known as the "Gorilla Murderer." After committing a score of murders across the United States, he made his way up into Canada, where the police finally apprehended him. Nelson was taken to Killarney jail, stripped of his boots, and tossed into a double-locked cell. Left unguarded for fifteen minutes, he somehow managed to escape, setting off a citywide panic and the largest manhunt in Manitoba history, which ended when he was recaptured less than twelve hours later.

Perhaps the most fear-provoking escape ever engineered by a serial killer occurred in 1967 when Albert **DeSalvo**, the "Boston Strangler," slipped out of custody. Countless women barricaded themselves in their homes as terror gripped New England. As it turned out, however, DeSalvo's escape was a symbolic act, not a serious attempt to break free and resume his career of crime. DeSalvo was unhappy with his lack of psychiatric treatment, and the escape was his way of protesting. When police finally caught up with him, he made no effort to resist.

Just one year earlier, a psychopathic runt named Charles Schmid, who came to be known as the "Pied Piper of Tucson," was sentenced to fifty-five years in prison for the rape-murder of a fifteen-year-old girl, one of his three teenaged victims. Five years after his conviction, Schmid managed to break out of prison. Before he was recaptured a few days later, there were some very nervous people in Arizona. At his trial, Schmid had vowed to "get the people" who had testified against him.

One of the most cunning of all modern serial killers was Ted **Bundy.** In January 1977, Bundy was extradited to Colorado to stand trial for murder. Since Bundy (who had been a law student in Utah) insisted on overseeing his own defense, he was allowed access to the law library at the Pitkin County courthouse in Aspen. On the morning of June 7, 1977, after being left alone in the library for a few minutes, Bundy leapt to freedom through an open second-story window. He was back in custody a few days later, but in late December of that year, he managed to saw a hole in the ceiling of his jail cell and escape. This time, he eluded the authorities for more than a month. Before he was captured again, in mid-February 1978, he had made his way to Florida and brutally murdered three more young women.

EXECUTIONS

Back in the old days—when public executions were a major form of popular entertainment—putting a serial killer to death was quite a production. When the fifteenth-century cutthroat Sawney Beane was finally brought to justice, he and all the other male members of his cannibal clan had their hands and legs chopped off. Then the women were tossed into three blazing bonfires after being forced to watch their men bleed to death. All this, of course, took place before a large crowd of eager spectators. (For more details on the bestial Beanes, see **Clans.**)

A century or so later, in the late-sixteenth century, a German serial killer named Peter Stubbe committed such unspeakable deeds that he was regarded as a literal werewolf. (Among his other atrocities, Stubbe murdered his own son, then cracked open the boy's skull and devoured his brain.) When Stubbe was finally arrested, authorities meted out a punishment commensurate with his crimes. After being tortured on the rack, he was broken on the wheel. Then red-hot pincers were used to tear out chunks of his flesh, his arms and legs were crushed with an axe head, then his head was cut off and his body incinerated.

As everyone knows, of course, we live in a much less barbarous age. Nowadays, even a creature like John Wayne **Gacy** ends up being treated like a beloved, ailing pet—put to sleep by lethal injection. Still there have been exceptions. Unsurprisingly, one particularly nasty exception occurred under the most barbarous regime of modern times. Between 1928 and 1943, a German laundry deliveryman named Bruno Ludke murdered as many as eighty women. Nazi officials repeatedly bungled the investigation, but when they finally caught up with Ludke, they reacted with characteristic brutality. Bypassing the usual channels, they shipped him off to a "research hospital" in Vienna, where he was used as a human guinea pig. Only when the Nazi torture doctors were done with him was Ludke excuted by lethal injection.

Of course, when you're dealing with serial killers, it's not always clear that putting them to death is a form of punishment. Some of these maniacs actually look forward to the experience. Ludke's countryman Peter **Kürten**—the so-called "Monster of Düsseldorf"—couldn't wait to be beheaded; the sound of his own gushing blood, he claimed, would be a source of ultimate pleasure. The American child-killer Albert **Fish** seemed to feel the same way. Fish was not only a sadistic killer but also a world-class masochist, who enjoyed shoving sewing needles into his groin (among other extravagant forms of self-abuse). When Fish was given the death sentence for the savage murder of a twelve-year-old girl, the newspapers quoted him as saying, "What a thrill it will be to die in the electric chair! It will be the supreme thrill—the only one I haven't tried!"

FAN CLUBS

Though many serial killers, even some of the most repugnant, have attracted **Groupies**, few possess enough broad-range appeal to generate fan clubs. The single exception (so far as we know) is Ed **Gein**, Wisconsin's most notorious native son. Undoubtedly because of his unique status as the most influential psychokiller since **Jack the Ripper**, Gein—whose ghoulish crimes inspired *Psycho*, *The Texas Chainsaw Massacre*, and *The Silence of the Lambs*—has attracted a sizable worldwide cult-following.

Evidence of Gein's appeal is the burgeoning membership of the Official International Ed Gein Fan Club, founded by the enterprising Damon Fox of Foxx Entertainment (see **Cards, Comics, and Collectibles**). For a modest induction fee of $9.95, each new member receives a rare facsimile of Gein's official death certificate, Xerox copies of his obituaries, a scholarly monograph comparing Gein to his splatter-movie counterpart, Leatherface, and a handsome, suitable-for-framing membership certificate personally signed by President Fox. Membership benefits include advance notification of upcoming Gein-related events and the opportunity to correspond with other Gein-o-philes around the globe.

For information, write to: Foxx Entertainment Enterprises, 327 West Laguna, Tempe, Arizona 85282.

FANTASY

Though we're sometimes loath to admit it (even to ourselves), everyone harbors socially unacceptable thoughts—forbidden dreams of sex and violence. There's a big difference, though, between the fantasies of serial killers and those of ordinary people. For one thing, the former are a whole lot sicker. An average guy might imagine himself making love to a super-model. The serial killer, on the other hand, will think obsessively

CERTIFICATE OF MEMBERSHIP

This certifies that _____ is a member
in good standing of

THE
OFFICIAL INTERNATIONAL
ED GEIN FAN CLUB

and has been registered as an Official Member entitled to all
membership benefits.

Certified this _____ day of _____ .

President
Official International
Ed Gein Fan Club

OFFICIAL MEMBER
ED GEIN FAN CLUB

Official Ed Gein Fan Club membership certificate and lapel pin. *(Courtesy of Damon Fox)*

about shackling her to a wall, then slicing up her body with a hunting knife.

There's a second, even scarier difference: unlike a normal person (who might indulge in an occasional daydream about, say, hiring a hitman to bump off his boss), serial killers aren't satisfied with *thinking* about taboo behavior. They are compelled to act out their fantasies—to turn their darkest imaginings into real-life horrors.

People who grow up to be serial killers begin indulging in fantasies of sadistic activity at a disturbingly young age—sometimes as early as seven or eight. While their peers are pretending to be sports stars or superheroes, these incipient psychopaths are already daydreaming about murder and mayhem. Interviewed in prison after his arrest, one serial killer explained that as a child he spent so much time daydreaming in class that his teachers always noted it on his report cards. "And what did you daydream about?" asked the interviewer. His answer: "Wiping out the whole school."

Another serial killer recalled that his favorite make-believe game as a little boy was "gas chamber," in which he pretended to be a condemned prisoner undergoing an agonizing execution. Fantasizing about a slow, painful death was a source of intense boyhood pleasure to this budding psycho.

Unlike other people, the serial killer never outgrows his childhood fantasies. On the contrary. Cut off from normal human relationships, he sinks deeper and deeper into his private world of grotesque imaginings. From the outside, he might appear perfectly well adjusted—a hard worker, good neighbor, and all-around solid citizen. But all the while, bizarre, blood-drenched dreams are running rampant inside his head.

Since psychopaths lack the inner restraints that prevent normal people from acting out their hidden desires, there is nothing to keep a serial killer from trying to make his darkest dreams come true. Eventually, this is exactly what happens. His perverted fantasies of dominance, degradation, and torture become the fuel that sets his crimes in motion. For this reason, former FBI agent Robert K. Ressler—the man who coined the term "serial killer"—insists that it is not child abuse or early trauma that turns people into serial killers. It is their dreams.

As Ressler puts it, creatures like Ted **Bundy**, John Wayne **Gacy**, and their ilk are "motivated to murder by their fantasies."

FBI

J. Edgar Hoover's G-men earned their reputation by battling such Depression-era outlaws as John Dillinger and Pretty Boy Floyd. But compared to today's serial killers, those tommy gun-toting badmen of yore seem almost quaint. To combat the growing threat of random violence in America, the Bureau has had to come up with sophisticated new crime-fighting techniques.

Beginning in the late 1970s, agents of the FBI's Behavioral Science Unit (BSU) (headquartered at the Bureau's Training Academy on the Quantico marine base in eastern Virginia) embarked on the Criminal Personality Research Project—an ambitious effort to probe into the minds of serial murderers. Traveling to prisons throughout the United States, these agents (whose forensic feats have been immortalized in the megahit movie *The Silence of the Lambs*) interviewed nearly forty of America's most notorious figures, including Ed **Gein**, Charles **Manson**, Richard **Speck**, David **Berkowitz**, John Wayne **Gacy**, and Ted **Bundy**. Flattered by the Bureau's attention, most of these killers were happy to chat about themselves. The insights gained from this survey enabled the BSU to devise a revolutionary "criminal personality profiling" method that has proven to be a major new weapon in the fight against violent crime (see **Profiling**).

With serial killings multiplying at an alarming rate, the FBI perceived the need for a national clearinghouse that would provide assistance to police officers throughout the country in their efforts to solve the most monstrous and baffling of murders. The result was the creation of the National Center for the Analysis of Violent Crimes (NCAVC), designed for the express purpose (as Ronald Reagan put it when he announced its establishment in June 1984) of "identifying and tracking repeat killers." Administered by the Behavioral Science Unit, NCAVC not only offers its Criminal Profiling service to stymied police agencies throughout the country but also serves as the world's leading resource center for the pursuit and capture of serial killers.

Besides profiling, the most powerful weapon in NCAVC's arsenal is the Violent Criminal Apprehension Program (VICAP), the brainchild of a former Los Angeles homicide detective named Pierce Brooks. Back in the late 1950s, Brooks was investigating a brutal murder that seemed to be the work of a veteran killer who kept on the move. Having hit a dead end in his investigation, Brooks decided to see if there were other unsolved homicides in the country with similar characteristics. Unfortunately, there was only one way to check—by going to the public library during his off-hours and plowing through newspapers from around the United States. It took him a solid year to find what he was looking for—a case in Ohio that bore all the earmarks of the the LA crime.

Perceiving the need for a more efficient way of tracking America's growing population of elusive, highly mobile killers, Brooks came up with the concept of a nationwide, computerized network designed to collate and provide leads on thousands of unsolved crimes. As a result of Brooks's efforts, VICAP finally became operational in 1985.

VICAP has had some problems: serious underfunding and the reluctance of local police to fill out the hellishly complex forms on their unsolved crimes. But the forms have been simplified, and the program received a major infusion of money from Con-

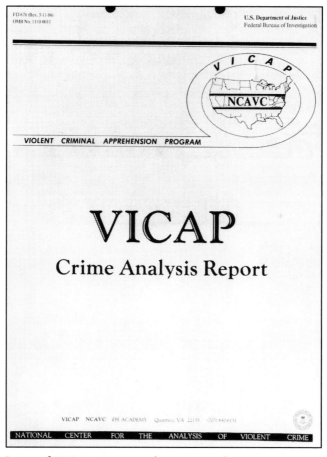

Cover of VICAP crime analysis report form

gress in 1994. If VICAP lives up to its potential, creatures like Ted **Bundy** might soon go the way of other obsolete scourges, like leprosy and the black plague.

TALES OF THE "PSYCHE SQUAD"

Two founding members of NCVAC—Robert K. Ressler and John Douglas—have published gripping accounts of their experiences. Readers interested in learning more about the Bureau's crack team of criminal personality profilers (aka the "Psyche Squad") shouldn't fail to check out *Whoever Fights Monsters* by Robert K. Ressler and Tom Schachtman (New York: Simon & Schuster, 1992) and *Mindhunter: Inside the FBI's Elite Serial Crime Unit* by John Douglas and Mark Olshaker (New York: A Lisa Drew Book/Scribner, 1995). Also recommended: H. Paul Jeffers's *Who Killed Precious?* (New York: St. Martin's, 1992), a lively, behind-the-scenes look at the history and operations of the FBI's Behavorial Science Unit.

FETISH OBJECTS

See **Trophies.**

ALBERT FISH

Albert Fish; from *True Crime Trading Cards Series Two: Serial Killers and Mass Murderers;* art by Jon Bright *(Courtesy of Jon Bright and Valarie Jones)*

ALBERT FISH

Albert Fish has been called "America's boogeyman"—and for good reason. A cannibal ogre in the guise of a kindly old man, he was every parent's worst nightmare: a fiend who lured children to destruction with the promise of a treat.

The crime that brought Fish to public attention was the 1928 kidnapping-murder of a pretty twelve-year-old girl named Grace Budd. After befriending her parents, Fish made up a diabolical lie. He said that his niece was having a birthday party and asked if Grace would like to go. Mr. and Mrs. Budd—who had no way of knowing that the grandfatherly old man was a monster—agreed.

Dressed in her Sunday finest, the trusting little girl went off with Fish, who led her to an isolated house in a northern suburb of New York City. There, he strangled her, butchered her body, and carried off several pounds of her flesh. Back in his lodgings, he turned her "meat" (as he called it) into a cannibal stew, complete with carrots, onions, and bacon strips. He spent the next nine days locked in his room, savoring this unholy meal and compulsively masturbating.

For the next six years, Fish remained at large, but throughout this time he was doggedly pursued by a New York City detective named William King, who had made the Grace Budd case his personal crusade. Even so, Fish probably would have gotten away with the crime if it hadn't been for his own inner demons. In 1934, he felt compelled to send Mrs. Budd one of the sickest **Letters** ever written. In the end, King was able to track down his quarry through the letterhead stationery Fish had used.

Once Fish was in custody, authorities quickly realized that they had their hands on a killer of unimaginable depravity, one who had spent his whole lifetime inflicting pain—on himself as well as on others. Like a number of serial killers, Fish was a religious maniac, and he subjected himself to grotesque forms of torture as penance for his sins—flagellating himself with leather straps and nail-studded paddles, eating his own excrement, shoving sewing needles up into his groin. The children he mutilated and murdered were, in his demented eyes, sacrificial offerings to the Lord. Noted New York City psychiatrist Dr. Frederic Wertham—who was called in by the defense to examine Fish—declared that the old man had practiced "every sexual perversion known," as well as a few that no one had ever heard of (among his grotesque pleasures, Fish liked to insert rose stems into his urethra). X rays of his pelvic region taken in prison revealed that there were twenty-nine needles lodged around his bladder.

Though the jury at his 1935 trial acknowledged that he was insane, they believed he should be electrocuted anyway. After receiving the death sentence, the bizarre old man reportedly exclaimed, "What a thrill it will be to die in the electric chair! It will be the supreme thrill—the only one I haven't tried!"

On January 16, 1936, the sixty-five-year-old Fish went to the chair— the oldest man ever put to death in Sing Sing.

FOREIGNERS

America may no longer be the world's leading manufacturer of cars, cameras, and color TVs, but we're still way ahead of the pack when it comes to serial killers. Not only do we turn them out in far greater quantity than any other civilized nation; we've also produced most of the really big-name psychos of the late twentieth century: **Manson**, **Bundy**, **Gacy** et al. Still, it would be the height of chauvinism to believe that the United States of America is the only country capable of creating homicidal sex-maniacs.

From the days of **Jack the Ripper**, England has been home to lots of serial killers (see **Rippers**). France, too, has produced its fair share—from Joseph **Vacher** to Dr. Marcel **Petiot** to Thierry Paulin (the "Monster of Montmartre," who murdered at least twenty old ladies in the mid-1980s). Some of the most monstrous lust murderers in history, including Peter **Kürten** and Fritz **Haarmann**, were born and bred in Germany. And—though Soviet officials like to claim that serial murder was strictly a function of capitalistic decadence—their position was somewhat undermined when the victims of Andrei **Chikatilo**, the "Beast of Rostov," began piling up.

For such a sparsely populated country, Australia has turned out a surprising number of serial killers, including "Granny Killer" John Wayne Glover, Edward Leonski (aka the "Singing Strangler"), and William McDonald, the "Sydney Mutilator." Belgium would be the last place on earth you'd expect to find a serial killer, but during the 1930s, a serial poisoner named Marie Becker knocked off a dozen people. (Becker had a knack for picturesque descriptions. During her trial, she told the judge that one of her female victims resembled "an angel choked on sauerkraut.")

Perhaps the most prolific killer in history was South American Pedro Lopez, the "Monster of the Andes," who was responsible for the deaths of as many as three hundred young girls in Ecuador, Colombia, and Peru. The Japanese take justifiable pride in the safety of their society, but during the 1940s a former naval officer named Yoshio Kodaira confessed to the rape-murder of seven women.

From the Netherlands to New Zealand, Scotland to South Africa, serial murder is clearly an international phenomenon. To paraphrase the song, it's an appalling world after all.

HORROR IN SOUTH AFRICA

In the fall of 1995, the bodies of a dozen women were found in a field in Boksburg, South Africa, a suburb of Johannesburg. The field was strewn with a bizarre assortment of objects—knives, mirrors, crosses, burned Bibles, dead birds stuck with pins like voodoo dolls.

Police immediately suspected that these so-called "Boksburg Murders" were connected to other recent atrocities: the slaying of fourteen women and a child near Pretoria the preceding spring, and the murder of sixteen more women in the suburb of Cleveland, just east of Johannesburg. In most of these cases, the victims were young black women who had apparently been abducted on the way to school or work, then raped and strangled with their own purse straps or clothing.

If one individual was indeed responsible for all these crimes, then—as of September 1995—he had already claimed a total of forty-three victims, making him one of the worst serial killers in history.

To help track down the unknown slayer, South African authorities called in former FBI Special Agent Robert K. Ressler, one of the founders of VICAP, who now works as a freelance consultant (see **Coining a Phrase**). Ressler—who felt convinced that the case would eventually be cracked—came up with the following profile: "a black male, twenty-five to thirty-five years old, an eye-catching dresser with a flashy car who charms his victims into entering the vehicle willingly."

Only the previous year, another South African serial killer—the so-called "Station Strangler," who was responsible for the murder of twenty-two boys—had been convicted. (He turned out to be a Cape Town schoolteacher.) And on the very day that the *New York Times* reported the discovery of the Boksburg Murders, the police were questioning a twenty-eight-year-old suspect in connection with yet another serial murder case, the killing of fourteen women near Donnybrook, two hundred miles southeast of Johannesburg.

As the *New York Times* reported in a piece on this sudden surge of serial murder: "South Africa has entered the big time of modern crime."

WAS JACK THE RIPPER REALLY A YANK?

Forget Shakespeare, Churchill, and the Beatles. As far as crime buffs are concerned, the most significant Englishman of all time was Jack the Ripper. There's only one problem with this belief. According to a pair of writers named Stewart Evans and Paul Gainey, Saucy Jack was really an American!

In their 1995 book, *The Lodger: The Arrest and Escape of Jack the Ripper*, Evans and Gainey argue that the legendary "Whitechapel Monster" was actually an Irish-American quack, Dr. Francis Tumberty. A bizarre personality who had once been arrested for the assassination of Abraham Lincoln, Tumberty was a self-confessed woman hater. He had developed a grudge against the opposite sex after discovering that his wife was moonlighting as a prostitute. Among his other eccentricities, he kept a personal collection of preserved female organs, which he liked to display to his guests during dinner parties.

While residing in London in the late 1880s, Tumberty became a prime suspect in the Ripper crimes. Arrested in mid-November, 1888—just days after what turned out to be the last of the Whitechapel murders—he was held for a week before being bailed out by loyal employees. Hopping a steamer back to the States, he holed up in his Manhattan apartment, then disappeared again with Scotland Yard inspectors still hot on his trail. Not long afterward, a series of grisly prostitute murders—identical in method to the Whitechapel slayings—occurred in Jamaica and later in Managua, Nicaragua. Evans and Gainey believe that Tumberty was responsible, making him "the world's first traveling serial killer."

John Wayne Gacy; from *Murderers!* trading card set *(Courtesy of Roger Worsham)*

13. JOHN WAYNE GACY

John Wayne Gacy was a man of many masks. There was the mask of masculinity. To live up to the two-fisted name bestowed by his tyrannical father, Gacy cultivated a gruff, swaggering air. There was the mask of middle-class respectability, symbolized by his tidy ranch-style house in a Chicago suburb. He even wore a literal mask, making himself up as a grinning clown called Pogo to entertain hospitalized children.

But Gacy was one of the most monstrously divided sociopaths in the annals of crime, and his masks concealed a hideous reality. Beneath his "man's man" persona, he was a tormented, self-loathing homosexual who preyed on young males. Beneath the smiling face, he was a leering, implacable sadist. Beneath the crawl space of his suburban house, more than two dozen corpses moldered in the slime.

Raised by an abusive, alcoholic father—who spent much of his time deriding his son as a sissy—Gacy grew up to be a pudgy hypochondriac whose homosexual drives were a source of profound self-hatred. He also possessed a terrifyingly antisocial personality.

For a long time, however, he managed to conceal his real character beneath the veneer of an ambitious middle-American businessman. By the time he was twenty-two, he was a married man and father, a highly respected member of the Junior Chamber of Commerce, and the successful manager of a Kentucky Fried Chicken outlet in Waterloo, Iowa. But he was also leading a secret life as a seducer and molester of young males. In 1968, after being arrested on a sodomy charge, he was hit with a ten-year sentence, though he proved to be such a model prisoner that he was paroled after only eighteen months.

Gacy—whose first wife had divorced him on the day of his sentencing—relocated to Chicago, where he soon reestablished himself as an apparent pillar of the community, remarrying, starting a thriving contracting business, becoming active in local politics (on one occasion, he was photographed shaking hands with First Lady Rosalynn Carter). Before long, however, his darkest impulses reasserted themselves—this time in an even ghastlier form. He became a human predator who tortured and murdered his young male pickups for his own depraved pleasure.

Cruising the streets for hustlers, drifters, and runaways, Gacy (who sometimes coerced them into his car by posing as a plainclothes cop) would bring them back to his house. There he would handcuff them and then subject them to hours of rape and torture before strangling them slowly. Their bodies would end up in the crawl space.

In 1978, police finally set their sights on the civic-minded contractor when a teenage boy dropped out of sight after telling friends that he was on his way to see Gacy about a job. Digging into Gacy's past, police uncovered records of his previous sex offenses. In the fetid muck of his crawl space, they exhumed the decomposing remains of twenty-seven victims. Gacy had buried two more elsewhere on his property and dumped another four corpses in a nearby river, bringing the number of his victims to thirty-three.

At first, Gacy maintained that he was the victim of multiple personality disorder, and that his atrocities were actually the work of an evil alter ego named Jack. But the ploy didn't work. He was given the death sentence in 1980. After fourteen years on death row, the "Killer Clown" was finally executed by lethal injection.

EDWARD GEIN

Ed Gein
(AP/Wide World Photos)

If a serial killer is defined as someone who murders at least three victims over an extended period of time, then—strictly speaking—Edward Gein was not a serial killer, since he appears to have murdered no more than two women. And yet his crimes were so grotesque and appalling that they have haunted America for almost forty years.

Gein was raised by a fanatical, domineering mother who ranted incessantly about the sinful nature of her own sex. When she died in 1945, her son was a thirty-nine-year-old bachelor, still emotionally enslaved to the woman who had tyrannized his life. Boarding up her room, he preserved it as though it were a shrine. The rest of the house, however, soon degenerated into a madman's shambles.

When Gein wasn't earning his meager living doing odd jobs for neighbors, he passed his lonely hours poring over lurid magazine pieces about sex-change opertions, South Sea headhunters, and Nazi atrocities. His own atrocities began a few years after his mother's death. Driven by his desperate loneliness—and burgeoning psychosis—he started making nocturnal raids on local graveyards, digging up the bodies of middle-aged

101

women and bringing them back to his remote farmhouse. In 1954, he augmented his necrophiliac activities with murder, shooting a local tavernkeeper named Mary Hogan and absconding with her two-hundred-pound corpse. Three years later—on the first day of hunting season, 1957—he killed another local woman, a fifty-eight-year-old grandmother who owned the village hardware store.

Ed Gein exhuming a corpse, art by Chris Pelletierre

Suspicion immediately lighted on Gein, who had been hanging around the store in recent days. Breaking into his summer kitchen, police discovered the victim's headless and gutted corpse suspended upside-down from a rafter like a dressed-out game animal. Inside the house itself, the stunned searchers uncovered a large assortment of unspeakable artifacts—chairs upholstered with human skin, soup bowls fashioned from skulls, a shoebox full of female genitalia, faces stuffed with newspapers and mounted like hunting trophies on the walls, and a "mammary vest" flayed from the torso of a woman. Gein later confessed that he enjoyed dressing himself in this and other human-skin garments and pretending he was his own mother.

The discovery of these Gothic horrors sent shock waves throughout Eisenhower-era America. In Wisconsin itself, Gein quickly entered local folklore. Within weeks of his arrest, macabre **Jokes** called "Geiners" became a statewide craze. The country as a whole learned about Gein in December 1957, when both *Life* and *Time* magazines ran features on his "house of horrors."

After ten years in a mental hospital, Gein was judged competent to stand trial. He was found guilty but insane and institutionalized for the rest of his life, dying of cancer in 1984.

By then, however, Gein had already achieved pop immortality, thanks to horror writer Robert **Bloch**, who had the inspired idea of creating a fictional character based on Gein—a deranged mama's boy named Norman Bates. In 1960, Alfred Hitchcock transformed Bloch's pulp chiller, *Psycho*, into a cinematic masterpiece. Insofar as *Psycho* initiated the craze for "slasher" movies, Gein is revered by horror buffs as the "Grandfather of Gore," the prototype of every knife-, axe-, and cleaver-wielding maniac who has stalked America's movie screens for the past thirty years.

ED GEIN, SUPERSTAR

ED GEIN

Ed Gein; from *True Crime Trading Cards Series Two: Serial Killers and Mass Murderers;* art by Jon Bright *(Courtesy of Jon Bright and Valarie Jones)*

Ed Gein's ghoulish crimes have served as the inspiration for the three most terrifying films of the past thirty years: *Psycho*, *The Texas Chainsaw Massacre*, and *The Silence of the Lambs*.

103

Though Robert **Bloch**, the original author of *Psycho*, insisted that his book was not simply a fictionalized version of Gein's crimes, his immortal character, Norman Bates, was clearly inspired by Gein. (Indeed, in Bloch's original novel, Norman himself points out the parallels between his own crimes and Gein's.)

Tobe Hooper, the director of *The Texas Chainsaw Massacre*, reportedly heard stories about Gein from midwestern relatives and grew up haunted by these tales. In his splatter-movie classic, the Gein-inspired character is not a mild-mannered motel keeper with a split personality but a bestial hulk named Leatherface, who sports a mask made of dried human flesh.

Thomas Harris researched the FBI's files on Gein before creating his fictional serial killer Jame Gumb (aka "Buffalo Bill"), a transsexual wannabe who attempts to fashion a suit from the flayed torsos of his victims. Jonathan Demme's Oscar-winning movie version relied on Harold Schechter's book *Deviant: The Shocking True Story of the Original "Psycho"* to create the squalid look of Gumb's Gein-inspred house.

Psycho, *Chainsaw*, and *Silence* all take considerable liberties with the Gein story. The film that sticks closest to the facts is a 1974 low-budget shocker called *Deranged*, which has developed a major cult following among horror buffs. Some video versions of *Deranged* are prefaced by a brief documentary on Gein called *A Nice Quiet Man*, which includes the only known footage of some of his hideous human-flesh artifacts.

GRAVE ROBBING

See **Necrophilia**.

> *"Every man to his own tastes. Mine is for corpses."*
> HENRI BLOT

GROUPIES

F ame can be a powerful aphrodisiac—even when a person is famous for committing serial murder. Celebrity killers have attracted groupies for at least a century. During a ten-day span in 1895, a handsome San Francisco medical student and Sunday school teacher named Theo Durrant—the Ted **Bundy** of his day—lured two young women into an empty church, then murdered them and raped their corpses, leaving one body inside the church library, the other in the belfry. Durrant's trial was a nationwide sensation, exerting a morbid fascination on people from coast to coast. A young woman named Rosalind Bowers, however, carried her fascination to what most observers felt was an unseemly extreme. Virtually every day of the trial, the dainty Miss Bowers appeared in court with a bouquet of sweet pea flowers, which she presented to the "Demon of the Belfry" as a gesture of support. Before long, Miss Bowers had gained a measure of celebrity herself, being dubbed by the papers the "Sweet Pea Girl."

In the century since the Durrant case, high-profile serial killers have continued to attract almost as many groupies as rock stars. While some of these murderers have possessed a certain superficial charm (like Bundy) others have been seriously repellent (John Wayne **Gacy**, for example) or just plain over-the-top bizarre (like Richard the "Night Stalker" **Ramirez**). But no matter how loathsome or grotesque the killer, there have always been women who considered him a dreamboat. Even Ed **Gein**—a dim-witted, middle-aged necrophiliac with the approximate sexual magnetism of Gomer Pyle—received frequent letters from women begging for locks of his hair.

One of the most startling examples of this strange erotic phenomenon came to light only recently with the publication of the book *Love Letters to Adolf Hitler*, culled from the collection of a man named William Emker. Shortly after the end of World War II, Emker—then a U.S. Army officer—was searching through Hitler's bombed-out headquarters when he came upon a trove of letters written to the Führer by female admirers. "Sweetest love," one typical letter begins, "favorite of my heart, my dearest, my truest and hottest beloved. I could kiss you a thousand times and still not be satisfied. My love for you is endless, so tender, so hot and so complete." Emker found thousands of missives like this one, addressed to "My darling, sugar-sweet Adolf," "My beloved Führer," or sometimes simply, "Dear Adi." The fact that the greatest mass murderer of the twentieth century could stimulate such overheated fantasies only confirms the disquieting point: there is something about monsters that just turns certain women on.

FRITZ HAARMANN

18: FRITZ HAARMANN:
"The Ogre
of Hanover"

Fritz Haarmann; from *Bloody Visions* trading cards *(© & ™ 1995 M. H. Price and Shel-Tone Publications. All rights reserved.)*

One of the most infamous lust slayers of the twentieth century, Haarmann was born to a working-class couple in Hanover, Germany, in 1879. He was a sullen and slow-witted child whose favorite pastime was dressing up like a girl. At seventeen, he was commited to an asylum after being arrested for child molesting. Six months later, he escaped to Switzerland and made his way back to Hanover.

For a while, he attempted to lead a respectable life, taking a job in a cigar factory, getting engaged to a young woman. But this period of relative normalcy didn't last. Deserting his fiancée, he ran off and joined the army. When he returned to Hanover in 1903, he launched into a life of petty crime. Throughout his twenties, he was in and out of jail for offenses ranging from being a pickpocket to burglary. He spent World War I behind bars.

Released in 1918, he returned to his native city and joined a postwar smuggling ring that trafficked, among other things, in black-market beef.

He also served as a police stool pigeon, a sideline that afforded him protection for his illicit activities. In 1919, however, after being caught in bed with a young boy, Haarmann was shipped back to prison.

It was after his release nine months later that Haarmann launched into his career of unparalleled depravity. Living in Hanover's seamy Old Quarter, he fell under the thrall of a homosexual prostitute named Hans Grans. Together, the two set about preying on the young male refugees who were flooding into the war-ravaged city. Though Haarmann was ultimately charged with twenty-seven murders, it seems likely he was responsible for as many as fifty. The method he employed to kill his victims was always the same.

After luring the hungry boy to his room, Haarmann would feed him a meal, then overpower him (often with Grans's assistance) and fall upon the boy's throat, chewing through the flesh until he had nearly separated the head from the body. Generally, he would experience a sexual climax while battening on the boy.

Afterward, Haarmann and Grans would butcher the body and dispose of the flesh by peddling it as black-market beef. The victim's clothes would also be sold, and the inedible portions of the body dumped in a canal.

As the number of missing boys mounted, police suspicion began to fall on Haarmann. A woman who had purchased one of his black-market "steaks" became convinced it was human flesh and turned it over to the police. In the summer of 1924, several skulls and a sackful of bones were found on the banks of the canal. Searching Haarmann's rooms, detectives discovered bundles of boys' clothing. The landlady's son was wearing a coat—given to him by Haarmann—that belonged to one of the missing boys.

In the end, Haarmann confessed. He was tried in 1924, found guilty, and sentenced to death. While awaiting execution, the "Vampire of Hanover" (as he'd been dubbed by the press) produced a written confession in which he described, with undisguised relish, the pleasure he had derived from his atrocities. At his own request, he was beheaded with a sword in the city marketplace. Afterward, his brain was removed from his skull and shipped to Goettingen University for study. Unfortunately, nothing came of this effort. Seventy years later, science is still no closer to comprehending the evil of monsters like Fritz Haarmann.

HEAD INJURIES

When faced with a phenomenon as incomprehensibly evil as serial murder, it's natural for people to search for some kind of rational explanation. After all, if researchers could only identify the sources of serial murder, then it might be possible to come up with a cure—or at least identify potential psychos before they have a chance to hurt anybody. In their urgent efforts to solve this problem, criminologists have come up with all sorts of theories, from "negative parenting" to screwed-up hormones (see **Causes**). Some specialists put the blame on "juvenile cerebral trauma"—or, in plain English, getting whacked on the head as a kid. The brain damage done by such an injury can, according to these experts, turn people into serial killers.

It's certainly true that a high percentage of serial killers have suffered head injuries during their childhoods. Earle Leonard **Nelson**, for example—the notorious "Gorilla Man" who murdered almost two dozen women in the mid-1920s—was thrown off his bike by a trolley when he was ten and lay comatose for nearly a week. He finally recuperated, but his behavior (which wasn't entirely normal to begin with) became even more bizarre from then on. The serial rapist and killer Bobby Joe Long—convicted in 1984 on nine counts of first-degree murder—must have set some kind of record for head injuries. At five he was knocked unconscious in a fall from a swing. At six, he had a bike accident that sent him flying headfirst into a parked car. At seven he fell off a pony and onto his skull. From that point on, he managed to avoid any more head traumas—until he reached his early twenties, when he got into a motorcycle accident, slamming headfirst into the asphalt with such force that his helmet was crushed. These are only two of many examples. The list of head-battered psychos includes some of the most infamous names in the annals of serial murder—John Wayne **Gacy**, Richard **Speck**, Charles **Manson**, and Henry **Lucas**.

Unfortunately, the cerebral trauma theory of serial murder has the same limitations as other reductive explanations. Head injuries are an everyday fact of childhood life. Millions of kids fall off bikes and swings and seesaws and land on their heads. But only a tiny fraction turn out to be psychopathic killers. On the other hand, combined with other predisposing factors, a serious head trauma may well contribute to incipient psychopathology.

So—can serial murder be caused by something as simple as a knock on the head? Probably not.

But it sure doesn't help.

GARY HEIDNIK

The average tabloid headline is the printed equivalent of a sideshow barker's pitch—a shrill, attention-grabbing come-on that tends to promise much more than it can possibly deliver by way of lurid thrills. On rare occasions, however, even the most sensational headlines fall short of the terrible truth. Such was the case on March 26, 1987, when papers from coast to coast trumpeted front-page phrases like "Madman's Sex Orgy" and "Torture Dungeon." Titillating as these headlines were, they couldn't begin to convey the shocking reality of Gary Heidnik's house of horrors.

Alerted by a frantic 911 call from a woman named Josefina Rivera—who claimed that she had been held captive for months in Heidnik's cellar—the cops entered the suspect's rundown home in North Philadelphia and found a scene that might have been dreamed up by the Marquis de Sade. In the dank and squalid basement, two naked women were shackled to pipes. Another sat quaking in a fetid pit that had been dug in the earthen floor. All three had been beaten, starved, tortured, raped.

Eventually, authorities would learn that Heidnik had abducted and imprisoned a total of six young women. Josefina Rivera had been lucky enough to escape. Two others had died. Heidnik had killed one by forcing her into the pit, filling it with water, then electrocuting her with a live wire. The other victim had perished after Heidnik left her dangling by the wrists for a week. He had dismembered her body, ground up some of her flesh in a food processor, and mixed it with dog food. Then he had forced the other captives to devour this unspeakable mush. Searching Heidnik's house, police discovered a charred human rib in the oven and a forearm in the freezer. Not surprisingly, Heidnik turned out to be a former mental patient and convicted sex offender with a history of preying on mentally retarded black women. In spite of his flagrant psychopathology, he was something of a financial whiz, who had parlayed a modest investment into a half-million dollar fortune. As one pundit put it, Heidnik was an expert in "stocks and bondage." He owned several expensive cars, including a Rolls-Royce. He had managed to avoid paying taxes on his income by founding his own church and appointing himself bishop.

Aspiring to the role of Old Testament patriarch, he had begun kidnapping women in late 1986, intending to assemble a personal harem of ten women who would provide him with a whole tribe of offspring. "We'll be just one big happy family," Heidnik told his captives, even as he was busily shoving screwdrivers into their ears, raping each one in turn while the others were forced to watch, and making them into unwitting cannibals.

At his arraignment, Heidnik offered a novel defense, claiming that the women were already there when he first moved into the house. For some reason, the judge failed to believe him. He was convicted of two counts of murder and currently awaits execution.

> "Any person who puts dog food and human remains in a food processor and calls it a gourmet meal and feeds it to others is out to lunch."
>
> **ATTORNEY CHUCK PERUTO JR.,**
> referring to his client Gary Heidnik

THE HILLSIDE STRANGLERS

When the corpses started piling up—young women who had been tortured, raped, and strangled—the papers blared the news: a serial killer was on the loose. They dubbed him the "Hillside Strangler" because the bulk of the bodies were deposited on hillsides around the Los Angeles area. But the newspapers were wrong. The grisly crimes weren't the work of a serial killer.

They were the demented teamwork of *two* serial killers.

The first to die was a black prostitute, whose naked corpse was dumped near Forest Lawn Cemetery in mid-October, 1977. Two weeks later, the body of a fifteen-year-old female runaway turned up in the Los Angeles suburb of Glendale. Over the next few months, eight more bodies would be found. The victims ranged in age from twelve to twenty-eight. All had been sexually violated (sometimes with objects like soda bottles), strangled, and tortured in a variety of ways. One had been burned with an electric cord. Another had been injected with cleaning solution. Yet another had been killed with voluptuous cruelty—strangled to the point of unconsciousness, then revived, then strangled again, and so on until her tormentor finally put her to death.

From early on in their investigation, police suspected that two killers were involved, since semen found inside the victims indicated that the women had been raped (often both vaginally and anally) by different men. That suspicion was confirmed when an eyewitness caught sight of two men forcing a young woman into their car.

As a rule, serial killers keep murdering until they are caught. In February 1978, however—four months after they started—the Hillside Stranglings abruptly ceased. The killers might well have gotten away with their atrocities—if it hadn't been for the twisted compulsions of one member of the unspeakable duo.

One year after the last of the Los Angeles murders, two young women were raped and strangled in Bellingham, Washington. Suspicion immediately lighted on a twenty-six-year-old security guard named Kenneth Bianchi, who had recently moved to Bellingham from Los Angeles. Before long, police had ferreted out the truth—Bianchi and his forty-four-year-old cousin, a brutish sociopath named Angelo Buono, were the Hillside Stranglers.

Though Buono led an outwardly respectable life as the owner of a successful auto upholstery business, he was also a sadistic pimp with a long history of violence against women. (He allegedly once sodomized his wife in front of their children after she refused to have sex with him.) Bianchi was a small-time con artist who had moved in with his cousin after relocating from Rochester, New York, in 1976. Separately, neither one had ever been known to commit murder—but together, they brought out the most monstrous impulses in each other.

For a while, Bianchi had authorities believing that he suffered from a split personality. Ostensibly, it was his evil alter ego, "Steve," who had participated in the murders. But a psychiatric expert finally established that "Steve"—a sadistic sex-killer who emerged under hypnosis—was a ruse.

In the end—in order to avoid a death sentence—Bianchi agreed to plead guilty to the murders and to testify against his cousin, who was convicted after a highly protracted trial. Both Hillside Stranglers are currently serving life sentences.

HISTORY

Reviewing the history of serial murder is a tricky proposition, since it's hard to know exactly where to begin. On the one hand, serial killing seems like a uniquely modern phenomenon, a symptom of the various ills afflicting late-twentieth-century America—alienation, social decay, sexual violence, rampant crime, etc. On the other hand, the savage, sadistic impulses that underlie serial murder are undoubtedly as old as humankind.

Any historical survey of serial murder would have to begin at least as far back as ancient Rome, when the Emperor Caligula was busily indulging his taste for torture and perversion. During the Middle Ages, depraved **Aristocrats** like Gilles de Rais (the original "Bluebeard") and Elizabeth Bathory (the "Blood Countess") fed their unholy lusts on the blood of hundreds of victims, while psychopathic peasants like Gilles Garnier and Peter Stubbe butchered their victims with such bestial ferocity that they were believed to be literal werewolves (see **Lycanthropy**). Other homicidal monsters of the premodern era include the Scottish cannibal Sawney Beane (see **Clans**) and Vlad the Impaler, the real-life Dracula (see **Vampires**).

Most crime buffs agree that the first serial sex-killer of the modern era was **Jack the Ripper**, whose crimes—the ghastly slaughter of five London streetwalkers—sent shock waves throughout Victorian England. One hundred years later, the serial slaying of prostitutes has become such a commonplace activity that (to cite just one of many examples) when, in July 1995, a former warehouse clerk named William Lester Suff was convicted of killing thirteen hookers in Southern California, the media barely noted the event. That shift sums up the history of serial murder in the twentieth century: its appalling transformation from a monstrous anomaly into an everyday horror.

Jack the Ripper's American contemporary, H. H. **Holmes**, who confessed to twenty-seven murders in the late 1890s, is regarded as America's first documented serial killer. Two full decades would pass before another one appeared on the scene: the unknown maniac dubbed the "Axeman of New Orleans," who terrorized that city between 1918 and 1919 (see **Axe Murders**).

Though it was a violent and lawless decade, the Roaring Twenties produced only two authentic serial killers: Earle Leonard **Nelson**—the serial strangler nicknamed the "Gorilla Murderer"—and the viciously depraved Carl **Panzram**. Serial killers were equally few and far between in the 1930s and 1940s. The cannibalistic pedophile Albert **Fish**, and the anonymous psycho known as the "Mad Butcher of Kingsbury Run" (aka the "Cleveland Torso Killer") are the only known serial killers of Depression-era America. The roster of 1940s serial killers is also limited to a pair of names: Jake Bird, a homicidal burglar who confessed to a dozen axe murders, and William Heirens, famous for his desperate, lipstick-scrawled plea: "For heaven's sake catch me before I kill more. I cannot control myself."

It wasn't until the post–World War II period that serial murder became rampant in this country. Its shadow was already beginning to spread during the sunny days of the Eisenhower era. The 1950s witnessed the depredations of Wisconsin ghoul Ed **Gein**; the voyeuristic horrors of Californian Harvey Murray Glatman (who photographed his bound, terrorized victims before murdering them); the crimes of homicidal scam artists Martha Beck and Raymond Fernandez (the "Lonely Hearts Killers"); and the bloody rampage of Charles Starkweather, who slaughtered a string of victims as he hot-rodded across the Nebraska badlands.

The situation became even grimmer during the 1960s, a period that produced such infamous figures as Melvin "Sex Beast" Rees, Albert "Boston Strangler" **DeSalvo**, Richard **Speck**, Charles **Manson**, and the still-unknown **Zodiac**. By the time the 1970s rolled around, the problem had become so dire that, for the first time, law enforcement officials felt the need to define this burgeoning phenomenon as a major category of crime (see **Coining a Phrase**). The 1970s was the decade of **Berkowitz** and **Bundy**, **Kemper** and **Gacy**, Bianchi and Buono (the "Hillside Stranglers"), and more.

By the 1980s, some criminologists were bandying words like *plague* and *epidemic* to characterize the problem. Though these terms smack of hysteria, it is nevertheless true that serial homicide has become so common in our country that most of its perpetrators stir up only local interest. Only the most ghastly of these killers, the ones who seem more like mythic monsters than criminals—Jeffrey **Dahmer**, for example—capture the attention of the entire nation and end up as creepy household names.

In view of this grim chronicle, it's hard not to agree with Voltaire's famous definition. "History," he wrote, "is little else than a picture of human crime and misfortune."

H. H. HOLMES

Dr. H. H. Holmes, the nineteenth-century "multi-murderer" (*Courtesy of the Illinois State Historical Society*)

At the same time that **Jack the Ripper** was terrorizing London, America was home to its own psychopathic monster. Calling himself Dr. H. H. Holmes, he was at least as notorious in his own day as "Saucy Jack." But while the latter's fame has grown through the years, Dr. Holmes—for unexplained reasons—has largely been forgotten. In the chronicle of American crime, however, he occupies a special place: he was our country's first documented serial killer.

Much about his life and crimes remains shrouded in mystery. We know that his real name was Herman Mudgett, that he was born in the tiny New

Hampshire village of Gilmanton Academy, and that—like other budding sociopaths—he enjoyed conducting "medical experiments" on small, living creatures during his childhood.

In his early twenties, he wed a young female acquaintance—the first of several wives he would acquire without ever bothering with the formality of a divorce. He abandoned her within a few years of the marriage. After a year of college in Vermont, he transferred to the University of Michigan at Ann Arbor, graduating with a medical degree in 1884. By then, he was already an accomplished swindler who had learned to bilk insurance companies of thousands of dollars. His method was simple. He would take out a life insurance policy for a fictitious person, obtain a corpse, claim that the corpse was the insured individual, and cash in on the policy. Of course, the scheme depended on Mudgett's ability to acquire dead bodies. But at this activity, too, he grew proficient.

In 1886, he showed up in Chicago under a new name—Henry Howard Holmes. Within a few months, he had taken a job as a druggist in the fashionable suburb of Englewood. The pharmacy was owned by an elderly widow, who mysteriously disappeared a few months later, leaving Holmes as the new proprietor. A consummate con artist, he had no trouble finagling large sums of cash from gullible investors. Combined with the proceeds from assorted scams, this money allowed him to construct a magnificient residence on a vacant lot across from his store. He called it "The Castle." It contained dozens of rooms, linked by secret passageways, hidden staircases, fake walls, concealed shafts, and trap doors. Some of the rooms were soundproofed, lined with asbestos, and equipped with gas pipes connected to a large tank in the cellar. From a control panel in his office, Holmes could fill these chambers with asphyxiating gas. A pair of chutes ran from the second and third floors to the basement, where Holmes kept a fully equipped dissection lab.

Inside the walls of this Gothic horror house, an indeterminate number of people disappeared—including a string of susceptible young women who had fallen under the spell of Holmes's insidious charm. During the 1893 Chicago World's Fair, Holmes also rented rooms to tourists, many of whom were never seen again. Throughout this period, local medical schools—in desperate need of high-grade anatomical specimens—purchased a regular supply of human skeletons from Dr. Holmes, no questions asked.

He was finally arrested for the murder of a confederate, Ben Pitezel. Holmes used Pitezel's corpse to try and pull off his favorite insurance scam, but he was caught by clever investigators. Following his trial—the most sensational of its day—he confessed to twenty-seven murders. The enormity of his deeds made him the most infamous criminal of his age, known throughout the land as "Holmes, the Arch Fiend." He was hanged in Philadelphia on May 7, 1896.

> *"I was born with the devil in me. I could not help the fact that I was a murderer, no more than the poet can help the inspiration to sing. . . . I was born with the Evil One standing as my sponsor beside the bed where I was ushered into the world, and he has been with me since."*
>
> From the confession of Dr. H. H. Holmes

HOMEBODIES

S ome serial killers range far and wide in search of their prey. Others, however, have a more domestic bent. Luring their victims to their houses or apartments, these psychos commit their gruesome murders in the comfort of their own homes—and sometimes even conceal the dead bodies right on the premises.

Shortly after a mousy little man named John Reginald Christie vacated his London flat in 1953, the new tenants began noticing an unplesant smell that seemed to be emanating from a hollow place in the kitchen wall. Tearing down the wallpaper, they discovered a concealed cupboard containing three female corpses. When police made a search of the premises, they found a fourth decomposed body—that of Christie's own wife—under the dining room floorboards, and the skeletal remains of two other victims buried in the backyard. (See **The Wrong Man**).

In the 1970s, both Dean Corll and John Wayne **Gacy** turned their homes into suburban torture chambers, committing dozens of atrocities on bound and helpless young men. Each of these sociopaths perpetrated over thirty at-home murders without ever arousing the suspicions of his next-door neighbors. Corll buried the corpses along the shore of a nearby lake (see **Partners**). Gacy likewise dumped some of his victims in a river—but not until he had run out of room on his property, where police eventually dug up twenty-nine bodies.

Jeffrey **Dahmer** was another homebody homosexual killer, who not only turned his cramped Milwaukee apartment into a death chamber but filled it with an appalling assortment of human remains. His British counterpart, Dennis **Nilsen**, played out twisted little scenes of domesticity with the dead bodies of his male victims—bathing them, snuggling with them in bed, propping them up in front of the TV, or seating them at the dinner table.

One of the most gruesome of all domestic serial killers was a deranged German innkeeper named Karl Denke. Denke was so reluctant to leave home that he didn't even bother to go out shopping for food. During the post–World War I era, he murdered almost three dozen lodgers, then butchered their carcasses, pickled the meat in brine, and stored it in his basement. When Denke was finally arrested in 1924, he told the police that he had been eating nothing but human flesh for the past three years (see **Cannibalism**).

HOMOSEXUALITY

In a tome called *A Casebook of Murder*, British crime maven Colin Wilson makes the rather remarkable statement that Ed **Gein**, the infamous Wisconsin ghoul, was "a sexually normal man." Since, among other things, Gein was guilty of digging up the bodies of elderly women, dismembering the corpses, and performing unspeakable atrocities upon them, it takes a moment to figure out that what Wilson really means is that, whatever other kind of creature Gein was, at least he wasn't a *homosexual*. While the implications of Wilson's remark are truly staggering (i.e., that grave robbing, necrophilia, dismemberment, etc. are more "normal" than homosexuality), he does manage to put his finger on a salient fact of serial murder. The great bulk of its pracitioners are, indeed, heterosexuals.

More specifically, criminologists estimate that at least 86 percent of male serial killers are heterosexual—meaning that they derive their deepest gratification from raping, mutilating, and murdering women. Still, though numerically inferior, gay serial killers include some of the foremost monsters of our time.

Throughout his two marriages, for example, John Wayne **Gacy** was busily having sex with teenage boys—twenty-seven of whom ended up buried in the crawl space beneath his suburban house. Likewise, Jeffrey **Dahmer** preyed exclusively on young males. So did the infamous British serial killer Dennis **Nilsen**,

whose murders—like Dahmer's—seemed at least partly motivated by a desperate desire to prevent his male pickups from leaving in the morning (see **Companionship**). Less well-known—though every bit as heinous—was California's so-called "Freeway Killer," William George Bonin, a Vietnam vet and truck driver responsible for torturing and then murdering twenty-one young men during the 1970s.

Serial sex murder, as practiced by men, is virtually unknown among **Women**, homosexual or otherwise. A recent exception is the lesbian hooker Aileen **Wuornos**, who killed a string of male motorists along a Florida highway in 1989 and 1990.

HOMOSEXUAL SERIAL KILLERS IN THE CINEMA

Aside from Nick Broomfield's prize-winning 1993 documentary, *Aileen Wuornos: Portrait of a Serial Killer*, the only movie ever made about a homosexual serial killer is William Friedkin's *Cruising*. (The character Buffalo Bill in *The Silence of the Lambs* is an aspiring *trans*sexual, which is a whole different kettle of fish.)

Friedkin's 1980 shocker was widely—and, to a large extent, deservedly—reviled by critics (in his most recent *Movie and Video Guide*, Leonard Maltin tosses around words like "distasteful," "sick," and "degrading"). Still, it's a deeply unsettling film, starring Al Pacino as a New York City cop on the hunt for a gay homicidal maniac in pre-AIDS Greenwich Village.

HOUSEKEEPERS

C ontrary to what some people claim, not all serial killers are men. Women commit serial murder, too—they just do it in a more, well, *womanly* way. Male serial killing is essentially old-fashioned phallic aggression carried to a monstrous extreme—the violent penetration of a victim's body with a sharp, pointed implement. Women serial killers, on the other hand, are like grotesque parodies of female stereotypes: **Black Widow** brides instead of adoring wives. Lethal **Nurses** instead of loving nurturers. And instead of happy homemakers, Housekeepers from Hell.

In the early years of the nineteenth century, an embittered German widow named Anna Zwanziger, who bore a striking resemblance to an oversized toad, hired herself out as a housekeeper and cook to a succession of middle-aged judges. Apparently, Zwanziger hoped that one of these worthies would become so dependent on her domestic skills that he would end up proposing. Of course, there was one small problem with Anna's plan—namely, the inconvenient fact that each of the men was already married or engaged to another woman. Anna hit on an ingenious solution: she poisoned two of the women with arsenic. For good measure, she also poisoned one of the judges, several servants, and a baby (who died after eating a biscuit soaked in arsenic-spiked milk). Just before her execution in July 1811, Anna told her jailers, "It is perhaps better for the community that I should die, as it would be impossible for me to stop poisoning people."

While Zwanziger appears to have been motivated by some lethal combination of desperation and crushed hope, other homicidal housekeepers have killed for more obscure reasons. Roughly ten years after Zwanziger's beheading, another German cook named Gessina Gottfried poisoned an entire family named Rumf—papa, mama, and five children—by sprinkling arsenic over every meal she prepared for them. Her admitted motive was sheer malevolent pleasure—at her trial in 1828, she confessed that the sight of her victims' death agonies threw her into a transport of ecstasy. Equally appalling was the French domestic Helene Jegado. Between 1833 and 1851, she fatally poisoned at least twenty-three and perhaps as many as thirty men, women, and children. her victims included several nuns and her own sister.

"Wherever I go," she was once heard to remark, "people die."

IMPOTENCE

Sigmund Freud argued that when normal sexual drives are warped, they tend to vent themselves as violence. The impulse to love turns into an urge to destroy. His theory is confirmed with brutal clarity in the behavior of serial killers, who commonly substitute murder for sex. This is especially evident in the cases of those psychopathic killers who suffer from sexual impotence.

John Reginald Christie, the "Monster of Rillington Place," was so plagued by impotence that he couldn't consummate his marriage for over two years. Murder was his sick way of compensating for this deficiency. Gassing and strangling women served as a sexual turn-on for Christie. Once his victims were dead he had no trouble raping them (see **The Wrong Man**).

Christie's potency problem probably wouldn't have surprised his acquaintances. Bald, bespectacled, and a known hypochondriac, he wasn't exactly a picture of self-confident virility. Paul John Knowles, on the other hand, cut an impressively masculine figure. Charming and ruggedly handsome, he became known in the mid-1970s as the "Casanova Killer." At least eighteen people who crossed his path—and perhaps as many as thirty-five—ended up shot, stabbed, or strangled. In the course of his deadly wanderings, Knowles met a British journalist named Sandy Fawkes who, like so many other young women, took an immediate fancy to him. The two ended up in bed, but Knowles was unable to perform sexually with a willing partner. When Fawkes abruptly broke off their short-lived relationship, Knowles reverted to the only kind of sex he was capable of, seeking out one of Fawkes's close friends and attempting to rape her at gunpoint.

Some serial killers, on the other hand, suffer from the opposite problem—not impotence but a sex drive of almost demonic intensity. When Bobby Joe Long, for example, was in his twenties, even the combination of twice-daily intercourse with his wife and compulsive masturbation couldn't slake his sexual hunger. Soon he began pursuing an additional outlet, raping at least fifty Florida women and murdering as many as ten.

INSANITY

When it comes to a killer who flays the skin from corpses, tans it like animal hide, and tailors it into a suit, the question of sanity would seem to be cut and dried (so to speak). And, in fact, Ed "Psycho" **Gein**—who actually did fashion garments out of human skin—was deemed officially insane and committed for life to a state mental institution.

Gein, however, represents the exception rather than the rule. Though at least one psychiatric expert has flatly declared that serial killers are "almost always insane," persuading a jury is another matter. Statistics tell the story. Of all the multiple murderers brought to trial in our century, fewer than 4 percent have resorted to an insanity plea. And of those, only one in three has been found NGRI ("not guilty by reason of insanity").

Still, the poor odds haven't stopped some notorious serial killers from trying. David "Son of Sam" Berkowitz, for example, did his best to persuade psychiatrists that his mind was controlled by his neighbor's dog, a black Labrador retriever that was ostensibly possessed by the spirit of a six-thousand-year-old demon named Sam. The "Voices from Beyond" gambit was also employed (unsuccessfully) by the so-called "Yorkshire Ripper," who slaughtered thirteen women in the late 1970s. The "Yorkshire Ripper" turned out to be a happily married truckdriver named Peter Sutcliffe, who insisted that he was simply acting on orders from God, whose voice he heard issuing from a grave in a local cemetery. Sutcliffe's countryman John George Haigh—the notorious "Acid Bath Murderer" of the 1940s—tried a different tack to impress jurors with his lunacy: he drank his own urine.

Other serial killers have tried their hands at the popular multiple personality ploy. William Heirens (famous for the lipstick-scrawled plea he left in a victim's apartment, "For heaven's sake catch me before I kill more") blamed his crimes on an alternate personality named "George Murman." Similarly, both John Wayne **Gacy** and Kenneth "Hillside Strangler" Bianchi claimed that their crimes were the handiwork of evil alter egos, named "Jack" and "Steve" respectively. None of these ruses worked.

The problem for defense lawyers with serial-killer clients is that even the most horrific acts—crimes no normal person could even imagine, let alone commit—are not necessarily proof of legal insanity. A killer like Jeffrey **Dahmer** can dismember his still-living victims, eat their flesh, store their heads in his refrigerator, etc. and still be deemed sane according to the law. Though legal definitions vary, most states rely on the McNaughton rule, which says, in essence, that the criterion for sanity is the ability to distinguish right from wrong. Since most serial killers go to great pains to cover up their crimes, it's hard to prove that they don't know they're engaged in wrongdoing.

The difficulty of a winning an NGRI verdict is vividly illustrated by the case of Albert **Fish**, certainly one of the most bizarre minds in the annals of American crime. A frighteningly sadistic child-killer and cannibal, Fish was a true psychiatric phenomenon, who indulged (according to expert testimony) "in every known sexual perversion and some perversions never heard of before." Though the jury agreed that Fish was suffering from severe mental derangement, they found him guilty and sentenced him to the chair. As one juror explained after the trial (expressing a sentiment that many people would endorse), "we believed he was insane, but we thought he deserved to die anyway."

> *"As a result of our psychiatric examination, we are of the opinion that this man at the present time is not insane."*
>
> From a 1930 Bellevue Hospital report on Albert Fish, who two years earlier had abducted, dismembered, and cannibalized a twelve-year-old girl

INTERNET

The Internet is rapidly becoming an excellent source of intriguing information. Web-browsing crime buffs might be interested in checking out the "Internet Crime Archives"—a lively and informative Web site, complete with gruesome graphics.

This "Digital Home of the Mass-Murdering Serial Killer" (as it calls itself) offers a varied menu that includes:

- A serial killer "Who's Who" ("Look for your favorite killer and check his or her standing on the Serial Killer Hit List! Savor their path of destruction!")
- A mass murderer "Greatest Hits List" ("Count down to Armageddon with these gun-toting, room-clearing maniacs!")
- An illustrated "Imagemap of Death" ("Look for your favorite psycho and find out why he or she really turns you on!")
- The "Death Net" ("Explore our digital atrocity exhibition. . . . Surf the links of death and mayhem at your disposal!")

All this and more can be found at the following address: http://www.mayhem.net/Crime/archives.htm

IQ

Though no real-life psychopath comes close to matching the evil genius of Dr. Hannibal Lecter, serial killers tend to be smart. When special agents of the FBI's Behavioral Science Unit began their criminal **Profiling** program, they discovered that the mean IQ for serial killers was bright normal.

The above-average intelligence of these psychopaths is one of the scariest things about them, making it possible for them not only to snare victims with relative ease but also to elude the police, sometimes forever (see **Whereabouts Unknown**). It also accounts for the striking number of serial killers who have done well in terms of worldly success. Ted **Bundy** was a law student, John Wayne **Gacy** ran a thriving business, Gary **Heidnik** made a fortune playing the stock market, and a considerable number of serial killers have been **Doctors**.

On the other hand, it's also true that because of their severe personality problems, many serial killers end up working at menial jobs that are far beneath their intellectual capacities.

JACK THE RIPPER

The horrors began in the early morning hours of August 31, 1888. At roughly 3:45 A.M., while walking down a deserted, dimly lit street in London's East End, a market porter named George Cross stumbled upon what he took to be a tarpaulin-wrapped bundle. Peering closer, he saw that the sprawling heap was the butchered body of a woman, later identified as a forty-two-year-old prostitute named Mary Anne Nicholls. Her throat had been slashed, her belly slit, her vagina mutilated with stab wounds.

Though no one could have suspected it at the time, the savaging of Mary Anne Nicholls was a grisly landmark in the history of crime. Not only was it the first in a string of killings that would send shock waves throughout London and, eventually, the world. But it also signified something even more momentous—the dawn of the modern age of serial sex-murder.

A week after the Nicholls atrocity, the mutilated remains of Annie Chapman, a wasted forty-seven-year-old prostitute suffering from malnutrition and consumption, were discovered in the rear of a lodging house a half mile from the site of the first murder. Chapman's head was barely attached to her body—the killer had severed her neck muscles and nearly succeeded in sawing through her spinal column. She had also been disembowelled.

The true identity of the killer would never be known. But several weeks later, the Metropolitan Police received a taunting letter by a writer who claimed to be the culprit and signed his note with a sinister nom de plume. The name caught on with the public. From that point on, the mad butcher of Whitechapel would be known by this grisly nickname—Jack the Ripper.

Two days after police received the Ripper's letter, the killer cut the throat of a Swedish prostitute named Elizabeth Stride. Before he could commit any further atrocities on the victim, he was interrupted by the sounds of an approaching wagon. Hurrying away, the Ripper encountered Catherine Eddowes, a forty-three-year-old prostitute who had just been released from a police station, where she had spent several hours sobering up after having been found lying drunk on the pavement. The Ripper lured her into a deserted square, where he slit her throat. Then, in the grip of a demoniacal frenzy, he disfigured her face, split her body from rectum to breastbone, removed her entrails, and carried off her left kidney.

The final crime committed by the Ripper was also the most hideous. On the evening of November 9, he picked up a twenty-five-year-old Irish prostitute named Mary Kelly, three months pregnant, who took him back to her rooms. Sometime in the middle of the night, he killed her in bed, then spent several leisurely hours butchering her corpse—disemboweling her, slicing off her nose and breasts, carving the flesh from her legs.

Following this outrage, the Whitechapel horrors came to an abrupt end. The Ripper vanished forever, stepping out of history into the realm of myth.

Since then, armchair detectives have proposed a host of suspects, from a Kosher butcher to an heir apparent to the English throne (see **Ripper Theories**). Most of these "solutions" make for colorful reading, but the Ripper's true identity remains what it has been for a hundred years—a tantalizing, probably insoluble mystery.

> *"The throat had been cut right across with a knife, nearly severing the head from the body. The abdomen had been partially ripped open, and both of the breasts had been cut from the body. . . . The nose had been cut off, the forehead skinned, and the thighs, down to the feet, stripped of the flesh. . . . The entrails and other portions of the frame were missing, but the liver, etc., were found placed between the feet of this poor victim. The flesh from the thighs and legs, together with the breasts and nose, had been placed by the murderer on the table, and one of the hands of the dead woman had been pushed into her stomach."*
>
> From an 1888 newspaper description of Jack the Ripper's final victim, Mary Kelly

RIPPER THEORIES

There is a basic (and disheartening) law of police work: if a case isn't cracked right away, then the odds of ever solving it rapidly shrink to zero. So the chances of coming up with the solution to a hundred-year-old crime are essentially less than nil. Still, that hasn't stopped a host of armchair detectives from offering up theories on the most tantalizing murder mystery of all—who was the knife-wielding serial prostitute killer known as

Jack the Ripper? For the most part, these theorists are harmless cranks, like the people who spend their time trying to prove that there was a second gunman on the grassy knoll, or that Amelia Earhart ended up in a Japanese nunnery. The most likely truth is that—like virtually every other serial killer in history—the Ripper was undoubtedly a complete nonentity whose only remarkable trait was a staggering capacity for violence. But—as is so often the case with reality—that simple explanation is infinitely less satisfying than more colorful alternatives. Following are some of the more entertaining hypotheses put forth by various "Ripper-ologists":

1. *The Mad Russian.* Supposedly Rasputin himself wrote a book called *Great Russian Criminals* in which he claimed that Jack the Ripper was actually a deranged Russian doctor named Pedachenko, who was dispatched to London by the tsarist police in an effort to create consternation in England and embarrass the British authorities.

2. *The Black Magician.* The Ripper was actually Dr. Roslyn D'Onston Stephenson, a self-styled conjurer obsessed with the occult, who supposedly committed the East End murders as part of a satanic ritual.

3. *The Jewish Slaughterman.* A *shochet*, or Kosher butcher, decided to use his carving skills on women of the night.

4. *Jill the Ripper.* The homicidal maniac was not a man at all but a demented London midwife.

5. *The Lodger.* An unnamed boarder in a London roominghouse acted suspiciously at the time of the Ripper murders and might have been the East End fiend. Although the vaguest of the Ripper solutions, this theory has distinguished itself as the basis for four entertaining movies, including an early Hitchcock thriller (see **Le Cinéma de Jack**).

6. *The Deadly Doctor.* A man named Dr. Stanley committed the murders as an act of revenge, after his son contracted syphilis from a prostitute.

7. *The Lethal Lawyer.* A failed attorney named Montague John Druitt committed the Ripper crimes, then drowned himself in the Thames.

8. *The Polish Poisoner.* A multiple murderer named Severin Klosowski (aka George Chapman), who poisoned three of his wives, presumably committed the Whitechapel slayings out of his pathological hatred of womankind in general.

9. *The Evil Aristocrat.* HRH Prince Albert Victor, Duke of Clarence— Queen Victoria's grandson and heir to the British throne—went on a killing spree after he was maddened by syphilis.

10. *The Crazed Cotton Merchant.* A diary that surfaced in the early 1990s "revealed" that the Ripper was a drug-addicted businessman named James Maybrick. Unfortunately, the diary was declared a hoax by renowned document experts.

LE CINÉMA DE JACK

It's not surprising that Jack the Ripper—the most famous of all serial killers—has been a long-time favorite of filmmakers. Following is a list of his most memorable big-screen appearances.

1. *Pandora's Box* (1928). Classic silent film by G. W. Pabst, starring screen legend Louise Brooks as the femme fatale Lulu, who ends up as a streetwalker in London. And guess who her very first (and last) customer is?

2. *The Lodger* (1944). Based on a 1913 novel by Marie Belloc Lowndes, this suspense thriller—about a family named Bunting who suspect that their new boarder is Jack the Ripper—had already been filmed by Alfred Hitchcock in 1926. But Hitchcock's version is like Hamlet without the prince, since it turns out that the Buntings are wrong. The 1944 version, directed by German émigré John Brahm, is more faithful to the original—Saucy Jack really is living in the Bunting house and taking a lively (or deadly) interest in their young daughter, Daisy.

3. *Room to Let* (1950). Adapted from a BBC radio play of the same title, this modest little thriller (in which Jack turns out to be a sinister physician named Dr. Fell) was an early production of the fledgling Hammer Film Company, beloved by horror buffs for the lurid fright films it began turning out in the late 1950s.

4. *Man in the Attic* (1954). Still another version of *The Lodger*, this one starring the inimitable Jack Palance as the Ripper. Talk about typecasting!

5. *Jack the Ripper* (1960). A low-budget British shocker with a memorable gimmick. Though the entire film is in black and white, the climactic sequence—in which Jack is crushed to death by a falling elevator—was shot in color so the audience could enjoy the vivid red of his gushing blood.

6. *A Study in Terror* (1965). What a concept! Sherlock Holmes battles Jack the Ripper in this brisk, entertaining thriller, produced with the cooperation of Adrian Conan Doyle, son of Holmes's creator.

7. *Hands of the Ripper* (1971). Suffering from the traumatic aftereffects of watching Daddy stab Mommy, Jack the Ripper's angelic daughter turns into a homicidal maniac whenever a guy kisses her. She ends up in treatment with an early disciple of Freud. A Hammer movie classic!

8. *Murder by Decree* (1979). Another Holmes vs. Ripper movie, this one with a stellar cast: Christopher Plummer, James Mason, Donald Suth-

erland, Genevieve Bujold, David Hemmings, John Gielgud, and Anthony Quayle.

9. *Time After Time* (1979). Nifty little fantasy written and directed by Nicholas Meyer in which Jack the Ripper travels from Victorian England to modern-day America via H. G. Wells's time machine.

10. *Jack the Ripper* (1988). Originally a two-part TV movie, this is a solid, lavish telling of the Ripper case, starring Michael Caine as a Scotland Yard inspector hot on the trail of Saucy Jack. Sticks to the facts except for its conclusion, when the hero succeeds in unmasking the killer.

JEKYLL/HYDE

Plenty of people lead double lives: suburban matrons with lovers on the side; happily married hubbies who sneak off at night to cruise the gay bars; successful corporate executives supporting costly heroin habits. But cases like these pale beside the lives of certain serial killers. Ted **Bundy** was so bright and personable that he could have run for elected office if he hadn't also been a sadistic sex-killer who murdered dozens of young women. John Wayne **Gacy** liked to dress up as a clown and entertain hospitalized children when he wasn't torturing teenage boys in his suburban home. And the Swedish physician Dr. Teet Haerm, who mutilated and killed at least nine young women, was a respected forensic pathologist who actually ended up performing the autopsies on some of his victims!

Killers like these possess such monstrously split personalities that they seem slightly unreal, as if they stepped from the pages of a horror story. More specifically, they seem like the flesh-and-blood incarnations of a figure first dreamed up by British writer Robert Louis Stevenson in the 1880s: Dr. Henry Jekyll, who spends half his life as an idealistic scientist and the other half as a hideous creature named Edward Hyde.

"Dreamed up" is not just a figure of speech, since the idea for the story reportedly came to Stevenson in a nightmare. He dashed off a first draft in just three days, but his wife was so shocked by this version that Stevenson burned it, then rewrote it in a slightly less sensational form. Like *Dracula* and *Franken-*

135

stein, *Dr. Jekyll and Mr. Hyde* is one of those stories that everyone knows, even if they've never read the original. This is largely because it's been made into so many movies, beginning with a 1920 silent version starring John Barrymore. It comes as a surprise, therefore, to discover that Stevenson's novelette is not so much a horror story as a mystery, revolving around the question of Edward Hyde's identity—who is this evil being and what is his relationship to the distinguished Dr. Jekyll? The answer to these questions isn't revealed until the very end, when readers discover that Hyde is really Jekyll's alter ego, the living embodiment of the good doctor's bestial, hidden self.

For people who only know *Dr. Jekyll and Mr. Hyde* from the movies there are other surprising aspects of the original story. On film, Hyde is typically portrayed as a fanged, hairy creature—a kind of werewolf in Victorian clothing. In the book, however, he is less overtly monstrous. There is something deeply repellent about him, but exactly where this quality comes from is hard to say. "He is not easy to describe," one character remarks. "There is something wrong with his appearance; something displeasing, something downright detestable. I never saw a man I so disliked, and yet I scarce know why. He must be deformed somewhere; he gives a strong feeling of deformity, although I couldn't specify the point. He's an extraordinary looking man, and yet I really can name nothing out of the way."

Furthermore, though Stevenson tells us that Hyde has a history of vile and violent deeds, he doesn't appear to be a homicidal maniac. Rather, he is the personification of the nasty, lawless impulses that lurk beneath our civilized veneers: what Sigmund Freud called the id. Indeed, in Stevenson's story, Edward Hyde commits only a single murder—the clubbing of a distinguished old gentleman named Sir Danvers Carew.

In short, though serial killers like Bundy and Gacy are often described as Jekyll-and-Hydes, they are really far worse. Compared to them, Stevenson's bestial creation was a pussycat.

JOKES

Serial murder is no laughing matter. But that hasn't stopped people from making fun of it—any more than it's kept them from swapping sick jokes about other lurid and sensational subjects, from O. J. Simpson to Lorena Bobbitt. The latter, in fact, costarred in this widely circulated rib tickler with one of America's premier serial killers, the late Jeff "The Chef" **Dahmer:**

What did Jeffrey Dahmer say to Lorena Bobbitt?
"You going to eat that?"

Dahmer's cannibalistic crimes inspired a host of sick jokes. One day, for example, his mother came over for dinner. "Jeffrey," she complained, halfway through the meal, "I really don't like your friends." "Then just eat the vegetables, Ma," Dahmer replied.

The phenomenon of serial-killer humor appears to have originated in relation to another celebrity psycho who (like Dahmer) resided in Wisconsin: Edward **Gein.** Not long after Gein's atrocities came to light, jokes about the "Plainfield Ghoul" began circulating throughout the Midwest. These crude riddles—known as "Geiners"—drew the attention of a psychologist named George Arndt, who published an article about them in a psychiatric journal. Among Arndt's examples were the following:

Why did Ed Gein's girlfriend stop going out with him?
Because he was such a cut-up.

What did Ed Gein say to the sheriff who arrested him?
"Have a heart."

Why won't anyone play poker with Ed Gein?
He might come up with a good hand.

Why do serial-killer jokes exist? Are they an expression of pure callousness and cruelty? Probably not. Like other gross and nasty jokes, serial-killer humor offers an outlet for our fears—in the same way that a child walking past a graveyard will whistle a lively tune to calm his nerves. It's a way of warding off terror with levity. As the saying goes, we laugh to keep from crying.

"A VISIT FROM OLD ED"

Woodcut portrait of Ed
Gein by Chris Pelletiere

Sick jokes about Ed Gein weren't the only kind of black humor circulating in the months following the discovery of his crimes. Researching local reaction to Gein's atrocities, psychologist George Arndt recorded this ghoulish parody of Clement Moore's "A Visit from St. Nicholas":

'Twas the night before Christmas, when all through the shed,
All creatures were stirring, even old Ed.

The bodies were hung from the rafters above,
While Eddie was searching for another new love.

He went to Wautoma for a Plainfield deal,
Looking for love and also a meal.

When what to his hungry eyes should appear,
But old Mary Hogan in her new red brassiere.

Her cheeks were like roses when kissed by the sun.
And she let out a scream at the sight of Ed's gun.

Old Ed pulled the trigger and Mary fell dead,
He took his old axe and cut off her head.

He then took his hacksaw and cut her in two,
One half for hamburger, the other for stew.

And laying a hand aside of her heel,
Up to the rafters went his next meal.

He sprang to his truck, to the graveyard he flew,
The hours were short and much work must he do.

He looked for the grave where the fattest one laid,
And started in digging with shovel and spade.

He shoveled and shoveled and shoveled some more,
Till finally he reached the old coffin door.

He took out a crowbar and pried open the box,
He was not only clever but sly as a fox.

As he picked up the body and cut off her head,
He could tell by the smell that the old girl was dead.

He filled in the grave by the moonlight above,
And once more old Ed had found a new love.

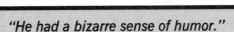

> *"He had a bizarre sense of humor."*
>
> **One of Jeffrey Dahmer's former schoolmates**

JUVENILES

Little boys who grow up to be serial killers tend to be extremely sadistic, but the targets of their cruelty are almost always small animals, not other children (see **Animal Torture**). An exception to this rule was the juvenile psychopath Jesse Pomeroy, one of the most unsettling criminals of nineteenth-century America.

Pomeroy suffered a difficult boyhood. He was raised in hardship by a widowed mother, who scraped together a meager living as a seamstress in South Boston. And he was cursed with a grotesque appearance—his mouth was disfigured by a harelip, and one eye was covered with a ghastly white film. Still, his contemporaries weren't inclined to attribute his atrocities to child-hood trauma. To them, he was simply a natural-born fiend.

Little is known about Pomeroy's early life until he reached the age of eleven—at which point, he began preying on other children. Between the winter of 1871 and the following fall, he attacked seven little boys, luring them to a secluded spot, then stripping, binding, and torturing them. His first victims were subjected to savage beatings. Later, Pomeroy took to slashing his victims with a pocketknife or stabbing them with needles.

Arrested at the end of 1872, Pomeroy was sentenced to ten years in a reformatory but managed to win probation after only eighteen months by putting on a convincing show of rehabilita-tion. No sooner had he been released, however, than he reverted to his former ways. But by this time, the teenage psychopath wasn't content merely to inflict injury. At this point, he was ho-micidal.

In March 1874 he kidnapped ten-year-old Mary Curran, then mutilated and killed her. A month later, he abducted four-year-old Horace Mullen, took him to a remote stretch of marshland, and slashed him so savagely with a pocketknife that the boy was nearly decapitated.

When Mullen's body was found, suspicion immediately lighted on Pomeroy, who was picked up with the bloody weapon in his pocket and mud on his boots that matched the soggy ground of the murder site. When police showed Pomeroy the victim's horribly mutilated body and asked if he had killed the little boy, Pomeroy simply said, "I suppose I did." It wasn't until July that Mary Curran's corpse was found, when laborers uncov-ered her decomposed remains while excavating the earthen cel-lar of the Pomeroy's house.

Pomeroy's 1874 trial was a nationwide sensation. Moral re-formers blamed his crimes on the lurid "dime novels" of the day (very much like those modern-day bluenoses who attribute the current crime rate to gangsta rap and violent action movies). Unfortunately, their position was undermined by Pomeroy's in-sistence that he had never read a book in his life.

In spite of his age, Pomeroy was condemned to death, but his sentence was commuted to life imprisonment with a harsh pro-viso: the so-called boy-fiend would serve out his sentence in soli-tary. And indeed, it wasn't until forty-one years later that he was finally allowed limited contact with other inmates. He died in confinement in 1932, at the age of seventy-two.

Pomeroy makes a brief but memorable appearance in Caleb Carr's best-selling 1994 novel, *The Alienist*, when the titular hero—seeking insight into the mind of an unknown serial killer—travels to Sing Sing to interview the former boy-fiend and finds him locked in a punishment cell, his head encased in a cagelike "collar cap."

"Despite both the shackles on the collar cap, Jesse had a book in his hand and was quietly reading. . . . 'Pretty hard to get an education in this place,' Jesse said, after the door had closed. 'But I'm trying. I figure maybe that's where I went wrong—no education. . . .'"

"Laszlo nodded. 'Admirable. I see you're wearing a collar cap.'

"Jesse laughed. 'Ahh—they claim *I* burned a guy's face with a cigarette while he was sleeping. . . . But I ask you—' He turned my way, the milky eye floating aimlessly in his head. 'Does that sound like me?'"

From *The Alienist*

EDMUND KEMPER

In August 1963, when Edmund Kemper was fifteen years old, he stepped up behind his grandmother and casually shot her in the back of the head. After stabbing her a few times for good measure, he calmly waited for his grandfather to return from work, then gunned him down, too. His motive? "I just wondered how it would feel to shoot Grandma," he explained to the police.

In retrospect, this homicidal outburst wasn't really very surprising. From his earliest years, Kemper had been what his mother euphemistically described as a "real weirdo." One of his favorite childhood games was to pretend that he was being asphyxiated in the gas chamber. He also enjoyed decapitating his sisters' dolls.

By the time he was ten, he had graduated to **Animal Torture,** chopping up a cat with a machete and stashing the dismembered parts in his closet. He buried another cat alive, then—after exhuming the corpse—cut off its head, which he proudly displayed in his bedroom.

Deemed mentally unsound after the double murder of his grandparents, Kemper was committed to a maximum-security mental hospital in 1963. Just six years later, he was released. Physically, he had undergone a striking change, having grown into a hulking, six-foot-nine, three-hundred-pounder. Psychologically, however, he was the same as ever—a sadistic psychopath obsessed with necrophiliac fantasies.

Two years after his discharge from the mental hospital, Kemper picked up a pair of hitchhiking co-eds, drove them to an isolated spot, and stabbed them to death. After smuggling their bodies back home, he amused himself for several hours with his "trophies"—photographing them, dissecting them, having sex with their viscera. Eventually, he bagged and buried the body parts and tossed the heads into a ravine.

Four months later, he abducted another teenage hitchhiker, strangled her, raped her corpse, then took it home for more fun and games. The same pattern would repeat itself with three more female victims, all of them hitchhiking students. Though Kemper clearly enjoyed the killing, it was the postmortem perversions that gave him the most satisfaction. He decapitated all of the women and enjoyed having sex with their headless bodies. He also liked to dissect the corpses and save various "keepsakes." On at least two occasions, he cannibalized his victims, slicing the flesh from their legs and cooking it in a macaroni casserole.

By January 1973, Santa Cruz authorities were aware that a serial murderer—dubbed the "Co-Ed Killer"—was on the loose, though they never suspected Kemper who, in fact, had befriended a number of local police officers. Several months later, on Easter weekend, Kemper committed matricide, hammering in the skull of his sleeping mother, then cutting off her head. After raping the decapitated body, he ripped out her larynx and jammed it down the garbage disposal. ("That seemed appropriate," he would later tell the police, "as much as she'd bitched and screamed and yelled at me over so many years.") Afterward, he telephoned his mother's best friend and invited her over for dinner. When she arrived, he crushed her skull with a brick and subjected her corpse to the usual postmortem outrages.

On Easter Sunday, Kemper got in a car and headed east. When he reached Colorado, he telephoned his pals on the Santa Cruz police force and confessed. Convicted of eight counts of murder, he was asked what he thought a fitting punishment would be. "Death by torture," was his reasonable reply. Instead, he was sentenced to life in prison.

Q. "What do you think when you see a pretty girl walking down the street?"
A. "One side of me says, 'I'd like to talk to her, date her.' The other side of me says, 'I wonder how her head would look on a stick?'"

EDMUND KEMPER, during a magazine interview

KIDNEY

This vital organ has a special significance for crime buffs, since it figures prominently in the case of the most famous serial killer of all time.

On the evening of September 30, 1888, the anonymous madman who would become known as **Jack the Ripper** committed two atrocities in quick succession. First, he slit the throat of a Swedish prostitute named Elizabeth Stride. Then—after being interrupted by an approaching wagon—he accosted a forty-three-year-old prostitute named Catherine Eddowes and lured her into a deserted square, where he slashed her windpipe and savaged her body, removing her left kidney.

Two weeks later—on October 16—a parcel arrived at the home of George Lusk, head of the Whitechapel Vigilance Committee, a group of local tradesmen who had organized to assist in the search for the killer. The parcel contained a ghastly surprise—a chunk of kidney (with an inch of renal artery still attached), accompanied by an equally appalling letter addressed to Lusk: "Sir I send you half the kidne I took from one woman prasarved it for you tother piece I fried and ate it was very nise I may send you the bloody knif I took it out if you only wate a whil longer." It was signed "Catch me when you can Mister Lusk."

The sender's address on the upper-right-hand corner of the letter said simply: "From Hell."

In the weeks since the Ripper first struck, the police had been inundated with letters from cranks claiming to be the killer, and at first, there were many who declared that this latest communication was nothing but a depraved hoax. The kidney, they proclaimed, had either been taken from a dog or removed from a dissecting room. Examination by a specialist from the London Hospital Museum, however, revealed not only that the kidney was human but that it had come from a middle-aged alcoholic woman who suffered (as did Catherine Eddowes) from Bright's disease. Moreover, the inch of renal artery still attached to the preserved piece of kidney precisely matched the severed arterial remains in Eddowes's eviscerated body.

There seemed little doubt that the ghastly human artifact sent to George Lusk was the real thing—or that the note that accompanied it was an authentic communication from the Whitechapel Butcher. To this day, the "From Hell" letter is regarded as the only apparently genuine message ever sent by the legendary killer.

KILLER COUPLES

Can a woman live with a man for many years without knowing he is a homicidal sex maniac? Apparently so. Some of the most infamous serial killers in history—among them Albert

"Boston Strangler" **DeSalvo,** Peter **Kürten,** and Andrei **Chikatilo**—were married to women who had no inkling of their husbands' sinister secret lives. It's possible to feel sorry for such women, who eventually discover, to their uttermost dismay, that they've been mated to monsters.

There is, however, another type of woman who—far from inspiring sympathy—elicits only loathing and disbelief. This is the wife or lover of a serial killer who is not only aware of the horrors her man commits but also actively participates in them.

Perhaps the most infamous of this breed is Myra Hindley. A shy, twenty-three-year-old typist from Manchester, England, Hindley led an unremarkable life until she hooked up with Ian Brady, a psychopathic creep with a taste for sadomasochistic porn and Nazi paraphernalia. Before long, Hindley was dressing up in S.S. regalia and posing for Brady's obscene photos—a kinky but relatively harmless pastime compared to the horrors that followed. Beginning in July 1963, the perverted pair murdered a series of children, then buried the corpses in the deso-

Myra Hindley and Ian Brady; from *Bloody Visions* trading cards *(© & ™ 1995 M. H. Price and Shel-Tone Publications. All rights reserved.)*

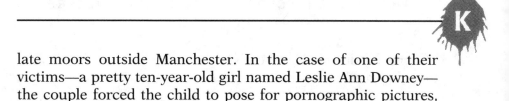

late moors outside Manchester. In the case of one of their victims—a pretty ten-year-old girl named Leslie Ann Downey— the couple forced the child to pose for pornographic pictures, then tape-recorded her tormented pleas before killing her. When the tape was played at the 1966 trial of the **Moors Murderers,** spectators and jurors alike wept uncontrollably.

Like Brady and Hindley, some deadly duos are unmarried lovers who enjoy serial murder the way other couples savor candle-lit dinners and romantic weekends at a country inn. The "Lonely Hearts Killers," Martha Beck and Raymond Fernandez, committed an indeterminate number of homicides in the late 1940s (they confessed to three but were suspected of twenty), including the murder of a two-year-old girl. Right to the bitter end, Beck persisted in seeing their vile affair as a storybook romance, vowing undying love for her sleazeball companion even as she was being led to the chair.

Carol Bundy took romantic devotion to even more hideous lengths. In the early 1980s, Bundy was the live-in lover of Douglas Clark, a psychopathic killer of prostitutes and necrophiliac dubbed the "Sunset Strip Slayer." Among his various pleasures, Clark liked to lure young women into his car, shoot them in the temple while they were fellating him, then carry their decapitated heads home for further fun and games. On at least one occasion, Bundy helped out by playing beautician—applying lipstick and makeup to one of the heads and giving it a pretty hairdo. As soon as she was done, her boyfriend took the head into the bathroom and used it for oral sex. "We had a lot of fun with her," Bundy later confessed. "I made her up like a Barbie."

There are also cases of husbands and wives who share a taste for serial murder—couples who add spice to their marriage by indulging in unspeakable crime. Between 1978 and 1980, Charlene Gallego helped procure teenage victims for her sadistic husband, Gerald, by luring them into his car with the promise of marijuana. She would then sit in the front seat and watch while he raped, sodomized, and beat them to death with a hammer. More recently, the British couple Fred and Rosemary West were charged with the grisly torture-murder of ten young women— including their own sixteen-year-old daughter! The monstrous Mrs. West, however, is no longer part of a killer couple. She became a widow on New Year's Day, 1995, when her abominable mate hanged himself in his jail cell.

THE "HONEYMOON KILLERS"

No.4

MARTHA BECK
Lonely Hearts Killer

MHPRICE
1994

Martha Beck; from *Bloody Visions* **trading cards** *(© & ™ 1995 M. H. Price and Shel-Tone Publications. All rights reserved.)*

The loathsome love story of Martha Beck and Raymond Fernandez made it to the screen in the 1970 sleeper *The Honeymoon Killers*, starring Shirley Stoler and Tony LoBianco. Writer/director Leonard Kastle does an outstanding job of capturing the creepy essence of this repugnant romance. In spite (or perhaps because) of its cheapness, this black-and-white low-budget chiller is extremely effective—just watching it makes you feel vaguely unclean.

A COUPLE OF CRAZY KIDS

Portrait of Charles Starkweather by Chris Pelletiere

Charlie "Little Red" Starkweather—a nineteen-year-old garbage collector from Lincoln, Nebraska—saw himself as a romantic young rebel like his teen idol, James Dean. In reality, he was a sociopathic punk with a grudge against everyone in the world except his fourteen-year-old sweetheart, Caril Ann Fugate. On December 1, 1957, Starkweather knocked over a gas station in Lincoln, abducted the twenty-one-year-old attendant, drove him out to the countryside, and gunned him down in cold blood.

That was just a warm-up for the most notorious murder spree of the 1950s.

Seven weeks later, Charlie went to visit Caril, who hadn't come home yet from school. Her mother—who had a justifiably low opinion of Stark-weather—let him know what she thought of him. Charlie shot her and her husband to death with his trusty .22 caliber rifle. Caril arrived home just as her psycho boyfriend was choking her baby sister to death by ramming the rifle barrel down her throat. After Caril tacked a note to the front door—

"Stay a Way. Every Body is Sick With the Flu"—the loathsome lovebirds settled in to watch TV, pig out on junk food, and screw.

When the food ran low and suspicious relatives began coming round, the pair made off in Charlie's jalopy. Stopping at a local farmhouse, they shot both the seventy-year-old owner and his dog, then hitched a ride with two high school sweethearts, Robert Jensen and Carol King. After abducting them at gunpoint, Charlie killed the boy, then raped the girl and shot her. In an apparent fit of jealousy, Caril reportedly mutilated the dead girl's genitals with a hunting knife.

Heading back to Lincoln, they invaded the home of a wealthy business-man, C. Lauer Ward, where Charlie tortured, raped, and killed Mrs. Ward and the fifty-one-year-old housemaid. After breaking the neck of the family dog, Charlie settled down to wait for Mr. Ward to return from work, blast-ing him as he stepped over the threshold.

Escaping in Ward's limousine, the pair headed for Washington state. By then, a 1,200-man posse was hunting for the killer couple. Deciding to switch vehicles, they stopped outside Douglas, Wyoming, where Char-lie shot a salesman named Merle Collison as he dozed in his car. Charlie was wrestling the corpse from behind the steering wheel when a passing motorist stopped and began to grapple with the little killer. Starkweather managed to leap into the limo and roar away just as the sheriffs arrived. Leading them on a high-speed chase, he surrendered after being grazed by a police bullet. The twenty-six-day murder spree, which left ten people dead, was over. Charlie was electrocuted on June 24, 1959. Caril was sentenced to life but was paroled in 1977.

Sordid as it was in reality, their story contained enough seductive ingre-dients—doomed young outlaw lovers on the lam—to give it romantic ap-peal. It has been told and retold in various forms, from Bruce Springsteen's song "Nebraska" to Terrence Malick's 1973 cult film, *Badlands*, and Oli-ver Stone's surrealistic update, *Natural Born Killers*.

KRAFFT-EBING

Anyone who thinks that serial murder is strictly a modern-day phenomenon will be quickly disabused of that notion by a glance at *Psychopathia Sexualis*, the classic nineteenth-century text on sexual deviation. Its author was Dr. Richard von Krafft-Ebing (1840–1902), a distinguished German physician who was regarded as the most important neuropsychiatrist of his day.

Krafft-Ebing's massive compendium covers every known perversion, from foot fetishism to necrophilia. For the student of serial murder, the most interesting portions are the case histories of notorious lust murderers. Krafft-Ebing covers all the big-name sex-killers of the nineteenth-century, including **Jack the Ripper** and Joseph **Vacher.** He also discusses a number of lesser-known, but seriously alarming, psychopaths, such as the English clerk "Alton" who—after dismembering a child—made the following entry in his personal diary: "Killed to-day a young girl; it was fine and hot."

Another obscure but horrifying case recorded by Krafft-Ebing is that of "a certain Gruyo, aged forty-one, with a blameless past life, [who] strangled six women in the course of ten years. They were almost all public prostitutes and quite old. After the strangling, he tore out their intestines and kidneys through the vagina. Some of the victims he violated before killing, others, on account of the occurrence of impotence, he did not. He set about his horrible deeds with such care that he remained undetected for ten years."

Krafft-Ebing's pioneering work makes it shockingly clear that though serial slaughter is unquestionably on the rise, the crime itself has always been with us.

> "I opened her breast and with a knife cut through the fleshy parts of the body. Then I arranged the body as a butcher does beef, and hacked it with an axe into pieces. . . . I may say that while opening the body, I was so greedy that I trembled and could have cut out a piece and eaten it."
>
> Lust murderer Andreas Bichel, as quoted
> by Professor Richard von Krafft-Ebing

PETER KÜRTEN

In his own words, Peter Kürten aspired to become "the most celebrated criminal of all time." He didn't quite make it—other criminals are more famous, including his role model, **Jack the Ripper.** Still, though Kürten fell short of that goal, he can lay claim to another distinction. In a century that has produced a slew of sadistic lust killers, Kürten, in the view of many experts, may have been the most appalling of all.

The household Kürten grew up in—a single room occupied by ten family members—was a hotbed of depraved sex. His father was a vicious drunk who habitually forced himself on his wife in front of the children and was jailed for the rape of his thirteen-year-old daughter. Kürten, too, engaged in sex with his sisters.

Young Kürten's favorite form of sexual activity, however, wasn't incest but bestiality. A neighbor who worked as a dog catcher taught the boy how to torture and masturbate animals, forging an early link in Kürten's already twisted psyche between sadistic cruelty and sexual release. Between the ages of thirteen and fifteen, he committed countless acts of bestiality with pigs, sheep, and goats, deriving particularly intense pleasure from stabbing the animal to death while having intercourse with it.

At fifteen, Kürten—already a habitual thief—was arrested and jailed, the first of a long string of prison sentences. Altogether, he would spend more than half of his forty-seven years behind bars. Between 1899 and 1928, during those periods when he managed to remain at large, he may have committed as many as three murders, though none was ever pinned on him. A raging pyromaniac, he also derived sexual satisfaction from torching barns, another of his favorite pastimes.

Kürten took a wife in 1921, winning the consent of his bride-to-be in an unconventional (if characteristic) way: he threatened to kill her if she refused to marry him. Until Kürten himself confessed to the unspeakable truth, his loyal, long-suffering wife remained completely unaware that she was wed to the infamous "Monster of Düsseldorf."

Kürten earned that nickname in 1929. During that year, he unleashed an unprecedented torrent of violence, attacking twenty-nine people between February and November. This blood spree came to an end with the strangling and frenzied stabbing of a five-year-old girl, Gertrude Alberman. A few days later—in emulation of his idol, Jack the Ripper—Kürten sent the police a letter. In it, he directed them to the savaged remains of the Alberman girl, as well as to the body of another of his victims, a housemaid he had stabbed twenty times and sodomized after death.

For more than a year, the citizens of Düsseldorf lived in terror. The police did everything possible to track down the killer, questioning nearly a thousand suspects and following hundreds of leads. But Kürten was hellishly difficult to track. Most lust killers prefer a single kind of weapon and a certain type of victim. But Kürten used axes, scissors, hammers, knives, and his bare hands to kill the young and old, male and female alike.

In May 1930, Kürten mysteriously let a young woman go after attempting to rape her. Seventy-two hours later, he was under arrest. In custody, he spilled out his unspeakable story in amazing detail. Among other facts, authorities learned that—besides his other perversions—Kürten was a **Vampire,** who drank the blood of various victims, and he had once experienced an ejaculation after cutting the head off a sleeping swan and guzzling the blood from the neck stump. Convicted of nine murders, he was guillotined in July 1931.

"In the case of Ohliger, I also sucked blood from the wound on her temple, and from Scheer from the stab in the neck. From the girl Schulte I only licked the blood from her hands. It was the same with the swan in the Hofgarten. I used to stroll at night through the Hofgarten very often, and in the spring of 1930 I noticed a swan sleeping at the edge of the lake. I cut its throat. The blood spurted up and I drank from the stump and ejaculated."

From the confessions of Peter Kürten

LADY-KILLERS

The conventional image of a serial killer is someone like Norman Bates—a guy so nice and harmless-looking that you'd never suspect he was a homicidal maniac. Clearly, this is a popular misconception. There have been plenty of scary-looking serial killers: hard-bitten losers like Henry Lee **Lucas,** wild-eyed madmen like Charles **Manson,** Mephistophelian creeps like Richard "Night Stalker" **Ramirez.** Still, stereotypes often possess a kernel of truth—and there have, in fact, been a number of serial killers who look not just normal but downright presentable. Unlike such psychotic dweebs as David **Berkowitz** and Edward **Gein**—who couldn't get the time of day from a woman—these debonair sociopaths are highly attracted to the opposite sex. They are genuine lady-killers—in more ways than one.

Though Ted **Bundy** is undoubtedly the best known of this breed, he certainly wasn't the first. A hundred years ago, another attractive young fellow who shared Bundy's first name—Theodore Durrant—earned nationwide notoriety as one of the most heinous killers of the century. A bright and personable twenty-three-year-old who still lived at home with his parents, Durrant appeared to be a paragon of young American manhood: a medical student, Sunday school teacher, and a member of the California militia signal corps. He was good-looking, too: tall, trim, and athletic, with fine, almost feminine features. Women found him hard to resist. On April 3, 1895, Durrant lured one of his lady friends into an empty church, then strangled her, raped her corpse, and hid it in the belfry. Nine days later, he dispatched another young woman in a similar way. It wasn't long before Durrant—who quickly became known as the "Demon of the Belfry"—was arrested, tried, and condemned to death. Public detestation of Durrant was so intense that, after he was hanged, no cemetery in San Francisco would agree to bury him. His parents had to take his body to Los Angeles for cremation.

Durrant's contemporary Dr. H. H. **Holmes,** was also catnip to the ladies. A dapper, smooth-talking sociopath, Holmes had no trouble working his seductive charm on scores of young women, an indeterminate number of whom met their ends in the depths of his infamous "Murder Castle." A model of Gilded Age enterprise,

159

TED BUNDY

Ted Bundy; from *True Crime Trading Cards, Series Two: Serial Killers and Mass Murderers;* art by Jon Bright *(Courtesy of Jon Bright and Valarie Jones)*

Theo Durrant hauls a victim to the belfry in this nineteenth-century engraving.

Holmes found a way to make a profit from his crimes by peddling the mounted bones of his victims to local medical schools.

Our own century has produced more than its share of lethal ladies' men. One of the most notorious was the English psycho-killer Neville Heath. Tall, handsome, and charming, Heath looked like a Hollywood version of a British war hero. He was, in fact, a military officer who saw action as an RAF bomber pilot in World War II. Unfortunately, he was also a sadistic sociopath whose taste for bondage and flogging blossomed into full-blown blood lust. In June 1946, a part-time actress named Margery Gardner accompanied Heath to his hotel room for a night of kinky sex. When Gardner's body was found the next day, the condition of her corpse shocked even hardened policemen. Tied up and suffocated with a gag, she had been savagely whipped with a riding crop. Her nipples had nearly been bitten off, and a poker had been thrust between her legs. Not long afterward, Heath murdered and mutilated another young woman he had met at a Bournemouth hotel. Arrested shortly afterward, he pleaded not guilty by reason of insanity at his trial, but the jury took less than an hour to convict him. He remained suave to the end. On the day of his hanging, he requested a double whiskey from the warden like a gentleman ordering a drink at a hotel bar.

> *"You feel the last bit of breath leaving their body. You're looking into their eyes. A person in that situation is God!"*
>
> TED BUNDY, on the joy of murder

LETTERS

There is some dispute as to whether the so-called "Unab-omber"—the antitechnological terrorist responsible for a string of letter bomb attacks since 1978—can be considered a serial murderer. Some people say he most certainly is: after all, he killed three people and seriously injured almost two dozen more. Others, however, see him as a revolutionary zealot who resorted to violence as a way of promoting his beliefs. This question remains a matter of debate, but one thing's for sure—the guy can write. In August 1995, he sent a letter to the *New York Times*, offering to refrain from violence if the paper agreed to publish his tract, "Industrial Society and Its Fate"—a 35,000-word manifesto that (however crackpot in some of its views) is a model of literacy, clarity, and coherence.

Unfortunately, the Unabomber also put his writing skills to less impressive uses. At the same time that he sent his letter to the *Times*, he also wrote to one of his victims, Dr. David Gelernter of Yale University, taunting the professor as a "techno-nerd." In this regard, the Unabomber is, in fact, typical of serial killers, a number of whom have taken delight in communicating through taunting missives.

During the height of the "Whitechapel Horrors," the London police were inundated with letters purporting to be from the shadowy killer. Almost all of these were hoaxes, but one was signed with a sinister pseudonym that would quickly become the most infamous name in criminal history:

> Dear Boss,
>
> I keep on hearing the police have caught me but they won't fix me just yet. I have laughed when they look so clever and talk about being on the right track. . . . I am down on whores and I shan't quit ripping them till I do get buckled. Grand work the last job was. I gave the lady no time to squeal. How can they catch me now. I love my work and want to start again. You will soon hear of me with my funny little games. . . . My knife is nice and sharp I want to get to work right away if I get a chance. Good luck.
>
> Yours truly
> **Jack the Ripper**

Ninety years later, the New York City psycho who, until that time, had been known as the ".44-Caliber Killer" received a new and permanent nickname when he left a ranting letter at a crime scene. Addressed to a Queens police captain, the letter began:

> I am deeply hurt by your calling me a wemon hater. I am not. But i am a monster. I am the "son of Sam." I am a little brat.
>
> When father Sam gets drunk he gets mean. He beats his family. Sometimes he ties me up to the back of the house. Other times he locks me in the garage. Sam loves to drink blood.

"Go out and kill," commands father Sam.

Behind the house some rest. Mostly young—raped and slaughtered—their blood drained—just bones now. . . .

I feel like an outsider. I am on a different wavelength then everybody else—programmed to kill.

In August 1969, another serial assassin who murdered with a gun—the California killer known only as **Zodiac**—mailed letters to three Bay area newspapers. Part of each letter was written in code. When these passages were deciphered, they formed one chilling message: "I like to kill people because it is so much fun. It is more fun than killing wild game in the forest, because Man is the most dangerous animal of all. . . . The best part will be when I die. I will be reborn in Paradise, and then all that I have killed will become my slaves. I will not give you my name because

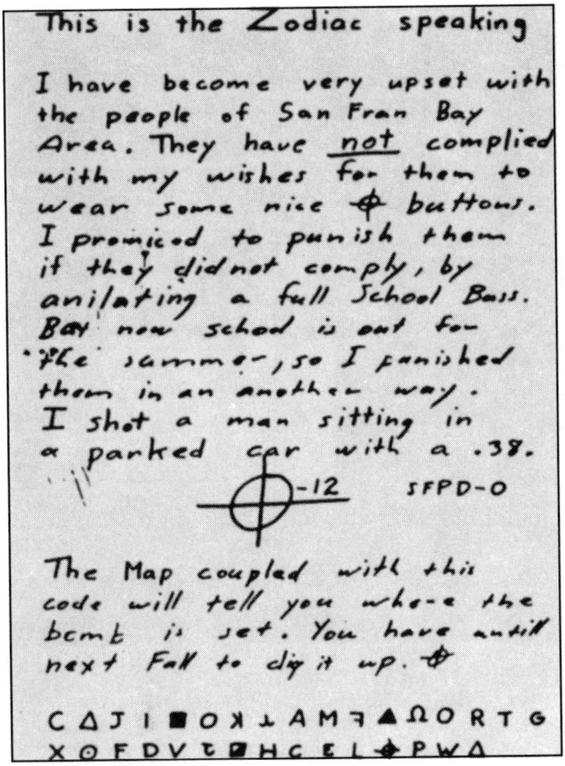
This is the Zodiac speaking

I have become very upset with the people of San Fran Bay Area. They have not complied with my wishes for them to wear some nice ⊕ buttons. I promiced to punish them if they did not comply, by anilating a full School Buss. Bay now school is out for the summer, so I punished them in an another way. I shot a man sitting in a parked car with a .38.

⊕-12 SFPD-0

The Map coupled with this code will tell you where the bomb is set. You have untill next Fall to dig it up. ⊕

"Zodiac" letter

you will try to slow or stop my collecting of slaves for my after-life." The following month, Zodiac sent another letter to the *San Francisco Chronicle*, threatening to "wipe out a school bus full of children"—a threat which, thankfully, he never carried out.

> *"I am deeply hurt by your calling me a wemon hater. I am not. But i am a monster. I am the 'son of Sam.' I am a little brat."*
>
> DAVID BERKOWITZ

THE SICKEST LETTER EVER WRITTEN?

Albert Fish in custody *(New York Daily News)*

Undoubtedly the most ghastly letter ever written by a serial murderer is the one that cannibalistic child killer Albert **Fish** mailed to the mother of his twelve-year-old victim Grace Budd. Fortunately, Mrs. Budd was functionally illiterate and so was spared the horror of reading this unspeakable document. The original of this letter is now part of the collection of artist Joe Coleman:

My dear Mrs. Budd,

In 1894 a friend of mine shipped as a deck hand on the Steamer Tacoma, Capt. John Davis. They sailed from San Francisco for Hong Kong China. On arriving there he and two others went ashore and got drunk. When they returned the boat was gone. At that time there was a famine in China. Meat of any kind of was from $1–3 Dollars a pound. So great was the suffering among the very poor that all children under 12 were sold to the Butchers to be cut up and sold for food in order to keep others from starving. A boy or a girl under 14 was not safe in the street. You could go to any shop and ask for steak—chops—or stew meat. Part of the naked body of a boy or a girl would be brought out and just what you wanted cut from it. A boy or girls behind which is the sweetest part of the body and sold as veal cutlet brought the highest price. John staid there so long he acquired a taste for human flesh. On his return to N.Y. he stole two boys one 7 and one 11. Took them to his home stripped them naked tied them in a closet. Then burned everything they had on. Several times every day and night he spanked them—tortured them—to make their meat good and tender. First he killed the 11 yr old boy, because he had the fattest ass and of course the most meat on it. Every part of his body was Cooked and eaten except head—bones and guts. He was Roasted in the oven (all of his ass), boiled, broiled, fried, stewed. The little boy was next, went the same way. At that time, I was living at 409 E. 100 St. near—right side. He told me so often how good Human flesh was I made up my mind to taste it. On Sunday June the 3—1928 I called on you at 406 W 15 St. Brought you pot cheese—strawberries. We had lunch. Grace sat in my lap and kissed me. I made up my mind to eat her. On the pretense of taking her to a party. You said Yes she could go. I took her to an empty house in Westchester I had already picked out. When we got there, I told her to remain outside. She picked wildflowers. I went upstairs and stripped all my clothes off. I knew if I did not I would get her blood on them. When all was ready I went to the window and Called her. Then I hid in a closet until she was in the room. When she saw me all naked she began to cry and tried to run down stairs. I grabbed her and she said she would tell her mamma. First I stripped her naked. How did she kick—bite and scratch. I choked her to death, then cut her in small pieces so I could take my meat to my rooms, Cook and eat it. How sweet and tender her little ass was roasted in the oven. It took me 9 days to eat her entire body. I did *not* fuck her tho I could of had I wished. She died a *virgin*.

LOVERS' LANE MANIACS

Driving home from the movies one Saturday night, a high school boy and his date pulled into their favorite lover's lane to do some necking. The boy turned on the radio for a little mood music. Suddenly, an announcer came on to say that a crazed killer with a hook in place of his right hand had escaped from the local insane asylum. The girl became scared and begged the boy to take her home. He got angry, stepped on the gas, and roared off. When they reached her house, the boy got out of the car and went around to the passenger side to let her out. There, hanging from the door handle, was a bloody hook!"

So goes the story of the "Hookman"—a homicidal maniac who preys on adolescents as they make out inside a parked car. Teenagers—who have been telling some version of this story for at least forty years—often accept it as the gospel truth. Folklore scholars, on the other hand, see it as an "urban legend" that reflects the anxieties of adolescent boys and girls who are just confronting the tricky issues of grown-up sexuality. While the folklorists make a valuable point, there may be more reality to the story than they realize. The fact is that the terrifying figure of a lovers' lane maniac is not purely a figment of the teenage imagination.

World War II had barely ended when the tiny southwestern town of Texarkana found itself under siege from a night-prowling gunman whose favorite targets were young, unwary lovers. In early March 1946, this masked maniac snuck up on a couple, ordered them out of the car, then—after pistol whipping the young man—subjected the girl to such vicious sexual torture that she begged to be killed. Precisely three weeks later, he struck again, this time shooting both young victims in the back of their heads. Following another three-week hiatus, the "Moonlight Murderer"—as the press dubbed him—killed yet another pair of sweethearts as they returned from a dance at the VFW hall. A massive manhunt was launched, involving local sheriffs, Texas Rangers, and homicide detectives disguised as teenage lovers. But the phantom gunman was never caught.

Equally elusive was the diabolical gunman known as **Zodiac,** whose victims included several young couples killed on deserted country roads. A third, notorious couple killer, David "Son of Sam" **Berkowitz,** was eventually apprehended—but not before he had shot over a dozen victims as they sat in their cars on the darkened streets of New York City.

TEEN TERROR LEGENDS

Young people love to give each other the chills with supposedly true stories about psychokillers. Though "The Hookman" is the most famous of these urban folktales, it's only one of many. Another is "The Boyfriend's Death," a story that the teller invariably swears is absolutely, positively true, since she heard it from an unimpeachable source, such as the next-door neighbor of her best friend's cousin. Typically, the story deals with a teenage couple whose car runs out of fuel one night as they are driving through some remote wooded area. The boy decides to hike into town for gas, telling the girl to make sure to keep the car doors locked, since there is a psycho on the loose. Huddling alone in the car, the girl waits anxiously for her boyfriend's return. But as the night passes, there is no sign of him. After a while, she hears a strange, scratching noise on the car roof. The next morning, a police cruiser arrives. As the girl is helped out of the car, she looks up and sees her boyfriend's butchered corpse, swinging upside-down from a tree branch, his fingernails scraping the roof!

A similar folktale, "The Roommate's Death," tells of two young women sharing a suite in a college dorm. Hearing that there is a serial killer at large, they lock themselves into their separate bedrooms. That night, one of the girls hears someone scratching ominously on the connecting door between the two bedrooms. In the morning, she musters up the courage to open the door—and discovers her murdered roommate, her throat cut from ear to ear. The scratching sound had been the victim's dying effort to get help.

Other teen folktales about psychokillers include "The Assailant in the Backseat"—about unwary women who discover that they have been driving along with a homicidal maniac hiding in the car—and "The Baby-sitter

167

and the Man Upstairs," which tells of a baby-sitter who gets menacing calls from a homicidal stranger, only to discover that the calls are coming from the upstairs telephone.

Anyone who hasn't heard these stories firsthand may have encountered them in another form, since many of them have been recast as low-budget horror movies like *Halloween*, *When a Stranger Calls*, and *Friday the 13th*. They have also been retold by folklorist Jan Harold Brunvand in his popular collections of urban legends, beginning with *The Vanishing Hitchhiker*.

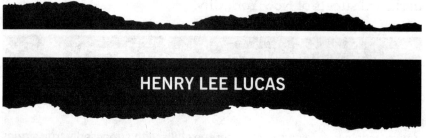

HENRY LEE LUCAS

**Portrait of Henry Lee Lucas
by Chris Pelletierre**

Henry Lee Lucas might be America's most prolific serial killer. On the other hand, he might be the biggest liar since Baron von Münchhausen. After experiencing a self-described "religious conversion" in prison, he decided to bare his soul and confess to an astronomical number of murders. Later, however, he recanted most of his testimony. Among law enforcement officials, the exact number of his crimes remains a matter of debate. Still, even if Lucas's final body count falls far short of the five hundred victims he originally claimed, he nevertheless ranks as one of the most depraved serial killers in history.

Subjected to untold horrors by his insanely abusive mother (see **Up-bringing**), Lucas began indulging in sadistic depravity while still a child. By thirteen, he was engaging in sex with his older half-brother, who also introduced Henry to the joys of bestiality and **Animal Torture.**(One of their favorite activities was slitting the throats of small animals, then sexually violating the corpses.)

One year later, he committed his first murder, strangling a seventeen-year-old girl who resisted his efforts to rape her. In 1954, the eighteen-year-old Lucas received a six-year prison sentence for burglary. Soon after his release in 1959, he got into a drunken argument with his seventy-four-year-old mother and stabbed her to death. (He also confessed to rap-ing her corpse, though he later retracted that detail.)

Receiving a forty-year sentence for second-degree murder, Lucas ended up in a state psychiatric facility. In spite of his own protestations—"When they put me out on parole, I said I'm not ready to go. I told them all, the warden, the psychologist, everybody, that I was going to kill"—he was released after only ten years. Eighteen months later he was back in prison for molesting two teenage girls.

Lucas was discharged from the state pen in 1975. Not long afterward, he met Ottis Toole, a vicious psychopath who became Lucas's partner in one of the most appalling killing sprees in the annals of American crime. For the next seven years, this deranged duo roamed the country, murder-ing and mutilating an untold number of victims. Like Lucas, the profoundly depraved Toole also had a taste for necrophilia. He also indulged in occa-sional cannibalism (an atrocity that Lucas tended to shun, since he found human flesh too gamy). For much of their odyssey, they were accompa-nied by Toole's preadolescent niece, Frieda "Becky" Powell, who became Lucas' lover, common-law wife, and—ultimately—victim.

Lucas was picked up on a weapons charge in 1983. A few days later, after apparently being stricken by an uncharacteristic attack of bad con-science, he summoned his jailer. "I done some pretty bad things," he muttered. With that, he began spilling his guts, admitting to a staggering number of murders. Some of these have been confirmed, others have proven false, many remain open cases. According to certain investigators, Lucas may have killed as many as sixty-nine victims; others put the num-ber at eighty-one or possibly even higher. At his 1985 trial, he was con-victed of ten homicides—more than enough to get him the death sentence.

Whatever the actual total, the horrific nature of Lucas's life and crimes was summed up in one of his own statements: "Killing someone is just like walking outdoors. If I wanted a victim, I'd just go and get one."

Viewers interested in subjecting themselves to a singularly disturbing cinematic experience should rush right out and rent *Henry: Portrait of a Serial Killer*, John McNaughton's brilliant (if harrowing) fictionalization of the Lucas-Toole story.

> *"Sex is one of my downfalls. I get sex any way I can get it. If I have to force somebody to do it, I do. . . . I rape them; I've done that. I've killed animals to have sex with them, and I've had sex while they're alive."*
>
> HENRY LEE LUCAS

LUSTMORD

For unexplained reasons, possibly having to do with their national character, Germans have a knack for coining colorful, descriptive words for nasty human behavior. The same folks who came up with the term *schadenfreude* (meaning "to take pleasure in another person's misfortune") also invented the word *lustmord*: to kill for joy, for the sheer, sexy fun of it.

Lustmord, in short, is really another, catchier name for sexual homicide. The classic lust murderer doesn't just kill his victims (usually women). He derives intense erotic pleasure from maiming and mutilating their bodies—gutting or beheading them, cutting out their vulvas, slicing off their breasts. "The presumption of a murder out of lust is always given when injuries of the genitals are found," writes Dr. Richard von Krafft-Ebing in his classic study, *Psychopathia Sexualis*, "and still more, when the body has been opened or parts (intestines, genitals) torn out."

Not only did the Germans invent the term *lustmord*, they pioneered its actual practice—at least according to one crime expert, Colin Wilson, who maintains that the earliest documented lust murderer in history was a sixteenth-century German named Nicklaus Stüller. Among his other atrocities, Stüller killed and cut open the bellies of three pregnant women, one of whom was carrying twins.

In our own century, Germany has continued its tradition of producing some of the world's most appalling lust murderers. During the years between the two world wars, no less than four of these monsters were at large in Germany: Fritz **Haarmann,** the "Vampire of Hanover," responsible for the slaughter of as many as fifty young men; Georg Grossmann, "The Berlin Butcher," charged with murdering and cannibalizing fourteen young women; Karl Denke, the "Mass Murderer of Münsterberg," another cannibal who butchered at least thirty people and stored their pickled flesh in the basement of his inn; and Peter **Kürten,** the "Monster of Düsseldorf," who murdered, raped, and mutilated a minimum of thirty-five victims, mostly women and children.

For a scholarly discussion of lust murder as a major theme in German art and literature during the years between the wars, readers are referred to Professor Maria Tatar's book, *Lustmord: Sexual Murder in Weimar Germany* (Princeton: Princeton University Press, 1995).

LYCANTHROPY

S erial murder has always existed, but the terminology used to describe this most heinous of crimes has changed over the centuries. Four hundred years ago, killers roamed the European countryside, slaughtering their victims with a bestial ferocity. But back then, they weren't known as "sociopaths" or "homicidal maniacs" or "lust murderers." They were known as *lycanthropes*, a term that derives from two Greek words—*lykos* (meaning "wolf") and *anthropos* (meaning "man"). In short, these maniacs were thought to be literal wolf-men or werewolves.

Some of these psychos were so deranged that they themselves might have actually believed they were supernatural monsters. The peasants they preyed on certainly did. So did the authorities, who openly believed in lycanthropy and regarded it as one of the most pressing social problems of the day.

In old-time movies like the 1941 classic *The Wolf Man*, lycanthropy is depicted as a terrible curse. Lon Chaney Jr. doesn't enjoy turning into a werewolf, but whenever the moon is full, he begins to sprout hair, claws, and fangs whether he likes it or not. Sixteenth-century people had a different view of things. Werewolves were regarded as malevolent men who had deliberately entered into a bargain with the devil. They *wanted* to turn into monsters.

In the late 1500s, a French hermit named Gilles Garnier was rumored to have cut just such a demonic deal. In exchange, he received a black-magic ointment that allowed him to turn into a ravenous, man-eating wolf. At roughly the same time, a German named Peter Stubbe supposedly peddled his soul for an enchanted belt that endowed him with lycanthropic powers.

The methods of transformation might have differed, but the killings committed by these two maniacs were remarkably similar and equally stomach churning—far more gruesome than the make-believe horrors in any wolf-man movie. Both Garnier and Stubbe were lust murderers and cannibals who preyed primarily on children. In two months, Garnier attacked and tore apart four little victims, using his bare hands and teeth. During a much longer period, Stubbe ravaged at least fifteen victims—including his own son. After ripping out the boy's throat, Stubbe allegedly cracked open his skull and devoured his brains.

Modern-day psychiatry has given us concepts like "antisocial personality disorder" to replace the medieval notion of lycanthropy. Even in our own century, however, a killer occasionally comes along whose crimes are so appalling that they seem like the work of a supernatural monster. Back in the late 1920s, for example, the cannibal-killer Albert **Fish** lured a twelve-year-old girl to an abandoned house known as Wisteria Cottage, then killed her, cut her to pieces, and removed several pounds of her flesh, which he turned into a stew. When this crime was discovered, tabloid writers wracked their brains to come up with sensational names for its perpetrator.

Among other lurid labels, they called him the "Werewolf of Wisteria."

CHARLES MANSON

Charles Manson trading card from *Bloody Visions* (© & ™ *1995 M. H. Price and Shel-Tone Publications. All rights reserved.*)

Manson is unique among homicidal maniacs. The killings that brought him lasting notoriety—the 1969 Tate-LaBianca murders, the most shocking crimes of the 1960s—were actually committed by others; he himself never fired a pistol or wielded a knife. But that's precisely the source of his dark fascination—the Svengali-like power he exerted over his slavish followers, who were prepared to do his most blood-crazed bidding.

Though Manson was little more than a clever con artist with a knack for occult babble, he made himself into an evil messiah, a malevolent guru, an embodiment of the darkest impulses of an era that began by preaching peace, love, and flower power and ended up awash in the satanic fantasy of *Rosemary's Baby*, *The Exorcist*, and "Sympathy for the Devil."

The illegitimate son of a dissolute mother who reportedly once tried to swap him for a pitcher of beer, Manson endured a nightmarish childhood of abandonment and abuse. His adolescence was essentially a continuous cycle of petty crime, arrest, incarceration, and escape. ("Truth is," Manson once said in a rare moment of insight, "I ain't never been anything but a half-assed thief who didn't know how to steal without getting caught.") At eighteen, he sodomized a fellow inmate at knifepoint, a deed that earned him a stint in a federal reformatory. Paroled in 1954, he spent the next dozen years in and out of various prisons for crimes ranging from check forgery to pimping. By the time he was released in 1967—against his own objections—the thirty-three-year-old Manson had spent the bulk of his life behind bars.

He emerged during the heady days of the so-called Summer of Love, when the counterculture was at its euphoric peak. In San Francisco's Haight-Ashbury district—the hotbed of hippiedom—Manson discovered psychedelic drugs, free love, and Aquarian Age occultism. Before long, his sinister charisma had attracted a "family" of drifters and dropouts.

Living with his followers on a dusty ranch outside LA, Manson developed a bizarre apocalyptic theory, partly inspired by—of all things—the Beatles' *White Album*, one of the most benign and whimsical rock and roll albums ever recorded. In particular, he interpreted the song "Helter-Skelter" (which referred to an amusement park kiddie-ride) as a prophecy about an impending race war, during which blacks would rise up and exterminate all white people, except for Manson and his chosen few, who would eventually rule the world. To instigate the war, Manson sent his followers on a deranged mission, ordering them to slay some prominent white people in a way that would implicate black revolutionaries. On the night of August 9, 1969, five of Manson's "family" members broke into the home of film director Roman Polanski and savagely butchered his pregnant wife, actress Sharon Tate, along with four other people. Before leaving, they used the victims' blood to scrawl incendiary grafitti on the walls. The following night, Manson himself led a party of his "creepy crawlers" to the home of a couple named LaBianca, who were similarly slaughtered and mutilated.

The killings set off a panic in Los Angeles and sent shock waves throughout the nation. Ultimately, Manson was arrested when one of his female followers—in jail on an unrelated charge—boasted of the murders to a cell mate.

Manson turned his 1970 trial into a circus (see **Courtroom Theatrics**), but the jury was not amused. He and four of his followers were slated for the gas chamber, but their sentences were commuted to life imprisonment in 1972, when the California Supreme Court abolished the death penalty.

"Wow, what a trip!"

Manson "family" member Susan Atkins, after licking Sharon Tate's blood off her hands.

MARRIAGE

That some of the most notorious serial killers in history have been husbands and fathers is a striking testament to the grotesquely divided personalities of these psychopaths—their ability to lead outwardly "normal" lives while secretly engaged in the most depraved activities imaginable. The roster of homicidal family men includes Albert **Fish,** John Wayne **Gacy,** Albert **DeSalvo,** and Andrei **Chikatilo.** It comes as no surprise to learn that their marriages weren't exactly made in heaven.

Though DeSalvo's wife never divorced him, his unslakable sex drive (reputedly, he insisted on love making as often as six times a day) turned her life into an unremitting ordeal. Other women haven't displayed Mrs. DeSalvo's tolerance. After being driven to distraction by his incessant sexual demands, Earle Leonard **Nelson**'s sixty-year-old wife finally kicked him out of the house (at which point he began venting his libido by raping and strangling elderly landladies from coast to coast).

Three wives abandoned Angelo Buono—one of the **Hillside Stranglers**—in rapid succession because of his brutal sex habits (one wife alleged that Buono sodomized her in front of the children). After putting up with his "peculiarities" for almost twenty years—such as his tendency to stroll around the house naked while screaming, "I am Christ!"—Fish's first wife, Anna, finally ran off with a young lover. Fish proceeded to woo and wed a string of desperate widows, each of whom dumped him the moment she discovered his fondness for such nuptial pastimes as flagellation and coprophagy.

John Wayne Gacy's first wife filed for divorce on the day he was sentenced to prison on sodomy charges. His second marriage likewise fell apart after it became clear that Gacy's preferred form of sex involved young male pickups. His wife had no idea, of course, that the crawl space beneath their suburban home contained the corpses of several dozen of these victims. She herself escaped unscathed. The wife of British sex-slayer John Reginald Christie wasn't as lucky. She ended up as one of his victims, her body stashed beneath the dining room floorboards of their London flat (see **Homebodies**).

By contrast, some serial killers actually manage to remain contentedly married to women who never suspect that their husbands are anything other than ordinary, if slightly eccentric, individuals. This was true of Peter **Kürten,** one of the most appalling lust murderers of the twentieth century, whose devoted wife had no inkling that her husband was the infamous "Monster of Düsseldorf."

Even more unbelievable are those cases in which the wives are not only aware of their husbands' depravities but also actively participate in them. Gerard Gallego's seventh wife, Charlene, helped lure young female victims into his clutches by promising them free marijuana. And the British sex-slayer Rosemary West allegedly helped her husband, Fred, torture and murder ten people—including their own sixteen-year-old daughter (see **Killer Couples**).

"MASK OF SANITY"

The Mask of Sanity is the title of a classic 1976 study of the psychopathic personality by psychiatrist Hervey Cleckley. The phrase itself refers to the psychopath's most chilling characteristic: his ability to appear perfectly ordinary, to conceal his cold-blooded nature beneath a normal facade.

Not all psychopaths are criminals. Some are highly successful people. After all, they are masters of manipulation. They can make you believe that they are the most caring, sensitive, charming people in the world. But it's all a show. Under the surface, they're hollow to the core—complete egocentrics who care about nothing except their own greedy desires.

The serial killer is the most frightening of all psychopaths. The most basic human emotions—empathy, conscience, remorse—are completely missing from his emotional makeup. Behind his "mask of sanity," he is utterly evil. And yet, he's so good at dissembling that it's almost impossible to see his true, monstrous face.

Not, at any rate, until it's too late.

For more on this phenomenon, see **Jekyll/Hyde.**

MASS MURDER

Although some people use the terms "mass murder" and "serial killing" synonymously, there are major differences between the two types of homicide. These differences have to do with matters of *time*, *place*, and *manner of killing*.

Serial killers typically commit their atrocities over a considerable span of time—sometimes years. Between each killing there is an emotional **Cooling-off Period,** similar to the sated lull that follows sex. Having satisfied his blood lust, the serial killer subsides into a more-or-less ordinary existence—at least for a while. Eventually, his monstrous cravings begin to grow again until they build into an unbearable need. At that point, he sets out in search of a fresh victim.

Though some serial killers limit themselves to a favorite hunting ground (like the prostitute killer who haunts a particular red-light district), others range freely over a wide territory. Earle Leonard **Nelson,** Ted **Bundy,** and Henry Lee **Lucas,** for example, all murdered women from coast to coast. Once he manages to capture his prey, the serial killer often subjects the victim to unspeakable acts of sadism.

By contrast, the mass murderer is a man who suddenly goes completely berserk, slaughtering a large number of random victims (at least four, according to an FBI criterion) in a single eruption of violence that takes place in one location (like a post office or fast-food restaurant). In short, if the most apt image for a serial killer is the "hunter of humans," the appropriate analogy for a mass murderer is the "human time bomb." He detonates without warning, destroying everyone in the vicinity (including himself, since most mass murderers either kill themselves to avoid capture or are gunned down by police in climactic shoot-outs).

The "classic" case of mass murder is that of Charles Whitman, the twenty-five-year-old architectural student who barricaded himself in a bell tower at the University of Texas in August 1966 and began firing at everyone within rifle range, slaying twenty-one people and wounding another twenty-eight.

As Whitman's case shows, mass murderers often claim more victims than serial killers (Jeffrey **Dahmer,** for example, slew seventeen people as compared to Whitman's twenty-one). And yet, the serial killer is an infinitely more terrifying figure. This is largely because we tend to perceive the mass murderer in human terms—as a deeply disturbed individual who snaps because of a crisis at home or on the job and goes on a wildly destructive rampage.

By contrast, the serial killer—the Jekyll/Hyde monster who coolly stalks his prey and derives his deepest pleasure from torture, mutilation, and butchery—seems like something straight out of a nightmare. Something hardly human.

MEDIA

See **X-rated.**

MODELS

At least one notorious serial killer—Harvey Murray Glatman, who enjoyed taking pictures of his terrified victims before killing them—specialized in preying on photographic models (see **Photographs**). But that's not the kind of models we mean. We mean the plastic, assemble-it-yourself kind. Yes, for those hobbyists who wish to add handsome serial-killer figurines to their collection of hand-painted polystyrene airplanes, automobiles, and battleships, a company called Von Then Productions (497 Westside Avenue, Suite 140, Jersey City, NJ 07304) offers both Charles Manson and Ed Gein model kits. Both of these kits, plus dozens of other creepy models (freaks, demons, zombies, and ghouls) are also available through the Catalogue of Carnage,

America's leading mail-order source of macabre merchandise (see **Cards, Comics, and Collectibles**).

Anyone inclined to condemn these products as a symptom of the total breakdown of moral values in this country might keep in mind that back in the 1960s the Aurora company—America's premier manufacturer of model kits—put out a line of monster figures (Dracula, Frankenstein, the Wolfman, the Mummy) that proved enormously popular. In fact, these kits were so successful that Aurora followed up with a line of do-it-yourself torture and execution devices (starvation cages, gallows, guillotines, etc.), provoking so much parental outrage that the company was forced to withdraw them from the marketplace—much to the distress of horror-happy boomer boys everywhere.

Advertisement for Charles Manson model kit
(Courtesy of Damon Fox)

THE MOORS MURDERERS

Myra Hindley

Ian Brady

Myra Hindley and Ian Brady; from *52 Famous Murderers* **trading cards** *(Courtesy of Roger Worsham)*

The most shocking crimes in modern British history were committed by a pair of perverted lovebirds named Ian Brady and Myra Hindley, aka the "Moors Murderers." Not since Saucy Jack prowled the backstreets of Whitechapel had a series of killings provoked such outrage and horror in England.

A child of the tough Glasgow slums, Brady (whose young, unwed mother had little time for him) was in trouble with the law by the age of thirteen. His sadistic tendencies also showed themselves early on. One boyhood acquaintance recalled the time that little Ian dug a deep pit in a graveyard, tossed in a live cat, then sealed up the opening with a stone. Brady wanted to see how long it would take the animal to die of starvation.

In his early twenties, Brady developed an obsessive fascination with Hitler and the Marquis de Sade. Before long, he was collecting Nazi paraphernalia and indulging in fascistic fantasies and sadistic daydreams. Only one thing was needed to make those daydreams come true—a slavish, masochistic follower.

He found her in Myra Hindley, an attractive twenty-four-year-old working girl who—until she fell under Brady's sway—had showed no signs of deviancy. Soon after they started dating, however, her puppy dog devotion turned into complete emotional submission. In obedience to Brady's needs, the quiet, seemingly well-adjusted young woman transformed herself into a Nazi fetishist's wet dream, a jack-booted dominatrix/sex-slave who loved to wield—and submit—to the whip and to strike pornographic poses for the delectation of her führer. Brady's pet name for her was "Myra Hess" (an homage to Hitler's henchman Rudolph Hess), and he fondly compared her to Irma Grese, the notorious female guard at Belsen concentration camp who took keen delight in torturing inmates.

But acting out Nazi-inspired sex fantasies wasn't enough for Brady. He had other—and far worse—things in mind.

For several years from the early to mid-1960s, the depraved couple abducted and killed at least four children, ranging in age from ten to sixteen. Generally, it was Hindley who lured the victim into her car. Exactly how much she participated in the actual killing remains a matter of debate, though Brady clearly took the more active role. Their final murder was, in many ways, the most appalling. After snatching a ten-year-old girl named Lesley Ann Downey, they brought her back to Hindley's house, bound and stripped her, compelled her to pose for pornographic pictures, and then—before killing her—tape-recorded her heart-wrenching screams, cries, and pleas for mercy. Like their other victims, Downey's corpse was buried on the moors.

The "Moors Murderers" were finally caught when Brady attempted to recruit a second follower, his teenage brother-in-law, David Smith. In the fall of 1965, Brady picked up a young homosexual, brought him home, and bludgeoned him to death in front of Smith. In effect, this was an act of ritual slaughter—a blood initiation intended to bring Smith into Brady's murderous fold. But the plan backfired. Smith was so horrified that he notified the police.

At their 1966 trial, Brady and Hindley had to sit behind bulletproof shields to protect them from an outraged public. When the tape recording of Lesley Ann Downey's final moments was played in court, not only the jury and spectators but hardened police officers as well wept openly.

The "Moors Murderers" were sentenced to life in prison.

MOTIVES

I n Shakespeare's tragic masterpiece *Othello*, the villainous Iago sets out to destroy the noble hero for no apparent reason.

After all, Iago has nothing to gain from wrecking Othello's life. And he isn't really acting out of either envy or revenge. In attempting to explain this character's vicious behavior, one famous scholar coined the memorable phrase "motiveless malignity." Iago does terrible things for one reason only— because he's the embodiment of absolute evil.

Some people tend to see serial murder in the same way—as pure, unprovoked malignity. And indeed—in terms of such traditional, easily identifiable causes as jealousy and greed—serial killing does appear to be a "motiveless" crime.

In actuality, however, there is no such thing as a motiveless murder. Everyone has his reasons—even if those reasons are not immediately obvious. What drives the serial killer are dark, psychological impulses—perverted passions and monstrous lusts. The twisted needs that dominate his psyche are every bit as real and compelling as more "objective" motives, such as the coveting of wealth or the desire to punish an unfaithful lover.

Insofar as serial killing is synonymous with lust murder, the primary motive, according to some experts in the field, is rage against women and the desire to inflict pain and suffering on them—in short, sexual **sadism.** Other specialists, however, insist that the dominant motive behind serial murder is not sex but power—even when the murder involves extreme sexual cruelty. As one sadistic serial killer explained to Special Agent Roy Hazelwood of the FBI's Behavioral Science Unit: "The wish to inflict pain on others is not the essence of sadism. One essential impulse: to have complete mastery over another person, to make him/her a helpless object of our will, to become the absolute ruler over her, to become her God. The most important radical aim is to make her suffer, since there is no greater power over another person than that of inflicting pain on her."

For this reason, some criminologists have begun to regard Ted Kaczynski, the alleged "Unabomber," not as the antitechnological terrorist he claims to be but as a genuine serial killer. According to John Douglas, former head of the BSU, the Unabomber's demands—as expressed in the lengthy manifesto he sent to the media—suggest a "desire for manipulation, domination, and control typical of serial killers."

MOVIES

People have always been intrigued by the kind of homicidal maniacs we now call serial killers, and every time a new mass medium has been invented, it's been used to gratify this primal fascination. In pre-electronic days, the "penny press" dished up wildly lurid accounts of grisly crimes, complete with graphic engravings of the murder victims. One of the earliest recordings produced for the Edison phonograph featured an actor reading the shocking confessions of H. H. **Holmes,** the notorious nineteenth-century "Torture Doctor." When radio became popular, listeners thrilled to such programs as Arch Obler's *Lights Out* (which also paid tribute to Holmes in a famous episode called "Murder Castle"). And ghoulish killers began stalking the screen virtually from the moment that motion pictures were invented.

With almost a century's worth of maniac movies to choose from, narrowing the list down to a mere handful is a thankless task. But if we were organizing the First Annual Serial Killer Film Festival, here—in alphabetical order—are the dozen we'd select:

Deep Red (1976). A truly unsettling gore film from Italian horror-maestro, Dario Argento. David Hemmings (looking highly dissolute) stars as a British pianist on the trail of a deranged killer in Rome. The soundtrack alone is scary enough to give you nightmares for a week.

Dirty Harry (1971). True, this is a classic Clint Eastwood vigilante-hero movie, not a psycho film in the strict sense of the term. But it demands inclusion thanks to Andy Robinson's unforgettable turn as a sniveling psycho modeled on the real-life **Zodiac** killer.

185

Fear City (1984). A shamefully under-rated thriller by director Abel Ferrara, about a serial killer stalking topless dancers in the sleazy heart of Manhattan. The first-rate cast includes Tom Berenger, Billy Dee Williams, Melanie Griffith, Rae Dawn Chong, Michael Grasso, and Maria Conchita Alonso.

Frenzy (1972). After a severe falling off with such turkeys as *Torn Curtain* and *Topaz*, Alfred Hitchcock returned to form in his penultimate film, a witty, stylish, and genuinely shocking thriller about a serial strangler on the loose in London.

Halloween (1978). John Carpenter draws on every teen horror legend ever told in this brilliant low-budget chiller that was followed by several lesser sequels and countless rip-offs.

Henry: Portrait of a Serial Killer (1990). Very possibly the most deeply disturbing—not to say harrowing—serial-killer movie ever made. A cinematic tour de force, but definitely not for everyone. Based on the appalling exploits of Henry Lee **Lucas** and his deranged sidekick, Ottis Toole.

M (1931). Fritz Lang's riveting masterpiece about a serial child-killer terrorizing Weimar Berlin. Loosely based on the career of Peter **Kürten,** the movie made an international star of Peter Lorre as the pudgy personification of psychopathic evil who is hunted down and tried by the criminal underworld.

Maniac (1980). A truly repulsive movie but—for that very reason—worth seeing, since it does such an effective job of capturing the sickening, sordid reality of serial murder. Starring the late lamented Joe Spinnell as a Norman Bates–like character who decks out his private collection of mannequins with the bloody scalps of his murder victims. Gore specialist Tom Savini served up the stomach-churning effects.

Peeping Tom (1960). The movie that effectively ended the career of British director Michael Powell (best known for his ballet fantasy, *The Red Shoes*). A young, psychopathic voyeur films his victims while impaling them with a blade concealed in his camera tripod. Vilified upon release, the movie is now acknowledged as a classic of psychocinema.

Psycho (1960). Not only a certified cinematic masterpiece but the seminal work from which the entire genre of so-called slasher movies springs. The crème de la crème of psychofilms.

Silence of the Lambs (1991). Jonathan Demme's deluxe, Oscar-winning version of Thomas Harris's brilliant best-seller. In Hannibal "The Cannibal" Lecter, the film created a genuine pop myth. Like *Psycho* and *The Texas Chainsaw Massacre*, *Silence* owes a large debt to the true-life crimes of Wisconsin ghoul Ed **Gein.**

The Texas Chainsaw Massacre (1974). The *Citizen Kane* of dismemberment movies. Tobe Hooper—who, sadly, has never been able to duplicate (or even approximate) his greatest achievement—creates the scariest interpretation of the Ed Gein story ever put on film. The movie achieves its shocks through a potent combination of relentless brutality, sickening atmosphere, rampaging sadism, and even a dash of black humor (which first-time viewers tend to miss, since they are generally covering up their eyes with their hands).

> *"Watching him act like a psychopathic killer with a mommy complex is like watching someone else throw up."*
>
> **New York Times** film critic Vincent Canby on Joe Spinell's performance in *Maniac*

MULTIPLE PERSONALITY

Ever since a mild-mannered motel keeper named Norman Bates became possessed by the evil spirit of his dear, departed mother, people have associated serial killers with split personalities. In reality, however, multiple personality disorder (or **MPD,** as it's known in the psychology biz) is an extremely rare condition. Still, that hasn't kept a whole string of serial killers from trying to blame their crimes on their ostensible alter egos.

William Heirens—the so-called "Lipstick Killer," who is best known for the desperate message he scrawled on the bedroom wall of one murder scene ("For heaven's sake catch me before I kill more")—claimed that an alternate personality named George Murman was responsible for the three vicious sex murders he committed in 1945 and 1946. Likewise, John Wayne

Gacy insisted that his thirty-three torture killings were actually the work of an evil personality he called "Jack."

Kenneth Bianchi—one of the **Hillside Stranglers**—was so convincing in inventing a second homicidal personality (named "Steve") that he managed to bamboozle several psychiatrists before being exposed as a fraud.

Indeed, despite all claims to the contrary, there hasn't been a single authenticated case of a split-personality serial killer (see **Insanity**). Crime maven Colin Wilson, however, does describe the apparently genuine case of a serial *rapist* named Billy Milligan who suffered from MPD. Sexually brutalized in childhood by his stepfather, Milligan's traumatized psyche responded by splitting itself into no less than twenty-two separate personalities—including a sixteen-year-old painter named Tommy; a fourteen-year-old boy named David (who claimed that he had once been buried alive); a twenty-two-year-old Englishman named Arthur who spoke fluent Arabic; a Serbo-Croatian thief called Regan; and a nineteen-year-old lesbian named Adalana, who took responsibility for the rapes.

MURDER RINGS

For the most part, serial killing is a solitary business, though simpatico psychos will occasionally bond in lethal pairs (see **Killer Couples** and **Partners**). Much rarer, though not entirely unheard of, are cases where three or more killers join together to commit murder for fun and profit.

For Dr. Morris Bolber and his confederates, Paul and Herman Petrillo, murder was strictly business. Operating in Philadelphia's Italian ghetto during the Great Depression, these enterprising reprobates found a way of turning bodies into bucks by persuading disgruntled housewives to take out hefty life-insurance policies on their hubbies. Then—after orchestrating the "accidental" deaths of the insured—Bolber & Co. split the proceeds with the widows. Between 1932 and 1937, Dr. Bolber and his associates were responsible for the deaths of at least a dozen victims.

While the Bolber-Petrillo organization was driven by good old-fashioned greed, other, far more unsettling motives lurked behind one of the most bizarre murder rings in the annals of crime. Though historically factual, the case has all the earmarks of a classic horror story—a kind of *Stepford Wives* in reverse, involving a quiet little town where the housewives were really homicidal maniacs.

Between 1919 and 1929, at least twenty-six women in the small Hungarian town of Nagyrev found a novel way to rid themselves of tiresome relatives. Led by a murderous midwife named Julia Fazekas—who taught them how to obtain arsenic by boiling flypaper and skimming off the poisonous residue— these fatal females disposed of boorish husbands, sickly children, ailing parents, obnoxious siblings—at least forty-five victims in all before the "Angel-Makers of Nagyrev" (as the newspapers dubbed them) were finally brought to trial.

NAZI BUFFS

C ritics of media violence complain that hard-core "splatter" films like *I Spit on Your Grave* and *Maniac* put bad ideas into the minds of budding psychopaths. But aspiring serial killers don't need movies to inspire them. All they have to do is open a history book.

Published accounts of Nazi atrocities were a common source of inspiration for killers who came of age in the post–World War II era. Graham Young, a British sociopath born in 1947, was a boyhood admirer of Hitler and his genocidal policies. Young also loved to read about the notorious English **Poisoners** of the nineteenth century. When Young was just fourteen, he set about poisoning his own family with all the dispassion of a concentration camp commandant. After a nine-year stint in a mental asylum, Young took a job at a photographic supply firm and immediately reverted to his old exterminative ways, poisoning a bunch of his co-workers before being caught.

Another postwar Briton who embraced Nazi philosophy was Ian Brady, the male half of the notorious **Killer Couple** known as the **"Moors Murderers."** Captivated by the concept of the Aryan Übermensch—the "superman" who is entitled to exert his will on lesser mortals—Brady recruited a willing sex slave, Myra Hindley, who played obedient storm trooper to his two-bit führer. Together this vile pair abducted and murdered four children and left their mangled bodies buried on the moors.

In America, a tormented Chicago teenager named William Heirens was similarly infatuated with Nazism. Both an honor student and a compulsive burglar, Heirens nursed a simmering obsession with violence, sex, and totalitarian power. Besides a stockpile of firearms and a stash of stolen female panties (which he liked to wear around the house), he collected photographs of Hitler, Himmler, and other Nazi bigwigs. In 1945 and 1946, Heirens's obsessions finally boiled over. He murdered two women and a six-year-old girl, leaving an infamous lipstick-scrawled message on the bedroom wall of one crime scene: "For heaven's sake catch me before I kill more. I cannot control myself."

At roughly the same time in Wisconsin, Edward **Gein** was feeding his own demented fantasies with magazine stories about Nazi atrocities. A deranged do-it-yourself-er, Gein was inspired by accounts of concentration camp officials who turned human skin into lampshades. When investigators broke into Gein's horror house in 1957, they found a staggering collection of similarly constructed ghastly artifacts—chair seats, lamp shades, wastebaskets, and more—all crafted from the flesh of corpses Gein had been stealing from local graveyards.

NECROPHILIA

In *Psychopathia Sexualis*, his classic study of aberrant behavior, Richard von Krafft-Ebing calls necrophilia the most monstrous of all perversions. Since necrophilia (from the Greek, meaning "love of the dead") is the practice of having sex with corpses, this is not a surprising assessment. Nor is it surprising that this most monstrous of acts should be common among the most monstrous of criminals—serial killers.

Many infamous psychopaths, from Earle Leonard **Nelson** to Ted **Bundy,** occasionally raped the bodies of their freshly slain victims. Still, some experts in the field of criminal psychology distinguish between this type of outrage—which is motivated by the malevolent desire to completely dominate and violate a victim—and the behavior of the "true necrophiliac," the man who is deeply infatuated with death, who derives his greatest sexual satisfaction from making love to a cadaver. This sort of necrophiliac is much rarer among serial killers. But there have been some notable cases.

Jeffrey **Dahmer's** love affair with dead things began as a child, when his favorite hobby was collecting and dissecting roadkill. By the time he was a grown-up, this morbid obsession had metastasized into an unspeakable perversion. Dahmer told psychiatrists that he routinely cut open the abdomens of his murder victims and masturbated into their viscera. He also confessed to anally raping the corpses. His British counterpart, Dennis **Nilsen,** was also driven by necrophiliac urges, though he tended to treat his victims more tenderly, masturbating as he snuggled beside them in bed.

The most infamous of all American necrophiliacs is Ed **Gein.** Like all classic necrophiliacs, Gein was completely uninterested in living women. He found his sex partners in local cemeteries, which he plundered periodically for more than a dozen years. In general, necrophiliacs are regarded as less of a menace than serial killers because the victims they prey on are already dead.

Gein was no exception. He was more ghoul than serial killer. Still, he was not, by any means, harmless. When the local graveyards ran low on available females, he simply went out hunting for a likely looking prospect and turned her into the kind of woman he loved best—a dead one.

> *"I took her bra and panties off and had sex with her. That's one of those things I guess that got to be a part of my life—having sexual intercourse with the dead."*
>
> HENRY LEE LUCAS, describing his reaction to the death of his beloved common-law wife, twelve-year-old Becky Powell, whom he had just stabbed in the chest during an argument

EARLE LEONARD NELSON

Earle Leonard Nelson; from *Bloody Visions* trading cards *(© & ™ 1995 M. H. Price and Shel-Tone Publications. All rights reserved.)*

In the annals of U.S. crime, Earle Leonard Nelson—aka the "Gorilla Man"—holds a historic position. He was the first American serial sex killer of the twentieth century. In February 1926, he began a frenzied, eighteen-month odyssey that took him from one end of the country to the other and up into Canada. Along the way, he slaughtered no less than twenty-two women—a grisly record that would remain unbroken for another fifty years.

Orphaned in infancy when his young parents both died of syphilis, Nelson was taken in and raised by his mother's family. He was a withdrawn, moody child with bizarre personal habits. (Among his other peculiarities, he would regularly set off for school in neat, freshly laundered garments and return in foul rags, as though he'd swapped clothes with a derelict.) As a result of a severe head injury—sustained when his bicycle collided with a cable car—his behavior became even more erratic.

By his early teens, he was already a habitué of the brothels and bars of San Francisco's Barbary Coast. He had also taken to petty thievery. In 1915—just a few months after this eighteenth birthday—he was arrested for burglary and sentenced to two years in San Quentin. America had just entered World War I when Nelson emerged. He enlisted in the navy, but—after refusing to do anything but lie on his cot and babble about the Great Beast of Revelations—he was confined to a mental institution. He remained there for the duration of the war.

Discharged in 1919, the twenty-two-year-old Nelson met and married a sixty-year-old spinster and proceeded to make her life a daily hell. Shortly after she left him, he attacked a twelve-year-old girl and was returned to the mental asylum. Discharged in 1925, he soon embarked on his deadly career.

He started in San Francisco, working his way up the Pacific Coast to Seattle, then headed eastward. At first, the tabloids dubbed him the "Dark Strangler"; later, he became known as the "Gorilla Man"—a nickname that had less to do with his appearance (he was actually quite ordinary-looking) than with the savagery of his crimes. For the most part, his targets were middle-aged or elderly landladies who had placed "Rooms to Let" ads in their local papers. Nelson—who could be ingratiating when he wanted to—would show up at their homes and ask to see a room. Once alone with his victims, he would undergo a Jekyll/Hyde–like transformation.

Typically, he would choke the women to death, commit postmortem rape, then conceal the corpses in bizarre hiding places. One of his victims was stuffed into an attic trunk. Others were crammed behind the basement furnaces. His final victim was discovered when her husband knelt to say his evening prayers and found her body shoved under the bed.

With the police departments of a dozen different cities on the alert, Nelson headed into Canada, where he finally reached the end of his corpse-strewn trail. After killing two more victims, he was captured in Manitoba. He managed to escape from jail, setting off a widescale panic and massive manhunt. Twelve hours later, he was back in custody—this time for good.

Several months later, Earle Leonard Nelson went to the gallows. His final words were: "I forgive those who have wronged me."

NICKNAMES

With the advent of tabloid newspapers in the 1800s, crime reporters began wracking their brains to come up with catchy nicknames for sensational killers—a tradition that continues to this day. Following is a list of notorious serial murderers along with their sinister pseudonyms:

Richard Angelo, "The Angel of Death"
Elizabeth Bathory, "The Blood Countess"
Kenneth Bianchi and Angelo Buono, "The Hillside Stranglers"
William Bonin, "The Freeway Killer"
Ian Brady and Myra Hindley, "The Moors Murderers"
Gary Carlton, "The Stocking Strangler"
Harvey Louis Carnigan, "The Want Ad Killer"
David Carpenter, "The Trailside Killer"
Andrei Chikatilo, "The Mad Beast"
Douglas Clark, "The Sunset Strip Slayer"
Albert DeSalvo, "The Boston Strangler"
Theo Durrant, "The Demon of the Belfry"
Albert Fish, "The Moon Maniac"
John Wayne Gacy, "Killer Clown"
Ed Gein, "The Plainfield Ghoul"
John Wayne Glover, "The Granny Killer"
Cleo Green, "The Red Demon"
Vaughn Greenwood, "The Skid Row Slasher"
Fritz Haarmann, "The Butcher of Hanover"
William Heirens, "The Lipstick Murderer"
H. H. Holmes, "The Torture Doctor"
Edmund Kemper, "The Co-Ed Killer"
Richard Macek, "The Mad Biter"
Earle Leonard Nelson, "The Gorilla Murderer"
Thierry Paulin, "The Monster of Montmartre"

Heinrich Pommerencke, "The Beast of the Black Forest"
Richard Ramirez, "The Night Stalker"
Melvin Rees, "The Sex Beast"
Vicytor Szczepinski, "The Doorbell Killer"
Peter Sutcliffe, "The Yorkshire Ripper"
Coral Eugene Watts, "The Sunday Morning Slasher"

Thomas Harris acknowledges this tradition in his best-selling thrillers, *Red Dragon* and *The Silence of the Lambs*, whose FBI heroes are on the hunt for two terrifying figures: a serial killer nicknamed the "Tooth Fairy" (because he bites his victims with a special set of dentures) and another dubbed "Buffalo Bill" (because he "always skins his humps").

DENNIS NILSEN

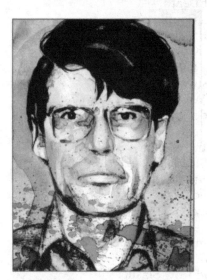

Dennis Nilsen; from
*True Crime Trading
Cards Series Two: Serial
Killers and Mass
Murderers;* art by Jon
Bright *(Courtesy of Jon
Bright and Valarie Jones)*

DENNIS NILSEN

Nilsen—the "British Jeffrey **Dahmer,**" responsible for the grisly murders of fifteen young men—never fit the standard profile of a serial killer. As a child, he recoiled from cruelty to animals. Even bird hunting seemed wrong to him. In his adult life, he devoted himself to helping the downtrodden in his work for the Manpower Services Commission. Even his murders were motivated less by psychopathic rage than by a grotesque form of love. In the phrase of writer Brian Masters, Nilsen "killed for company."

From early adolescence onward, Nilsen's sexuality was marked by a necrophiliac strain. As a teenager, he liked to stretch out in front of a mirror and masturbate while imagining that the body reflected in the glass was a corpse. During a brief homosexual affair in 1972, he took home movies of his lover—an eighteen-year-old army private—while the young man pretended to be dead.

During his eleven-year stint in the military, Nilsen worked for a time as a butcher (an occupation that provided him with skills he would later put to appalling use). After leaving the army in 1972, he joined the London police, lasting just a year. Before long, he had begun his civil service career at a government-run Job Centre. For a time, he had a contented relationship with another young man, but when it finally broke up, the reclusive Nilsen was plunged into a despairing loneliness. He reverted to bizarre autoerotic rituals. Applying powder and paint to his naked body—to make it look like the corpse of a gunshot victim—he would masturbate while regarding his own ghastly flesh in a mirror.

A few days after Christmas, 1978, Nilsen began to kill. After picking up a teenage boy in a pub, Nilsen brought him back to his apartment in the Cricklewood section of London. Frantic for companionship, Nilsen did not want the young man to leave. While the teenager slept, Nilsen garroted him with a necktie, then finished the job by submerging the boy's head in a bucketful of water. Afterward, Nilsen stripped the corpse, gave it a tender, ritual bath and laid it out on his bed. He kept it around the flat for the next few days, caressing it, cleaning it, masturbating over it. Eventually, he stashed it under the floorboards.

Over the next three years, the same ghastly pattern repeated itself another eleven times in Nilsen's Cricklewood apartment. The accumulating bodies posed a problem, which Nilsen dealt with in increasingly sickening ways. At first, he stored the corpses in and around his flat—in his cupboard or under the floorboards or in a garden shed. Eventually, however, he was compelled to dismember the decaying bodies and incinerate them in a backyard bonfire. He tossed an old tire onto the blaze, hoping that the smell of burning rubber would disguise the stench of burning flesh.

In 1981, Nilsen moved to a different apartment, where he murdered three more young men and got rid of the bodies by chopping them up and flushing the chunks down the toilet. (To remove the flesh from the skulls, he boiled the heads in a big soup pot.) Eventually, this method of **Disposal** led to his downfall. When the toilets in the entire building became clogged up, neighbors called a plumber, who discovered human bones and gobs of decomposed flesh blocking the pipes.

Inside his fetid flat, police found a ghastly assortment of human remains—heads and limbs, torsos, bones, and viscera. Nilsen, who confessed freely to fifteen murders, was sentenced to life imprisonment at his 1983 trial.

*"I wished I could stop but I could not.
I had no other thrill or happiness."*

DENNIS NILSEN

NOMADS

Here's a sobering statistic: nearly three-quarters of all known serial killers in the world—74 percent to be exact—come from the United States (as opposed to a measly 19 percent for all of Europe). Clearly, there is something about American culture that is conducive to serial murder. Theories range from our Puritanical attitudes about matters of the flesh—which presumably produce all kinds of sexual pathology—to our steady diet of media violence.

Whatever other factors are involved, one aspect of our cultural life surely exacerbates the problem—the extreme mobility of Americans. Ever since the time of the early pioneers, we've been a people on the go. While this cultural characteristic has undoubtedly been a source of strength (our unique freedom of movement has helped our nation develop at an extraordinary pace), it has also contributed to our notoriously high crime rate. From the days of John Wesley Hardin and Billy the Kid, highly mobile outlaws have been able to get away with murder for years by staying a few steps ahead of the law.

As early as the 1920s, however, a new and even more frightening phenomenon appeared on the criminal scene: the nomadic killer who exploited modern modes of transportation (primarily cars and trains) to keep constantly on the move, leaving behind a trail of corpses (and little else in the way of traceable clues). Earl Leonard **Nelson**—the so-called "Gorilla Murderer" who strangled nearly two dozen women during an eighteen-month, coast-to-coast killing spree—was one of the first of this deadly breed. Another was Carl **Panzram**, the globe-trotting sociopath who bragged of having committed over one thousand homosexual rapes and twenty-one murders in the course of his extraordinarily hard-bitten life. Twenty years later, a homicidal drifter named Jake Bird racked up an even higher body count during his career of peripatetic **Axe Murder.**

It wasn't until the late 1970s and early 1980s, however, that Americans began to perceive nomadic serial murder as a growing public menace, thanks largely to the crimes of monsters like Ted **Bundy** (who committed his lust killings in four different states) and—even more unnervingly—Henry Lee **Lucas,** who may have slaughtered as many as one hundred people during his life of aimless travel. In our mobile, fast-paced society, such itinerant psychopaths can go on killing for years, depositing corpses in quiet stretches of woods, along deserted coastlines, and beside isolated highways—preying on hitchhikers, roadside hookers, casual pickups, and other easy victims as rootless (and often as difficult to trace) as the killers themselves.

For a contrast to the nomadic style of serial murder, see **Homebodies.**

NURSERY RHYMES

As everyone knows, little children are fascinated by violence and horror (if you want to read something *really* scary, check out *The Complete Grimm's Fairy Tales*). So it's not surprising that homicidal maniacs frequently pop up in children's verse.

An anonymous axe-murderer is the subject of this cheerfully grisly nursery rhyme:

> Here comes a candle to light you to bed.
> Here comes a chopper to chop off your head.

A different "chopper"—the one belonging to the infamous German lust murderer and cannibal, Fritz **Haarmann**—features in this German nursery rhyme:

> Just you wait 'til it's your time,
> Haarmann will come after you,
> With his chopper, oh so fine,
> He'll make mincemeat out of you.

The bloody deeds of other real-life killers have also been celebrated in nursery rhymes. Everyone, of course, knows the one about Fall River's most notorious daughter:

> Lizzie Borden took an axe
> And gave her mother forty whacks.
> And when she saw what she had done,
> She gave her father forty-one.

Lizzie's near-contemporary the British "Queen Poisoner," Mary Ann Cotton (see **Black Widows**), was also immortalized in a kiddie rhyme:

> Mary Ann Cotton
> She's dead and she's rotten.
> She lies in her bed
> With her eyes wide oppen.

The English, in fact, seem to specialize in turning lurid crimes into nursery rhymes. Two of the most notorious murderers in British criminal history were the nineteenth-century miscreants Thomas Burke and William Hare. Up until 1832, British law forbade the dissection of human corpses, except for those of executed murderers. As a result, there was a serious shortage of medical school cadavers. To fill this scientific need, some physicians turned to professional body snatchers, who would plunder fresh graves and peddle the bodies. Burke and Hare added a new twist to the body-peddling business by murdering lodgers in the boardinghouse they ran, then selling the corpses to an Edinburgh surgeon named Robert Knox. Their story has been retold many times and in various forms, from street ballads to Robert Louis Stevenson's "The Body Snatcher" (made into a 1945 Boris Karloff movie). It also inspired this little rhyme:

> Burke's the murderer, Hare's the thief,
> And Knox the boy who buys the beef.

And, of course, there's this whimsical couplet about the legendary "Butcher of Whitechapel":

> Jack the Ripper stole a kipper,
> Hid it in his father's slipper.

More recent British murderers have also served as the subject for children's verse. In the mid-1930s, a physician named Buck Ruxton murdered his wife, Isabella, and a witness to the crime, his housemaid, Mary Rogerson. Then he dismembered both corpses and dumped the remains in a ravine near Moffat, Scotland. Before long, British schoolchildren were chanting this little ditty:

> Red stains on the carpet, red stains on your knife
> Oh Dr. Buck Ruxton, you murdered your wife.
> The nursemaid she saw you, and threatened to tell.
> Oh Dr. Buck Ruxton, you killed her as well.

Today, of course, we live in less poetic times. Instead of verse, horrific crimes tend to be transformed into grisly jokes. Still, every now and then some humble versifier will compose a tribute to a serial killer. The atrocities of Edward **Gein,** for example, inspired not only a spate of sick riddles (see **Jokes**) but also these immortal lines:

> There once was a man named Ed
> Who wouldn't take a woman to bed.
> When he wanted to diddle,
> He cut out the middle,
> And hung the rest in a shed.

NURSES

It's bad enough when a law student (like Ted **Bundy**) or a policeman (like G. J. Schaefer, the Florida "Sex Beast" linked to twenty sadistic murders) turns out to be a serial killer. It seems even worse when the psycho is affiliated with the healing arts—someone who has pledged his or her professional life to the care of other human beings. Deadly **Doctors** fall into this category. So do lethal nurses—those homicidal health-care workers who prey on the sick and the helpless, administering not succor and comfort but suffering and death.

In Cincinnati during the 1930s, a German immigrant named Anna Marie Hahn made a reputation for herself as a kindly, devout nurse, an angel of mercy who looked after sickly old men— all of whom happened to have very healthy bank accounts. In one way or another, Hahn managed to get her hands on their money, either by asking for "loans," getting herself written into their wills, or stealing it outright. Then she dispatched her patients with a dose of lethal medication. Over five years, she poisoned at least eleven of the trusting old souls. She became the first woman ever electrocuted in Ohio.

While Hahn was in it strictly for the money, other lethal nurses have been motivated by even darker impulses. The notorious turn-of-the-century multi-murderer Jane **Toppan** declared that her deepest desire was to become the most prolific killer of her day. Though Toppan was accused of eleven murders, she claimed to have committed thirty-one, and some crime buffs believe that the real total was closer to one hundred. If so, then Toppan certainly achieved her ambition.

Much more recently, in the late 1980s, a sociopathic nursing home aide named Gwendolyn Graham and her lesbian lover, Catherine Wood, devised a demented game. They decided to smother six elderly patients, selecting victims whose last initials, when strung together, spelled out the word *murder*. As it happened, the "game" became too complicated to complete, but Graham and Wood kept killing old people anyway, largely because it provided the two depraved lovers with such a powerful sexual thrill.

Not all lethal nurses are women. Richard Angelo—Long Island's so-called "Angel of Death"—had perhaps the weirdest rationale of all for multiple medical murder. Obsessed with the need to be recognized as a hero, the one-time Eagle Scout and volunteer fireman got his degree as a registered nurse, then went to work in the intensive care unit of Good Samaritan Hospital, where (aptly enough) he worked the graveyard shift. Before long, postoperative patients began dropping like flies. Eventually, the authorities discovered the cause of the mysterious deaths. Between mid-September and late October, 1987, Angelo had been injecting an average of two patients per week with Pavulon and Anectine, drugs that induced paralysis and heart failure. His reason? So that he could rush to their rescue and prove that he was a hero. Unfortunately, his plan had its flaws: out of the nearly forty patients he injected, at least ten—perhaps as many as twenty-five—died.

ORCHARDS

B ack in the early 1800s (according to legend) a wandering folk hero named Johnny Appleseed roamed across the land, turning empty fields into fertile orchards. Of course, fertility isn't the only quality connected with apple orchards. Ever since the days of Adam and Eve, the apple tree has also symbolized sin and corruption. In real life as in myth, orchards have been associated with both goodness and crime—not only with the delicious fruits of God's earth but also with the deadly fruits of man's evil.

In the spring of 1873, the citizens of Labette County, Kansas, were concerned about the alarming number of travelers who had vanished while passing through the region. A posse investigating the recently abandoned farmstead of a family named Bender noticed something peculiar about the apple orchard behind the house. Depressions in the soil between the blossoming seedlings were rectangular in shape—and approximately the size of human graves. By the time the posse finished digging up the orchard, they had uncovered the bodies of a dozen people. Most of them were men, their skulls crushed with a sledgehammer. One was a baby girl who had been buried alive with her father's corpse. As it turned out, the "Bloody Benders" had been preying on unwary travelers for years, having turned their ramshackle farmhouse into a kind of hotel-from-hell where overnight guests rarely survived to see the light of day (see **Clans**).

An apple orchard also featured prominently in the most sensational crime of the 1920s, the Hall-Mills murder case. On a September morning in 1922, a young couple out for a stroll in New Brunswick, New Jersey, stumbled upon two corpses, male and female, lying side by side in a crabapple orchard. The woman's throat had been slashed so ferociously that she was nearly decapitated. She had also been shot three times in the face at point-blank range. Though the dead man had not been subjected to the same mutilations, he had been killed with chilling deliberation—executed with a single bullet to the brain. What made the murders especially lurid was the identity of the victims: the Reverend Edward Wheeler Hall, pastor of New Brunswick's most fashionable Episcopal church, and his choir-girl mistress, Mrs. Eleanor Mills. The subsequent trial of the reverend's betrayed wife and her two eccentric brothers was the O. J. Simpson affair of its day—a frenzied, three-ring media circus followed with prurient fascination by the whole country. (As in the O. J. case, the defendants were acquitted and the case remains officially unsolved.)

The orchard where the bodies had been found turned into a major tourist attraction, where vendors hawked soft drinks and popcorn to the curious hordes, who stripped every leaf and crabapple from the branches as morbid souvenirs.

Fifty years later, orchards of another kind—the peach orchards surrounding Yuba City, California—became the site of one of the most gruesome discoveries in American criminal history. In May 1971 a farmer discovered a hacked-up corpse buried between two fruit trees. Other discoveries in nearby orchards soon followed. One by one, the corpses of migrant workers and male transients were unearthed until the body count reached a staggering twenty-five. All of the victims had been savagely slashed with a knife and machete, and a number of them bore the signs of sexual assault. Evidence eventually led police to someone very familiar with the orchards of Yuba City, a farm labor contractor named Juan Corona, whose conviction on twenty-five counts of murder in 1973 marked him as the nation's most prolific serial killer. Unfortunately for America, that record has since been eclipsed several times.

ORGANIZED/DISORGANIZED

See **Profiling.**

OVENS

Few fairy tales are more chilling to children than "Hänsel and Gretel"—the story of a cannibal witch who plans to feast on two fattened children but ends up incinerated in her own oven. Perhaps that's what adds a special dimension of horror to serial killers who use ovens to dispose of their victims. The whole situation seems like something from a childhood horror story—a real-life, exceedingly grim fairy tale.

Henri Landru, the so-called "Bluebeard of Paris," even *looked* like a fairy-tale villain, with his bald head, bristling brows, and spiky red beard. In spite of his unprepossessing appearance, however, he became infamous as one of the world's leading ladykillers, marrying and murdering no less than ten women (see **Bluebeards**). Believing (incorrectly) that, without a corpse, the authorities could not convict him of murder, he reduced all his victims to ash in an outdoor oven. Even without a single identifiable body, however, the authorities were able to assemble enough circumstantial evidence to send Landru to the guillotine.

Dr. H. H. **Holmes**—the turn-of-the-century serial killer and another notorious ladykiller—disposed of dozens of victims in the same way. When investigators finally broke into his rambling "Horror Castle" in a suburb of Chicago, they discovered both a basement crematorium and an oversized office stove that still contained the charred remnants of one of his ill-fated mistresses. Holmes's most heinous crimes, however, were the cold-blooded murders of three young siblings—the children of his

Perhaps the most appalling of Holmes's many crimes was the murder of two young girls, Alice and Nellie Pitezel, who were gassed to death inside a steamer trunk—an atrocity portrayed in this nineteenth-century book illustration.

accomplice, Ben Pitezel. Two of these little ones were asphyxiated and buried in a basement crawl space. The blackened remains of the third, a ten-year-old boy, were found in the belly of a coal-burning oven.

Of course, disposing of victims isn't the only use to which ovens have been put by deranged psychokillers. When German police arrested the cannibalistic sex-killer Joachim Kroll in 1976, they found something cooking on his stove—the chopped-off hand of a four-year-old girl, simmering in a saucepan with sliced potatoes and carrots.

CARL PANZRAM

Portrait of Carl Panzram by Joe Coleman

During his final prison stretch in the late 1920s, Carl Panzram confessed to twenty-one murders, countless felonies, and more than one thousand acts of sodomy. "For all these things," he declared, "I am not the least bit sorry." It was a typical statement by one of the most incorrigible criminals in American history. Some sociologists have blamed Panzram's vicious nature on the penal system, which subjected him to countless brutalities in an effort to break his spirit, but only filled him with a hatred for all humankind. Others have a different explanation—that he was simply born bad.

Whether Panzram's badness was acquired or innate is a matter of debate. One thing is certain—his criminal career started early. His first conviction was for drunk and disorderly conduct—when he was eight years old. Three years later, a string of burglaries landed him in reform school. During his time there, he torched one of the buildings, causing an estimated $100,000 worth of damage. The thirteen-year-old Panzram was released from the institution in 1904 with knowledge that would last him a lifetime—"how to steal, lie, hate, burn, and kill" (as he would write in his autobiography).

Paroled to his mother's custody, he promptly ran away to lead the life of a hobo. While hitching a ride in a boxcar, he was gang raped by four "burly bums," who taught him another lesson he would continue to live by: "force and might make right."

He joined the army at sixteen, but military discipline was not Panzram's long suit. He was court-martialed and sentenced to three years in Leavenworth. Following his release, he embarked on a career of spectacular brutality. Traveling around the world—to South America, Europe, Africa, and finally back to the United States—he left a trail of corpses in his wake.

In the 1920s, Panzram committed two of his most infamous crimes. With the proceeds from an especially profitable heist, he purchased a yacht and lured ten sailors aboard with the promise of free bootleg liquor. After the sailors drank themselves into a stupor, Panzram raped them, shot each one in the head, then dumped their bodies in the ocean.

Later, after shipping out as a merchant seaman to West Africa, he hired eight native bearers, presumably to help him hunt crocodiles. Panzram ended up killing and raping the Africans, then feeding their corpses to the crocs.

By 1928, Panzram was back in America, where he was arrested for a series of burglaries in the vicinity of Washington, D.C. Sentenced to twenty years in Leavenworth, he announced that he would "kill the first man that bothers me." He made good on his threat the following year, smashing in the skull of a laundry foreman. It was this crime that finally got Panzram a long-overdue death sentence. He was hanged on September 5, 1930. Consistent to the end, he went to his death with a curse on his lips. "Hurry it up, you Hoosier bastard," he snarled as the executioner prepared the noose. "I could hang a dozen men while you're fooling around!"

> "I sat down to think things over a bit. While I was sitting there, a
> little kid about eleven or twelve years old came bumming around.
> He was looking for something. He found it, too. I took him out to
> a gravel pit about one-quarter mile away. I left him there, but
> first committed sodomy on him and then killed him.
> His brains were coming out of his ears when I left him,
> and he will never be any deader."
>
> CARL PANZRAM

PARAPHILIA

Paraphilia—which literally means "abnormal love"—is the technical term for sexual deviation or perversion. It need hardly be said that when it comes to paraphiliac behavior, serial killers are as sick as they come.

The average foot fetishist, for example, might assemble a sizable collection of stolen spike-heeled shoes. By contrast, at least one serial killer gratified his fetish by cutting off the feet of his victims and storing them in his refrigerator. Clipping and saving tufts of female pubic hair is another common fetish. Serial killers, on the other hand, are just as likely to remove the entire vulvas of their victims.

Voyeurism is another paraphilia that serial killers practice with a singular malevolence. The typical Peeping Tom enjoys spying on people who are having sex. Voyeuristic serial killers, on the other hand, like to watch while their partners or accomplices rape, sodomize, and torture helpless victims. Among the other paraphilias favored by serial killers are bestiality, S-M, and exhibitionism.

Undoubtedly the single most perverted serial killer in the annals of American crime was Albert **Fish**. According to the psychiatric experts who examined him, Fish had spent his lifetime indulging in every known paraphilia, plus a few no one had ever heard of before. (For example, he liked to insert long-stemmed roses into his penis and look at himself in the mirror. Then he would remove the roses and eat them.) His more commonplace paraphilias included: sadism, masochism, flagellation, exhibi-

217

Painting of Albert
Fish flagellating
himself with a nail-
studded board; art
by Michael Rose

tionism, voyeurism, piquerism (deriving sexual pleasure from
jabbing himself with sharp objects), pedophilia, analingus (oral
stimulation of the anus), coprophagia (eating feces), undinism
(sexual preoccupation with urine), fetishism, and cannibalism.

PARTNERS

S erial killers have their own special form of male bonding.
Instead of bowling with a buddy, they will occasionally link
up with a partner and go prowling in pairs. It is estimated that

approximately 28 percent of all serial homicides in this country are committed by such deadly duos.

Though the bisexual Henry Lee **Lucas** and his homosexual partner, Ottis Elwood Toole, were occasional lovers, the true basis of their friendship was not sex but a shared passion for serial slaughter. Shortly after meeting in a Florida soup kitchen, they launched into a life of random, nomadic violence, traveling the highways and preying on an untold number of victims—hitchhikers, vagrants, women with car trouble. They killed with appalling cruelty. (In one typical instance, they attacked a forty-six-year-old woman in her mobile home, Lucas raping her while Toole strangled her with a telephone cord; after she was dead, Toole ripped off her nipples with his teeth.) When the pair ran low on cash, they would knock over a convenience store and kill the clerk (whose corpse was generally raped by the necrophiliac Toole).

Both Lucas and Toole had committed homicide before hooking up with each other. Other cases, however, are examples of what the French call a folie à deux—a shared psychopathology that only operates when the two individuals come together. Separately, each man—however potentially violent—might never commit murder; together, they bring out each other's most monstrous impulses. This was the case, for example not only with the **Hillside Stranglers,** but also with Leonard Lake and Charles Ng, a pair of ex-marines with a common interest in automatic weapons and sadomasochistic pornography. In the early 1980s, this depraved duo abducted at least three women and kept them as "sex slaves" in an underground bunker on Lake's remote, wooded compound in Calaveras County, California. The victims were videotaped while being subjected to extreme sexual torture, then murdered when their captors grew tired of them. (Ng awaits trial on these charges and maintains his innocence to this day.) Other depraved twosomes include Lawrence Bittaker and Roy Norris (a pair of degenerates who cruised the California roads in a van they called Murder Mack, abducting, torturing, and killing a string of young girls), Dean Corll and Wayne Henley (who conspired to lure dozens of young males to Corll's home in Pasadena, Texas, where the boys were drugged, shackled, tortured—sometimes for days—then killed), and Theodore Simmons and Milton Jones of Buffalo, New York (who teamed up to torture and kill Catholic priests).

Some serial killer teams have more in common than their psychopathology—they are actually related by blood. This was true of the "Hillside Stranglers," Kenneth Bianchi and Angelo Buono, who were cousins; the Haley brothers of Los Angeles, who committed no less than five hundred burglaries, sixty rapes, and eight murders in the early 1980s; and the wildly psychotic Joseph Kallinger, who enlisted the aid of his own twelve-year-old son in his six-month campaign of murder and mutilation.

Of course, even the closest of companions can sometimes disagree. Rudolph Pleil—arguably the most monstrous German lust murderer of the post–World War II era—had a voracious appetite for rape, mutilation, and murder but objected when an accomplice insisted on beheading a victim. Though Pleil slaughtered at least two dozen victims with hammers, hatchets, and knives, he evidently drew the line at decapitation. And Henry Lee Lucas disapproved of his partner's cannibalistic proclivities, refusing to participate when Toole indulged his taste for human flesh.

MARCEL PETIOT

The smoke spewing from the chimney of 21 Rue Le Sueur on March 11, 1944, was so thick, black, and foul smelling that it might have been coming from a Nazi crematorium. A neighbor telephoned the Parisian authorities. When firemen broke into the building, they made an appalling discovery—a stack of dissected and dismembered human bodies, more than two dozen in all. These would later prove to be the remains of Jewish men and women. Inside the furnace, the firemen found a pile of burning limbs—the source of the billowing stench.

There was a good reason why the chimney smoke carried the stench of a Nazi crematorium. In effect, that's what the building's owner—a physician named Marcel Petiot—had turned his basement furnace into.

When Petiot was confronted with the evidence of his crimes, however, he had a ready explanation. A psychopath of unusual—even flamboyant—audacity, he insisted that far from being a criminal, he was actually a patriot. The remains, he claimed, were those of Nazi collaborators, killed by the Resistance and entrusted to himself for disposal. The gullible gendarmes swallowed this whopper whole and released Petiot, who immediately fled Paris with his wife.

He remained at large for seven months, during which time he sent regular, pseudonymous letters to the newspaper *Resistance*, repeating his claim that the bodies were those of Nazis and traitors. In Paris, however, police were entertaining a different theory—that Petiot himself was a collaborator who had been murdering patriots on behalf of the Gestapo.

The truth finally came to light when Petiot was arrested after seven months on the lam. Though perceived by his Parisian neighbors as a prosperous, benevolent physician, the forty-seven-year-old Petiot had a history of criminal behavior going back to World War I, when he was convicted of black marketeering. Later, as mayor of the town of Villeneuve, he had been arrested for drug peddling. He was also a suspect in the mysterious disappearance of a pregnant servant girl. But nothing in his past compared to the outrages he had been perpetrating in his Rue Le Sueur residence.

The murders, it turned out, had nothing to do with politics at all. The victims were neither Nazis nor French patriots. Greed was the sole motive behind Petiot's atrocities. The victims were wealthy Jews desperate to flee occupied France. Posing as a Resistance leader, Petiot offered to smuggle them out of the country—for a fee. When the unsuspecting victims showed up at his house—laden with all their valuables—Petiot administered a "typhoid inoculation" that was spiked with strychnine. Then he placed them in a sealed chamber. After observing their death agonies through a peephole, he disposed of their remains in his furnace. The valuables he netted through this unspeakable swindle amounted to nearly a million English pounds.

Petiot's 1946 trial was one of the most sensational in modern French history. The defendant himself—by turns witty and withering, charming and arrogant—put on quite a show, though his histrionics failed to beguile the judge and jury. The "greatest criminal affair of the century" (as the French papers dubbed it) ended on May 26, 1946, when Marcel Petiot, still maintaining his innocence, went to the guillotine.

For an interesting (if overly arty) dramatization of the case, curious viewers might check out the 1992 French movie *Docteur Petiot*, starring Michel Serrault.

> *"There is a legend that you all know well: the story of the ship-wreckers. Cruel men placed lanterns on the cliffs to lure ashore ships in distress. The sailors, confident, never suspecting that such evil deceit could exist, sailed onto the reefs and died, and those who had pretended to lead them to safety filled their coffers with the spoils of their foul deeds. Petiot is just that: the false savior, the false refuge. He lured the desperate, the frightened, the hunted, and he killed them by turning their instincts for self-preservation against them."*
>
> PIERRE VÉRON, lawyer at the trial of Dr. Marcel Petiot

PHASES

The step-by-step pattern that the typical serial killer follows—from the time he first starts brooding on his crime through the inevitable letdown of its aftermath—has been charted by Dr. Joel Norris, one of the country's leading experts on the subject. According to Norris, the seven "key phases" of serial murder are as follows:

1. *The Aura Phase.* The process begins when the potential killer starts to withdraw into a private world of perverted fantasy. From the outside, he may appear to be perfectly normal. Inside his head, however, he exists in a kind of twisted twilight zone. His grasp on reality loosens as his mind becomes increasingly dominated by daydreams of death and destruction. Gradually, the need to act out his demented fantasies becomes an overwhelming compulsion.

2. *The Trolling Phase.* Like a fisherman casting out his line and trolling for a catch, the killer now begins to seek out a victim, focusing on those places where he is most likely to encounter the precise kind of person that his sick needs require. He may stake out a schoolyard, cruise a red-light district, patronize a popular pickup spot, or stalk a local lovers' lane. Eventually, he will zero in on a target.

3. *The Wooing Phase.* In some cases, the killer will simply strike without warning—snatching a victim off the street or breaking into a house and slaying everyone inside. Often, how-

ever, the killer will derive a depraved satisfaction from luring his victims into his clutches—lulling them into a false sense of security, tricking them into lowering their defenses. Ted **Bundy** seemed so disarmingly clean-cut and normal that he had no trouble talking young women into his death car. Other killers, like John Wayne **Gacy**, seduce their victims with the promise of money or a job or a place to spend the night. In November 1995, a drifter named Glen Rogers allegedly committed five murders during an interstate killing spree. According to those who knew him, Rogers was a master at wooing his victims. "He could talk a person into anything," one acquaintance told the police. "A ride home from the bar. A place to crash for a few days. A woman's affections." (Rogers has not yet been tried and denies the charges.)

4. *The Capture Phase.* The next step is to spring the trap that the killer has set for his victims. Seeing their terrified reactions as the true horror of their situation suddenly hits home is part of his sadistic game. This is the moment when—having accepted a lift from an affable stranger who has offered you a ride home—you suddenly notice that the car is headed in the wrong direction and that the door handle on the passenger side has been removed, so that there is no possibility of escape. Or when the handsome one-night stand who has handcuffed you to the bedposts for some kinky fun and games smilingly tells you that he has no intention of releasing you—ever.

5. *The Murder.* If killing is a substitute for sex, as it is for so many serial murderers, then the moment at which they put a victim to death is the climax, the acme of pleasure toward which the whole process has been building ever since they began fantasizing about the crime. (Indeed, it's not uncommon for sexual psychopaths to experience an orgasm while murdering their victims.) And just as normal people have their particular sexual pleasures—their favorite positions or ways of being touched—serial killers have their own homicidal preferences, some enjoying strangulation, others bludgeoning or slashing or death by slow torture.

6. *The Totem Phase.* Like a sexual climax, the murder is an intense but transient pleasure for the serial killer. To prolong the experience and help him relive it in fantasy during the fallow period before his next crime, he will often remove a souvenir or

"totemic" object associated with the victim. This may be anything from a wallet to a body part (see **Trophies**).

7. *The Depression Phase.* In the aftermath of the murder, the serial killer often experiences an emotional letdown that is the equivalent of what the French call postcoital *tristesse*. This state can be so severe that the killer may actually attempt suicide. Unfortunately, a more common response is a renewed desire to commit murder again—a growing need for a fix of fresh blood (see **Post-Homicidal Depression**).

PHOTOGRAPHS

In his chilling 1971 book, *The Family*, Ed Sanders reveals that Charles Manson and his creepy-crawly followers allegedly made snuff movies with stolen super-8mm cameras—real-life splatter films depicting human sacrifice, decapitations, and other atrocities. Though Sanders was never able to confirm this story (he was offered a reel of reputed Manson porn by one unnamed source but couldn't come up with the $250,000 asking price), the rumor itself embodies an unnerving truth about serial killers. In the same way that ordinary people like to record life's special moments on film (weddings, birthday parties, family vacations) many serial killers enjoy taking pictures of their victims, dead and alive, to keep as twisted souvenirs—morbid mementoes to help them relive the thrill of their murders.

When police entered the squalid apartment of Jeffrey **Dahmer**, they were staggered to find a cache of Polaroid pictures showing male corpses in various stages of dismemberment. One photo was of a body slit from breastbone to groin like a gutted deer. Another showed a corpse eaten away by acid from the nipples down. Perhaps the most shocking of all was described by Milwaukee journalist Anne E. Schwartz: a photograph of "a bleached skeleton [with] the flesh on the head, hands, and feet . . . left perfectly intact."

In the mid-1960s, the British **Killer Couple** Ian Brady and Myra Hindley—aka **The Moors Murderers**—kidnapped a ten-year-old girl and forced her to pose for pornographic snapshots before strangling her to death. They also made an audiotape of the child's piteous pleas for mercy—a recording so heart wrenching that when it was played in court during the murder trial, even hardened policemen wept openly.

As technology has progressed over the years, the recording techniques of serial killers have become increasingly sophisticated. Twenty years after the "Moors Murders" case, Leonard Lake and Charles Ng began kidnapping women and imprisoning them in an underground bunker in Northern California (see **Partners**). The bunker was outfitted with a set of state-of-the-art video equipment, which Lake had stolen from the home of a San Francisco photographer named Harvey Dubs. Lake and Ng used the equipment to record the rape, torture, and murder of three young women—including Dubs's wife, Deborah.

HARVEY MURRAY GLATMAN, SNUFF PHOTOGRAPHER

Harvey Murray Glatman; from *52 Famous Murderers* trading cards *(Courtesy of Roger Worsham)*

In 1960, the distinguished British director Michael Powell—renowned for his beautiful ballet fantasy, *The Red Shoes*—released a film that so incensed both the public and critics that it effectively ended his career. It was called *Peeping Tom*, a movie about a sadistic voyeur who films his victims as he is stabbing them to death with a lethal camera-tripod (see **Movies**). What sort of sick mind—asked the outraged reviewers—could have dreamed up such a story? But, in fact, just a year before *Peeping Tom* came out, an American psycho named Harvey Murray Glatman had been put to death at San Quentin for crimes shockingly like the ones depicted in the film.

Even as an adolescent, Glatman showed twisted sexual tendencies. His favorite form of masturbation was autoerotic asphyxiation—achieving sexual release while dangling by his neck from a rope tied to an attic rafter. A family physician assured Glatman's mother that her son would outgrow this bizarre practice. As Glatman matured, however, he continued to be obsessed by fantasies of bondage, sadism, and strangulation. At the age of twenty-nine, he set about making his depraved dreams come true.

Posing as a professional photographer, he managed to persuade a series of struggling young models that he was going to take their photos for the covers of the kind of sleazy detective magazines that were so popular back in the 1950s. Since these covers typically featured bound and helpless young women, the models allowed Glatman to truss them up and gag them. They were further disarmed by his appearance—Glatman looked like a creepy but essentially harmless nerd. (If a movie were ever made about his case, Rick Moranis would be the inevitable casting choice.)

Once he had the women in his power, Glatman proceeded to strip and photograph them, rape them at gunpoint, and take more photos of their terrified looks as the true horror of their situation finally dawned on them. Then he strangled them with a length of rope and disposed of their bodies in the desert.

Altogether, Glatman murdered three young women in this way. He tried to set up a fourth deadly photo session—but this time, the intended victim proved to be more than he could handle. When Glatman pulled his pistol on her in his car, she lunged at him, wrestled the weapon away, and held him at gunpoint until the police arrived.

In custody, Glatman confessed in lengthy detail. He was convicted after a three-day trial in November 1958 and received his death sentence with a philosophical shrug. "It's better this way," he remarked.

Few people would have argued with him.

PLUMBING

C logged pipes have proven to be the undoing of more than one serial killer. In February 1983, residents of a small

North London apartment house complained that their toilets wouldn't flush. When a plumber showed up to check out the problem, he opened a nearby manhole and descended into the sewer. As expected, he found a blocked drainpipe leading from the building. What he couldn't possibly have anticipated was the nature of the obstruction—a reeking mass of putrifying flesh, mixed with human fingerbones. It didn't take long for police to discover the source of this nightmarish glop. It had come from the upstairs flat of a thirty-seven-year-old **Civil Servant** named Dennis **Nilsen,** who—just several days earlier—had murdered and butchered his fifteenth homosexual victim, then flushed the remains down his toilet.

A similar, grisly discovery had been made in West Germany seven years earlier. In July 1976, police in the city of Duisburg were conducting a door-to-door search for a missing four-year-old girl. In the course of interviewing one old man, they heard a bizarre story. According to the old man, a fellow tenant of his apartment building—a lavatory attendant named Joachim Kroll—had warned him not to use the communal bathroom on their floor because the toilet was backed up. What made the story so weird was Kroll's explanation of the plumbing problem. He had casually mentioned that the toilet was blocked "with guts."

The police summoned a plumber, who applied a plunger to the clogged toilet. Up came a mass of human entrails and other viscera. Inside Kroll's apartment, police found several freezer bags full of human flesh and a child's hand simmering in a saucepan. Like his British counterpart, Dennis Nilsen, Kroll had been murdering for a long time—since 1955. In all, the German **Cannibal** and sex-killer was responsible for fourteen homicides.

POETRY

Among the ranks of infamous serial killers there have been some rather creative individuals. John Wayne **Gacy** was a prolific painter whose works have become trendy collectibles (see **Art**). Charles **Manson** has composed dozens of **Songs,** some of which have been recorded by bands like Guns 'n' Roses and the Lemonheads. Ed **Gein** crafted everything from belts to wastebaskets to soup bowls out of the exhumed and dismembered corpses of middle-aged women. So it's not entirely surprising that some serial killers have tried their hands at poetry. It's also not surprising that their poetry is really bad.

Dennis **Nilsen** wrote a whole slew of verse in homage to the young men he strangled, dismembered, and flushed down the toilet. Here's a typical example, addressed to one of his dead victims: "I try to smile / Despite the vengeance looking at me, / Covered in your tomato paste, / A man of many parts / I try to forget. / Even the perfume of your passing / Lingers on. / More problems now / With all your bits and pieces. . . ."

As a teenager, Long Islander Joel Rifkin—who murdered and dismembered at least seventeen prostitutes—obviously saw himself as some sort of knight in shining armor, as this scrap of adolescent doggerel suggests: "A siren temptress calls me near / a stranger beyond darkness haze / pleading from within the shadows / and though I be helpless to help her / help her I must." And the ever-romantic Ted **Bundy** beguiled his lovers with greeting card verse like: "I send you this kiss / deliver this body to hold. / I sleep with you tonight / with words of love untold."

What woman could resist such lyrical power?

A PERVERSE VERSE

Dr. J. Paul de River's classic forensic text, *The Sexual Criminal,* (1949) includes a chapter called "The Poetic Nature of the Sado-Masochist," which reprints a number of works by convicted sex offenders. Reprinted below is one example, entitled "Uncensored Exotics." As poetry it's no "Gunga Din," but it does offer insight into the workings of one psychopathic mind:

> Vainly I crouch at the fireside,
> For the flames on the hearth cannot warm me.
> Vainly I put on coats
> Against the cold of the star winds . . .
>
> And my bones are chilled within me
> And my blood is become as water.
> And now from the void behind me

Comes the piping of the piper,
That senseless, complaining piping,
That tuneless, high, thin piping. . . .

Then, with a shout, I surrender,
And leap to do the bidding.
From the wall I snatch my weapons
And rush from the house to the forest.
Where the road winds down the mountain,
Panting I lie in ambush,
Waiting for some poor traveller
Who shall bring me my release.
When he comes with laggard footsteps,
Sudden and fierce is my onslaught.
Like a beast I overcome him
And utterly destroy him.
And I cut out his heart and eat it,
And I guzzle his blood like nectar,
And I cut off his head and scalp him,
And hang his scalp at my belt.
Homeward I walk through the snowdrifts,
And my heart is warm within me,
And my blood and bones are new again
And the star winds cease to chill me. . . .

POISONERS

Compared to the average lust murderer who goes in for torture, mutilation, and evisceration, serial killers who quietly dispatch their victims with poison seem like models of refinement. When it comes to racking up bodies, however, serial poisoners can be every bit as deadly as any blood-crazed psycho.

Particularly back in the 1800s—when forensic pathology was still in its infancy—poisoners could get away with murder for years, since their victims appeared to drop dead of natural causes. Homicidal **Housekeepers** like Anna Zwanziger and Helene Jegado knocked off dozens of people by serving them arsenic-spiked food. As late as the 1930s, a sociopathic **Nurse** named

Anna Marie Hahn was dishing out lethal doses of arsenic to her patients in Cincinnati's German community, murdering as many as eleven elderly men over a five-year period. (In 1938, Hahn became the first woman to die in Ohio's electric chair.)

Though women have a particular preference for poison, they certainly don't have a monopoly on this insidious murder method. In the latter half of the nineteenth century, England was home to a trio of men who left a trail of poisoned corpses in their wake: Dr. William Palmer (who used antimony tartrate and strychnine to get ride of bothersome relatives and insistent creditors); George Chapman (who poisoned a succession of lovers, also with antimony); and Dr. Thomas Neill Cream (who prescribed strychnine pills to four London prostitutes and claimed he was **Jack the Ripper**).

The deadly tradition of these Victorian villains was carried on by a twentieth-century British youth named Graham Young. Curious as to the effects of antimony tartrate on the human body, the fourteen-year-old chemistry buff (and psychopath) began lacing his family's food with the deadly substance, eventually killing his stepmother. Found guilty but insane in 1962, he spent the following nine years in a mental asylum. No sooner was he released in 1971 than he took a job at a photographic supply firm and began poisoning fellow employees with thallium. By the time investigators figured out what was going on, five of Young's co-workers had fallen violently ill and two of them had died after days of agony. "I could have killed them all if I wished," Young told the arresting officers.

Young's crimes were the basis of *The Young Poisoner's Handbook*, a 1996 film praised by *New York Times* movie critic Janet Maslin for its "assured style, malevolent wit, and uncompromising intelligence."

POLITICAL CORRECTNESS

Since PC etiquette requires language and behavior that are completely inoffensive, serial killers are about as *in*correct as it's possible for people to be. Bizarrely enough, however, at least one multiple murderer—a young Californian named John Linley Frazier—acted out of his own demented sense of political correctness. From his warped point of view, he was killing to protect the environment.

A high school dropout who worked as an auto mechanic, Frazier evolved into an ecological zealot, apparently under the influence of the psychedelic drugs he began ingesting in the late 1960s. Quitting his job (because he believed that cars contributed to "the death cycle of the planet"), he began drifting from commune to commune. His fierce, obsessive rants against environmental destruction, however, clashed with the mellowed-out sensibilities of his newfound hippie friends, and Frazier soon found himself living like a hermit in a six-foot-square shack in the Northern California woods.

About half a mile away from the shack stood the home of an eye surgeon named Victor Ohta. In the fall of 1970, Frazier broke into the Ohtas' house and—in his paranoia—decided that the family was the evil personification of American materialism in its most pernicious form. Returning shortly afterward with a .38 revolver, Frazier managed to tie up the entire family (father, mother, and two sons), plus Dr. Ohta's secretary. After lecturing them on the damage done to the environment by capitalistic society, Frazier shot and killed all five people and dumped their bodies in the swimming pool. Next, he typed out a note promising death to all those who would "ruin the environment," set the house on fire, and fled.

With the help of local hippies—who recognized the crackpot ideas in the note as Frazier's—police quickly nabbed the suspect. During his 1971 trial, Frazier showed up in court with one side of his head shaved completely bald, the other side sporting shoulder-length hair and half a beard. In spite of his flagrantly bizarre behavior, he was ruled sane and sentenced to the gas chamber. Frazier appeared to welcome the decision, since, as he said, he preferred death to spending his life under the control of "fascist pigs." When the Supreme Court abolished capital punishment, however, his sentence was commuted to life imprisonment.

PORNOGRAPHY

See **X-rated.**

POST-HOMICIDAL DEPRESSION

Sick as it sounds, the fact is that for many serial killers murder is a substitute for sex. The act of plunging a sharp, pointed object into the writhing body of another person is the equivalent of intercourse. Many lust murderers actually achieve orgasm while stabbing (or beating or strangling) their victims to death. So it's not surprising that, following a murder, many serial killers experience the equivalent of post-coital depression—the emotional letdown that sometimes descends after sex.

Indeed, so common is this experience among lust murderers that one expert on the subject, Dr. Joel Norris, actually describes depression as one of the standard **Phases** of serial murder. According to Dr. Norris, many serial killers suffer severe bouts of dejection following a murder because the killing fails to live up to their fantasies. Moreover, even the most cold-blooded killers can sometimes be hit with a belated sense of horror and guilt after perpetrating a particularly vicious crime. Occasionally, they suffer such intense despair that they actually attempt suicide (see **Death Wish**).

Whatever the cause of their depression, the response is often a binge of drinking or drug taking, which dulls their sense of emptiness and despair. Soon their inner compulsions rise up again. Like addicts who can't stop getting high—even though they know that they will suffer an inevitable crash—they go prowling for their next "fix" of blood.

POWER TOOLS

The chain saw is the favorite weapon of serial killers. At least that's what you'd think if your concept of serial killers came entirely from the movies. During the 1970s, Hollywood churned out a spate of low-budget splatter films with titles like *Driller Killer*, *The Toolbox Murders*, *The Bloody Mutilators*, and *The Ghastly Ones*. The psychos in these movies wielded more power tools than Tim Allen on *Home Improvement*: drills, bucksaws, chain saws, you name it. The power tool motif made it to the big

time in a pair of Brian de Palma movies from the early 1980s—
Body Double (featuring an electric drill bit large enough to qualify for *The Guinness Book of World Records*) and *Scarface* (which
contains what is arguably the most harrowing chain saw mutilation sequence in cinematic history).

Though the very first chain saw murder movie was Wes Craven's pioneering splatter film *The Last House on the Left* (1971),
the film that made this particular piece of equipment de rigueur
for cinematic psychos was Tobe Hooper's 1975 cult classic, *The
Texas Chainsaw Massacre*. Like *Psycho* and *The Silence of the
Lambs*, Hooper's masterwork was inspired by the horrific deeds
of the Wisconsin ghoul, Edward **Gein**. Indeed, the original advertisements for the film claimed that it was entirely factual.
"What happened is true! Now see the movie that is just as real!"
The real truth, however, is that Hooper's film is only loosely—
very loosely—based on reality. Among other things, Ed Gein
didn't even *own* a chain saw. The only tools he is known to have
employed were his trusty spade (for exhuming female corpses)
and a big-bladed hunting knife (for dismembering them).

It's easy to see why the makers of in-your-face splatter movies
are attracted to chain saws—they are big, loud, and exception-
ally scary-looking (the chain saws, that is, though the description undoubtedly applies to some of the filmmakers, too). For
those same reasons, however, chain saws do not make very suit-

able weapons for real-life serial killers. After all, it's hard to sneak into a house in a nice residential neighborhood and quietly dismember an entire family with a chain saw. Chain saws also make notoriously poor concealed weapons.

There is, however, at least one serial killer who used a power saw on his victims, albeit posthumously. In the 1980s, a Swedish physician named Teet Haerm, who worked as a medical examiner for the Stockholm police, was accused of the serial murder of seven prostitutes. But his outrages didn't stop there. After killing his victims, he beheaded and dismembered their bodies with a power saw.

Then—like another serial-killer physician, the fictional Hannibal "The Cannibal" Lecter—Dr. Haerm devoured portions of their flesh.

PROFILING

During the 1950s, New York was terrorized by an anonymous psycho—dubbed the "Mad Bomber" by the press—who planted dozens of homemade explosives around the city. Stymied in their investigation, police turned to a psychiatric whiz named James Brussel. After studying all the available evidence, Dr. Brussel deduced that the unknown madman would turn out to be a middle-aged paranoiac of Eastern European descent who lived in Connecticut with a maiden aunt or sister, was afflicted with a serious physical illness like tuberculosis, attended church regularly, went out of his way to behave in a polite, soft-spoken manner, and would be wearing a double-breasted suit (buttoned) when arrested.

Thanks in large part to Brussel's description, police were able to trace the bomber, who turned out to be a well-mannered, fifty-four-year-old bachelor of Polish immigrant stock named George Metesky, who lived in Connecticut with his unmarried sisters, was a weekly churchgoer, had been treated for TB, and suffered from severe paranoia. When Metesky was led off by police, he was dressed in a blue, double-breasted suit. Buttoned.

Brussel's amazing prediction is universally acknowledged as the pioneering example of a technique that now stands as one of the most potent weapons in the war against serial killers: the psychological profiling of "unsubs" (police slang for "unknown subjects"). Building on Brussel's groundbreaking work, agents of the FBI Behavioral Science Unit began visiting prisons in the late 1970s. They interviewed several dozen of America's most infamous killers in an effort to figure out what makes these monsters tick. The agents found that serial murderers can be roughly divided into two categories. The *organized* type is a methodical killer who carefully plans his crimes, stalks his prey, brings along his weapon of choice, then—once he has his victim in his power—engages in slow, sadistic murder. By contrast, the *disorganized* killer tends to be subject to sudden, overwhelming impulses, chooses his victims spontaneously, then quickly overpowers and kills them with whatever weapons are at hand.

Beyond these broad classifications, each case taken on by the FBI's crack team of "mind hunters" receives highly individualized attention. When local law officers are faced with a particularly savage and baffling crime, they can—as an ultimate resort—submit a request to the FBI's Criminal Personality Profiling Program. If the Bureau decides to accept the case, a profiler will make a close study of all the facts he receives, then send back a highly detailed, multipage report containing his analysis of the unsub. Since profiles are a form of highly educated guesswork, involving as much intuition as science, they sometimes miss their mark. But when they are accurate—which is surprisingly often—they can seem uncanny.

Stumped by the brutal murder of a twelve-year-old girl, for example, police in a small southern town contacted renowned FBI profiler John Douglas, who came up with this sketch of the unsub: a divorced white man who drove a black or blue car, worked at a "macho laborer's job," was dishonorably discharged from the military, knew the victim, and had a previous record of sex crimes. Following through on this lead, police soon arrested the culprit—a divorced white male who drove a blue Pinto, cut tree limbs for a living, had been kicked out of the army, had done work at the victim's house, and was implicated in an earlier rape case.

Sherlock Holmes couldn't have done it any better.

PROSTITUTES

I t comes as no surprise to learn that prostitutes are prime targets of serial killers. For one thing, hookers have no compunctions about going off to isolated places with strange men (indeed, it's part of the job description). For another, since so many working girls are runaways, drifters, and druggies, nobody becomes very concerned—or even notices—when they disappear or turn up dead. Finally—for those twisted, often impotent lust killers who see all women as "sluts"—prostitutes epitomize everything they most hate and fear about sex. In the demented view of these psychos, these prostitutes "deserve to die."

From the very beginning of modern serial murder, killers have seized on the vulnerability of prostitutes. In the 1880s, **Jack the Ripper** set the pattern for future generations of night-stalking butchers by slaughtering a series of harlots. His deadly descendants include Dr. Thomas Neill Cream (who deviated from the usual pattern by poisoning his victims instead of slashing them to pieces), the still-unidentified "Jack the Stripper," and Peter Sutcliffe, who believed he was doing the Lord's work in ridding the world of whores. Dr. Teet Haerm of Sweden also believed that he was engaged in a righteous cause. During the 1980s, he killed, dismembered, and occasionally cannibalized a string of Stockholm hookers in order—so he claimed—to clean the streets of sin.

One of the more sensational cases of the serial murder of prostitutes in recent years occurred in 1990, when a forty-five-year old man named Arthur Shawcross was accused of the mutilation and murder of ten hookers in Rochester, New York. According to Shawcross, he killed one woman because she bit him, another because she made too much noise during sex, a third for trying to steal his wallet, and a fourth because she called him a "wimp." Like a number of other serial killers, Shawcross insisted that he had **Multiple Personalities,** and was possessed by the reincarnated spirit of a thirteenth-century English cannibal named Ariemes, who had taught him to dine on human flesh. (Shawcross claimed to have eaten the body parts of several of his victims.)

Another bizarre case involving killing hookers took place in Manhattan in the fall of 1995. As the *New York Post* reported in its October 25, 1995, edition, a thirty-nine-year-old security guard named James Jones allegedly stalked and killed prostitutes because of a "bizarre foot fetish that made him want to turn them into dead ballerinas." After picking up a young streetwalker and bringing her to a sleazy hotel room, Jones reportedly would make the woman "do a grotesque dance of death before sexually attacking and choking" her. Jones was identified and arrested after allegedly attacking six women and killing two and as of this writing awaits trial.

> *"The women I killed were filth—bastard prostitutes who were littering the streets. I was just cleaning up the place a bit."*
> PETER "YORKSHIRE RIPPER" SUTCLIFFE

PYROMANIA

Along with **Animal Torture** and protracted **Bed-Wetting,** starting fires is one of the three early warning signals of future homicidal mania (see **Triad**). So it's not surprising that some serial killers continue their pyromaniac activities as grown-ups. After all, destruction is the serial killer's raison d'être. Human beings are his ultimate target, but when a living victim isn't readily available, an inanimate object will do. Torching a building or two is a common way for a serial killer to satisfy his urge to annihilate.

Back in the late 1800s, Thomas Piper—the "Boston Belfry Murderer," who fatally bludgeoned and raped four victims (including a five-year-old girl)—confessed that in between his frenzied outbursts of lust murder, he was fond of setting fire to some of the city's most prominent buildings, including Concord Hall. Since then, arson has been a favorite form of amusement for a long line of serial killers, from turn-of-the-century killer-nurse Jane **Toppan,** to the "Düsseldorf Monster," Peter **Kürten,** to such recent psychos as David "Son of Sam" **Berkowitz** and Ottis Toole (Henry Lee **Lucas**'s partner in crime).

The ferociously nihilistic Toole might have been speaking for all killers of this kind when he explained why he felt compelled to burn down houses. "I just hated to see them standing there," he said.

QUARRY

An obsessed big-game hunter—who has bagged everything from Bengal tigers to Alaskan grizzlies—grows bored of ordinary prey. He seeks an exciting new challenge, the ultimate thrill. He buys a small, South American island and stocks it with castaways and shipwreck survivors. He begins to hunt the only animal that possesses courage, cunning, and the ability to reason—man.

This is the premise of Richard Connell's prizewinning short story, "The Most Dangerous Game." At the time of its publication in 1924, the tale was perceived as an exercise in sardonic imagination, its kill-crazed villain—a Russian count named Zaroff—as a chilling embodiment of the hunting instinct gone mad.

Unfortunately, the hunting of humans has become an all-too-common reality, as serial killers stalk, trap, and butcher their human quarry with all the methodical madness of Connell's fictitious monster.

Serial killers of the so-called organized type (see **Profiling**) pursue their quarry in a frighteningly systematic way. Arming themselves with their chosen weapons, they stalk their favorite hunting grounds in search of the easiest prey—unescorted women, female hitchhikers, prostitutes of both sexes, unsupervised children. Then they pounce, snaring their victims by force or deception.

Perhaps the most unnerving parallel between serial killers and big-game hunters is their shared fondness for taking **Trophies.** Though some serial killers are satisfied with saving mementos like the wallets or photographs of their victims, others collect and preserve body parts. Edward **Gein**—the most notorious of all human-trophy hunters—kept the flayed, stuffed, and mounted faces of women hanging on his bedroom walls (very much in the manner of Connell's crazy Count Zaroff, who decorates his trophy room with the heads of his human victims).

Between 1973 and 1983, an Alaskan outdoorsman named Robert Hanson indulged in his own depraved version of "The Most Dangerous Game." Abducting prostitutes to the wilderness outside Anchorage, he would strip and rape them, then force them to flee through the woods while he stalked them with a knife, bow and arrow, or hunting rifle. Hanson was ultimately convicted of four savage murders, though his actual tally may have been as high as seventeen.

> " 'Oh,' said the general, 'it supplies me with the most exciting hunting in the world. No other hunting compares with it for an instant. Every day I hunt and never grow bored now, for I have a quarry with which I can match my wits."
>
> RICHARD CONNELL, "The Most Dangerous Game"

QUICKLIME

When Indiana police dug up the farmyard of Belle Gunness in April 1908, they uncovered more than a dozen bodies—the grisly record of years of profit-motivated murder, mostly of prospective husbands (see **Black Widows**). Most of the corpses were drastically decomposed. A chillingly practical woman, Gunness had devised a way to expedite the putrefaction process. She had chopped each of the bodies into six sections, then treated the pieces with quicklime, a highly caustic substance that eats away at organic matter. If the search of her farmyard had occurred any later, the bodies would have been decomposed beyond the possibility of identification.

Other murderers have employed quicklime for the same purpose—eliminating the corpus delicti. Dr. H. H. **Holmes** kept a vat of the stuff in the dungeon of his Chicago "Horror Castle," where untold victims disappeared at the tail end of the nineteenth century. Fifty years later, Dr. Marcel **Petiot**—who murdered dozens of would-be refugees during the Nazi occupation of Paris—used quicklime to dissolve the corpses buried in his backyard. (Only later did he turn to another method—cremation—as a more efficient means of disposal.) John Wayne **Gacy** periodically sprinkled lime into the crawl space beneath his house to dampen the stench of the rotting male bodies accumulating in the muck.

Of course, if you're going to use quicklime for this ghoulish purpose, it helps to know something about its chemical properties. In the mid-1980s, a sixty-year-old woman named Dorothea Puente began renting rooms in her San Francisco boarding house to elderly welfare recipients, who subsequently vanished without a trace. Alerted by suspicious social workers, police launched an investigation and eventually discovered seven headless corpses planted in Puente's backyard garden. Though Puente had taken care to sprinkle the bodies with quicklime, she was undone by her faulty knowledge of chemical reactions. Unless lime is mixed with water, it actually acts as a kind of preservative, slowing down instead of accelerating the decomposition process. As a result, medical examiners had no trouble discovering that the victims had died from massive doses of Valium and Dalmane—evidence that helped convict the lethal landlady and send her to prison for life.

RACISM

Though racism has undoubtedly been responsible for more violence (often on a genocidal scale) than any other form of human hatred, it rarely functions as a motive among serial killers, the vast majority of whom are driven by sexual sadism, not bigotry. According to FBI statistics, only one percent of serial murders kill because of racial hatred. Still, within that tiny fraction there have been some notably vicious cases.

The late 1970s and early 1980s were a boom time for serial murders based on race, as a handful of self-styled "Aryan warriors" launched homicidal crusades against minorities. In Cleveland, a Nazi transvestite named Frank Spisak killed one black man and two whites he believed were Jews. In western New York State, white supremacist Joseph Christopher hunted down and murdered a dozen African Americans over a three-month period (cutting out the hearts of two of his victims), while Hitler-worshipping Joseph Franklin roamed from state to state, slaughtering blacks, Jews, and interracial couples—more than thirteen victims in all.

On rare occasions, a serial killer will choose victims of color not because he is especially bigoted himself but in order to exploit the prevailing prejudices of society. Jeffrey **Dahmer,** for example, preyed mostly on African American and Asian young men, apparently in the belief that the police would pay less attention to crimes involving minority victims. And indeed, the discovery of Dahmer's atrocities set off major protests among black and Asian Milwaukeeans, outraged at the perceived racism of the city's police department.

Of course, racially inspired serial murder is not strictly a white phenomenon. In the early 1970s, a Black Muslim splinter group known as the "Death Angels" required that prospective members prove their zeal by murdering white people and taking Polaroids of the corpses. San Francisco's "Zebra" killings (so-called because the victims were white and the perpetrators black) were the horrific result: fifteen men and women slain in six months. A few years later, the Chicago area was the scene of a similar string of random killings. Calling themselves "De Mau

Mau," the culprits were a group of black Vietnam veterans who vented their rage against white society by slaughtering ten people, including two entire families.

RICHARD RAMIREZ

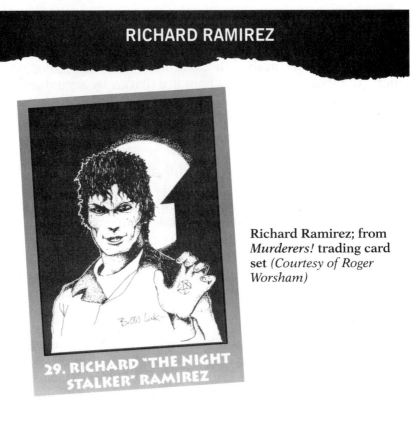

Richard Ramirez; from *Murderers!* trading card set *(Courtesy of Roger Worsham)*

They called him the "Night Stalker"—a shadowy fiend who would slip into darkened houses and savage the sleeping occupants. During his six-month rampage in the spring and summer of 1985, no one in Los Angeles felt safe.

Often, he would kill the husband first, then turn his depraved attentions to the woman. His victims—who ranged in age from thirty to eighty-three—were shot, slashed, bludgeoned, and viciously mutilated. In one case, he carved out the eyes of a forty-four-year-old woman and carried them off as **Trophies.** Sometimes, he daubed satanic pentagrams on the bodies before fleeing into the night.

By early August 1985, he was officially credited with more than a dozen homicides. A few weeks later, after attacking another couple—shooting the man in the head and raping the woman—he fled in their car. After recovering the stolen vehicle, police were able to lift a clear set of fingerprints, which turned out to match those of a small-time hood named Richard Ramirez. An all-points bulletin was issued for the suspect, and his mug shot was broadcast on local TV.

On August 31, Ramirez tried to yank a woman from her car in a Hispanic neighborhood in East LA. Her screams drew the attention of passersby, who recognized Ramirez and pounced on him. Only the timely arrival of the police saved the "Night Stalker" from the enraged mob.

At his trial, Ramirez (who had also been involved in numerous sexual assaults, including the abduction-rape of several small children) indulged in various bizarre antics. He enjoyed playing Satan, inscribing a pentagram on his left palm and flashing it to photographers, and making devil's horns with his fingers while intoning, "Evil, evil, evil . . ." He was ultimately convicted of thirteen murders and sentenced to death. "Big deal," he sneered when the judge handed down the sentence. "Death comes with the territory. See you in Disneyland."

According to his own estimate, the "Night Stalker" (who remains on death row) was responsible for even more murders than the thirteen he was convicted of. "I've killed twenty people, man," he told a fellow inmate. "I love all that blood."

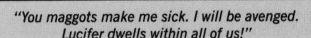

> *"You maggots make me sick. I will be avenged.*
> *Lucifer dwells within all of us!"*
>
> RICHARD "NIGHT STALKER" RAMIREZ,
> addressing the court after being convicted of thirteen murders

RECOMMENDED READING

Though the popularity of true-crime books has boomed in recent years, the genre itself dates back at least as far as 1621, when one of the best-selling tomes in England was a collection of real-life crime stories called *God's Revenge Against Murder and Adultery.* Clearly, a comprehensive history of crime books would require a lot more space than we have at our disposal. Even a history of books dealing only with American serial killers is beyond the scope of this entry. As long ago as 1896, Frank P. Geyer—the Philadelphia detective who followed the trail of the

249

notorious "multi-murder" Dr. H. H. **Holmes**—published an account of his investigation, *The Holmes-Pitezel Case*. Since that time, virtually every serial killer of note has been the subject of at least one book. Covering all of them would take a book of its own.

Still, there are some volumes that anyone interested in serial killers should be aware of. Some of these deal with the phenomenon as a whole. These include: Thomas S. Duke's *Celebrated Criminal Cases of America* (1910); L. C. Douthwaite's *Mass Murder* (1928); Eric Hickey's *Serial Murders and Their Victims* (1991); Jack Levin and James Alan Fox's *Mass Murder: America's Growing Menace* (1988); Elliott Leyton's *Hunting Humans* (1988); Michael Newton's *Serial Slaughter* (1992); Colin Wilson and Donald Seaman's *The Serial Killers*; and the volume *Serial Killers*, part of the "True Crime" series of Time-Life Books.

Capsule biographies of infamous serial killers are included in a number of encyclopedia-style collections. Jay Robert Nash's sweeping *Bloodletters and Badmen* (1973) is the best known of these, but it has to be approached with a certain amount of caution, since it is rife with inaccuracies. Others include: Michael Newton's *Hunting Humans* (1990); Brian Lane and Wilfred Gregg's *The Encyclopedia of Serial Killers* (1992); and David Everitt's *Human Monsters* (1993).

In terms of full-length studies of individual serial killers, the following is an alphabetical list of selected world-class psychos and the books that examine their crimes.

The Axeman of New Orleans
Robert Tallant and William Kimber. *Murder in New Orleans* (1953)

Martha Beck and Raymond Fernandez
Pearl Buck. *The Honeymoon Killers* (1970)

David Berkowitz
David Abrahamsen. *Confessions of Son of Sam* (1985)

Kenneth Bianchi and Angelo Buono
Ted Schwartz. *The Hillside Strangler* (1981)

Ian Brady and Myra Hindley (the "Moors Murderers")
Emlyn Williams. *Beyond Belief* (1967)

Ted Bundy
Ann Rule. *The Stranger Beside Me* (1988)

Andrei Chikatilo
Richard Lourie. *Hunting the Devil* (1993)

John Reginald Christie
Ludovic Kennedy. *Ten Rillington Place* (1961)

The Cleveland Torso Killer
Steven Nickel. *Torso* (1989)

Juan Corona
Tracy Kidder. *The Road to Yuba City* (1974)

Jeffrey Dahmer
Anne E. Schwartz. *The Man Who Could Not Kill Enough* (1992)

Albert DeSalvo
Gerold Frank. *The Boston Strangler* (1967)

Albert Fish
Harold Schechter. *Deranged* (1990)

John Wayne Gacy
Tim Cahill. *Buried Dreams* (1986)

Edward Gein
Harold Schechter. *Deviant* (1989)

Belle Gunness
Janet L. Langois. *Belle Gunness* (1985)

Gary Heidnik
Ken Englade. *Cellar of Horror* (1988)

William Heirens
Lucy Freeman. *Before I Kill More . . . .* (1955)

H. H. Holmes
Harold Schechter. *Depraved* (1994)

Jack the Ripper
Donald Rumbelow. *The Complete Jack the Ripper* (1975)

Jack the Stripper
Brian McConnell. *Found Naked and Dead* (1974)

Edmund Kemper
Margaret Chaney. *The Co-Ed Killer* (1976)

Peter Kürten
Margaret Seaton Wagner. *The Monster of Düsseldorf* (1932)

Henry Lee Lucas
Joe Norris. *Henry Lee Lucas* (1991)

Charles Manson
Vincent Bugliosi. *Helter Skelter* (1975)

Dennis Nilsen
Brian Masters. *Killing for Company* (1985)

Carl Panzram
Thomas Gaddis and James O. Long. *Killer* (1970)

Marcel Petiot
John V. Grombach. *The Great Liquidator* (1982)

Richard Ramirez
Clifford L. Lindecker. *Night Stalker* (1991)

Peter Sutcliffe ("The Yorkshire Ripper")
David A. Yallop. *Deliver Us From Evil* (1980)

Zodiac
Robert Graysmith. *Zodiac* (1986)

The Amok Bookstore in Los Angeles publishes a catalogue (or "Sourcebook for Extremes of Information in Print") that includes many of these books, plus hundreds of other astonishing publications on subjects ranging from post-mortem procedures to pulp fiction. For information, write to: Amok, P. O. Box 861867, Terminal Annex, Los Angeles, CA 90086-1867.

PSYCHO FICTION

It's virtually impossible to crack open a thriller these days without encountering a psychopathic sex-killer, so short-listing the best serial-killer novels is a pretty tricky affair. We've settled for brief descriptions of our ten personal favorites (a few of them golden oldies):

1. *Psycho.* The granddaddy of psychokiller novels. This pulp classic by the late great Robert Bloch transformed the real-life atrocities of Ed **Gein** into genuine myth and inspired one of the masterworks of American cinema.

2. *American Gothic.* Another lesser-known (but in certain ways even more suspenseful) novel by Bloch, based on the crimes of Chicago's nineteenth-century Bluebeard, Dr. H. H. **Holmes.**

3. *American Psycho.* At the risk of offending the entire membership of NOW, we have to say that Bret Easton Ellis's notoriously nauseating best-seller is actually a serious, if flawed, work that manages to make a point about the rapacious consumerism of Reagan-era America. Still, it's only recommended for the strong of stomach.

4. *Red Dragon.* Hannibal Lecter's debut appearance. This brilliant, harrowing page-turner by the inimitable Thomas Harris was made into a stylish (if slightly disappointing) film called *Manhunter,* directed by Michael Mann.

5. *The Silence of the Lambs.* The *Gone With the Wind* of psychokiller novels. A tour de force of horror-suspense, this novel stands as the yardstick against which all future fiction in the serial-killer genre must be measured.

6. *The Killer Inside Me.* The narrator of Jim Thompson's pulp classic—a small-town sheriff who is also a homicidal maniac—is not, strictly speaking, a serial killer. Still, this powerfully unsettling, darkly hilarious novel is one of the best psychological portraits of a psychopath in print.

7. *Slob.* The protagonist of Rex Miller's deeply disturbing novel is a hyperintelligent, five-hundred-pound psycho called Chaingang who has a penchant for tearing out and devouring the hearts of his victims. A favorite book among hard-core horror buffs.

8. *The Stranger Returns.* Michael Perry constructs a gripping suspense novel around a nifty premise: Ted Bundy engineers his escape by contriving to have another death row inmate electrocuted in his stead, then goes on a new rampage. Perry's fictionalized Bundy is a thoroughly creepy creation—an utterly convincing evocation of the legendary ladykiller.

9. *Ghoul.* Another over-the-top splatter fest from "Michael Slade," the nom de gore of three Canadian collaborators (Jay Clarke, John Banks, and Lee Clarke) who have also given us *Headhunter* and *Cutthroat.*

10. *Zombie.* Joyce Carol Oates crawls into the mind of a Jeffrey **Dahmer**–like psycho who dreams of creating his own personal **Zombie** by using ice picks to perform lobotomies on living victims. Not for the squeamish!

FOR BIBLIOPHILES ONLY

Patterson Smith, an antiquarian bookseller and social historian, specializes in rare and out-of-print crime volumes. Smith offers everything from hard-to-find reference works (like a reprint of Thomas S. Duke's 1910 classic, *Celebrated Criminal Cases of America*) to oddities like *Killer Fiction*, a collection of absolutely hair-raising stories by convicted sex-killer G. J. Schaefer.

For information, contact: Patterson Smith, 23 Prospect Terrace, Montclair, New Jersey 07402.

RECORDS

No, we're not referring to Guns 'n' Roses' version of Charlie Manson's "Look at Your Game, Girl" or "Heidnik's House of Horrors" by the Serial Killers (you'll find those catchy numbers covered under **Songs**). We're talking about something much grimmer: killers who can claim the deadly distinction of having slain the most victims.

The serial-murder rate has increased so alarmingly in recent years that some criminologists talk in terms of an "epidemic." One indication of how scary the situation has become is the escalating number of victims attributed to individual killers. In 1888, the Western world was horrified by the deeds of **Jack the Ripper**—but Saucy Jack's total of five victims wouldn't even rate a mention on the national news nowadays.

By 1896, Jack's record had already been eclipsed by Dr. H. H. **Holmes**, who killed a minimum of nine victims (he himself claimed twenty-seven, and some crime historians put the total in the hundreds). Thirty years later, Earle Leonard **Nelson** set the homicidal record in our country, strangling twenty-two women during a savage, cross-country killing spree. His contemporary Carl **Panzram** fell just short of that number, confessing to twenty-one murders (in addition to a slew of other crimes).

During the past twenty-five years, each new record has been broken almost as soon as it had been set. In 1973, Juan Corona officially became the most prolific serial killer in American history when he was convicted of slaying twenty-five California transients. But by the end of the decade, Ted **Bundy** had slain at least twenty-eight and John Wayne **Gacy** thirty-three.

And still the numbers kept rising. The still-unidentified "Green River Killer" murdered forty-nine victims in the early 1980s, while in Russia, Andrei **Chikatilo** was accused of fifty-two sadistic slayings and suspected of several more.

When it comes to killers who have *claimed* the highest totals, the all-time champions are America's own Henry Lee **Lucas** and the South American lust slayer Pedro Lopez (aka the "Monster of the Andes"), each of whom confessed to over three hundred murders. In both cases, however, the true totals have never been established.

Henry Lee Lucas; from
Murderers! trading card set
(Courtesy of Roger Worsham)

255

REFRIGERATORS

Serial killers have been known to use their household appliances for purposes that the friendly folks at Maytag and KitchenAid have never dreamed of—not even in their worst nightmares. Living in a decaying old farmhouse without electricity, Edward **Gein** was forced to rely on time-consuming tanning methods to preserve his collection of anatomical **Trophies.** Other serial killers, however—whose homes were equipped with all the modern conveniences—had a much easier time of it. To preserve a favorite body part, all they have to do is pop it in the fridge.

Douglas Clark—the so-called "Sunset Strip Slayer," who killed a string of Hollywood hookers in 1980—had a particular fetish for decapitated female heads. His girlfriend, Carol Bundy, indulged this perversion by applying makeup to the head of one of Clark's victims, a twenty-year-old streetwalker. Clark stored this grotesque keepsake in his apartment refrigerator, occasionally removing it for the purpose of oral sex.

Seven years later, in March 1987, Philadelphia police raided the home of a maniac named Gary **Heidnik** and discovered a trio of half-starved women chained up to the plumbing in his cellar. Heidnik, as it turned out, had abducted and enslaved a total of six victims altogether, subjecting them to months of rape and torture. Searching the rest of the house, the officers quickly discovered that the horrors were not confined to the so-called Torture Dungeon. In the freezer compartment of the kitchen refrigerator, they found a human arm, intended for a cannibal meal. Among his other atrocities, Heidnik liked to mix chopped-up human flesh with dog food and force his starving captives to devour the unholy meal.

Other serial killers, like the German lust murderer Joachim Kroll, had stocked their refrigerators with human flesh to satisfy their own cannibalistic cravings. The same was true of Jeffrey **Dahmer,** whose refrigerator contained a wide assortment of body parts, including heads, intestines, kidneys, lungs, livers, and a heart.

RELIGION

See **Zealots.**

RIPPERS

According to most crime historians, **Jack the Ripper** is the seminal psychokiller of the modern era—the granddaddy of all serial murderers. So it's only fitting that some of his descendants have been named after him.

His earliest namesake stalked the countryside of southern France: Joseph **Vacher,** the "French Ripper," who savaged almost a dozen victims in the late 1890s. Since that time, most of the killers christened with the Ripper name have been compatriots of the original.

During the London blitz of World War II, while Hitler's Luftwaffe rained terror from the sky, the city was confronted with a very different kind of menace—a homicidal fiend who stalked and slaughtered defenseless women. On February 9, 1942, this bloodthirsty butcher struck for the first time, strangling a female pharmacist in an air-raid shelter. The following day, he picked up a prostitute in Picadilly Circus, then—after accompanying her back to her Soho flat—slit her throat and mutilated her genitals with a can opener. Two more victims followed on succeeding nights, both subjected to hideous mutilations. The perpetrator of these atrocities—who turned out to be a twenty-five-year-old RAF cadet named Gordon Cummins—was caught after two more attempted killings, both of which he botched. His ghastly deeds, so reminiscent of those of the original "Whitechapel Horrors," earned him the moniker "The Blackout Ripper."

Another of Jack's homicidal heirs was Peter Sutcliffe, aka the "Yorkshire Ripper." A thirtyish truckdriver and former gravedigger, Sutcliffe—who believed he was acting on orders from God—conducted a five-year campaign of carnage that commenced in the mid-1970s. Using his favorite weapons—ball peen hammer, chisel, carving knife, and screwdriver—he attacked over two dozen women, killing thirteen. Though some of his victims were co-eds, his primary targets were prostitutes. When Sutcliffe was finally arrested in 1981 after the largest manhunt in British history, his younger brother, Carl, asked him why he had done it. "I were just cleaning the streets," Sutcliffe replied.

The crimes of Cummins and Sutcliffe were clearly in the tradition of the original "Whitechapel Horrors." But these two killers differed from Jack the Ripper in one important respect: both of them were eventually caught. One serial killer of prostitutes who eluded the police was the shadowy killer who strangled half a dozen women in the early to mid-1960s. After dispatching his victims, he dumped their naked bodies in various places around London—an MO that inspired his punning tabloid moniker. The killer (who has never been officially identified) was dubbed "Jack the Stripper."

RITUAL

Ritual killings committed by devil-worshipping cultists happen all the time in horror fiction and fantasy but rarely, if ever, in real life. The FBI has yet to document a single instance of such ceremonial sacrifice in America (see **Satanism**). On the other hand, bizarre ritualistic patterns are commonplace among serial killers. Though this behavior often appears random to an outside observer, it clearly possesses some deep, terrible significance to the killer himself, who is compelled to repeat it again and again.

Often the pattern involves a particular *way* of killing. Each of **Jack the Ripper**'s crimes culminated in a kind of ritual evisceration—as if he were enacting some primitive sacrifice in which the victim's entrails were removed and offered up to the gods. Another unidentified serial murderer, the 1930s madman known as the "Cleveland Torso Killer," methodically dismembered his victims and made off with their heads, which he apparently kept as ritual **Trophies**—in much the same way that aboriginal warriors collect the scalps and shrunken heads of their foes.

At other times, the killer will perform some compulsive ritual as an integral *part* of the crime. John Wayne **Gacy** turned his hideous murders into a grotesque ceremony by reciting the

Twenty-Third Psalm ("The Lord is my shepherd") while slowly garroting his victims. The so-called "Green River Killer"—who murdered a string of young women in the Seattle area during the early 1980s—left weird, pyramid-shaped stones in the vaginas of his victims. Ed **Gein**—in unwitting emulation of those Aztec priests who arrayed themselves in the flayed skin of sacrificial victims—liked to parade around in apparel fashioned from the human flesh of dissected female corpses. And Albert "Boston Strangler" **DeSalvo** ritualistically left his victims looking like grotesque, gift-wrapped holiday presents. After strangling a woman, he would tie the ligature—usually a scarf, stocking, or bathrobe sash—into a big, ornamental bow. In one case, he also left a greeting card propped up against the victim's foot.

RUSSIA

For decades, leaders of the Soviet Union maintained that crime was not a problem in their country. Thievery and murder, they insisted, were symptoms of Western-style capitalistic decadence. The collapse of communism in the early 1980s, of course, revealed all sorts of problems that had been hidden by the Iron Curtain. In particular, the 1992 trial of Andrei **Chikatilo**—the so-called "Rostov Ripper"—demonstrated that while the USSR might not be able to supply its citizens with basic consumer items, it could certainly produce serial killers every bit as terrifying as any American psycho. Moreover, though Chikatilo was undoubtedly the most savage of Russian sex-killers, he was not unique: multiple murderers had been prowling through the Soviet Union from the earliest days of the Communist regime.

In the early 1920s, thirty-three men fell victim to a sociopathic horse trader named Vasili Komaroff, aka the "Wolf of Moscow." After luring a prospective customer to his stable, Komaroff—assisted by his wife—would bludgeon or strangle the victim to death, strip him of his possessions, then truss up the body, stuff it into a sack, and deposit it an empty lot somewhere in the city. When authorities finally caught up with him, Komaroff claimed that he killed solely for money—an unlikely explanation, since his nearly three dozen murders netted him a grand total of

$26.40. Clearly, there were other, darker motives at work—but the Soviet authorities were much less interested in fathoming his psychology than in putting him to death as promptly as possible. Komaroff and his wife were executed by a firing squad in June 1923.

In more recent years, as the serial-murder rate started burgeoning in the West, the Soviet Union also had its share of grisly killers. In 1964, an unemployed Moscow actor named Vladimir Ionosyan butchered five people with an axe. Ten years later, a shadowy killer nicknamed "Ivan the Ripper" slaughtered eleven Moscow women. Authorities eventually arrested a man for the killings, but—in typically secretive Soviet style—they never divulged who the culprit was or how the case was resolved.

In the 1980s—while America was confronted with the gruesome likes of Henry Lee **Lucas** and Gary **Heidnik**—Soviet authorities caught up with Gennadily Mikhasevich, who used his position as an auxiliary policeman to trap and strangle thirty-three women. Another homicidal monster of that decade was Nikolai Dzumagalies—one of the most frightening and ferocious serial killers ever spawned in the USSR (or anywhere else, for that matter). Like Francis Dolarhyde, the terrifying psychocreep in Thomas Harris's novel *Red Dragon*—who savages his victims with a lethal set of dentures—Dzumagalies (or "Metal Fang," as he came to be nicknamed) sported scary, white metal false teeth. Luring women to a lonely riverbank at night, he proceeded to rape them, stab them, and carve up their bodies. Then, he roasted the flesh and shared it with friends, who—believing they were partaking of beef—were turned into unwitting cannibals.

SADISM

S ome criminologists define serial murder in strictly quantita-
tive terms: three or more homicides committed over an extended length of time, with an emotional "cooling-off" period
between each incident (see **Definition**). Other specialists in the
field, however, believe that serial murder in the strict sense of
the term always contains another element—a powerful streak of
sexual sadism.

Certainly, this is the aspect of serial killing that makes it such
a uniquely hideous crime—even worse than mass murder. After
all, it is one thing to be cut down by a crazed gunman in a convenience store; it is quite another to fall victim to a psycho who
calmly explains (as one serial killer actually did): "First, I'm
going to torture you in the most horrible and painful manner I
can think of. Then I'm going to abuse you sexually in the most
degrading way I can possibly think of. Then I'll kill you in the
slowest and most painful way I can. Any questions?"

Albert **Fish** liked to castrate teenage boys and watch them
bleed to death in agony. Leonard Lake and Charles Ng took
videotapes of the slow, sadistic murder of their bound and captive sex slaves. Another serial killer tortured a prostitute for
forty-three days before killing her. These are just a few of countless, unspeakable examples.

In this regard, serial murder can be seen as a kind of depraved
travesty of normal sexual functioning. Instead of looking for a
date at a singles bar or dance club, the serial killer goes trolling
for victims in some favorite hunting ground—a red-light district,
say, or a homosexual hangout. Once he has a victim in his
power, he achieves sexual release not through intercourse but
through torture, degradation, and finally murder (it is not uncommon for a lust murderer to reach orgasm during his victim's
death throes). The so-called cooling-off period corresponds to
the contented lull that normally follows sex, while the psychopath's growing need to kill again is the equivalent of building
sexual hunger—in effect, the serial killer gets increasingly horny
for blood.

Sexual psychopaths of this type tend to be victims of extreme physical and/or emotional childhood abuse (often sexual abuse). Subjected to vicious **Upbringings** that twist their erotic natures completely out of shape, they grow up equating sex not with love and tenderness but with aggression, dominance, and murderous rage. To cite just one of many examples: Joseph Kallinger—who tortured and mutilated a string of young boys (including his own son)—was raised by parents who routinely flogged him with a cat-o'-nine-tails and threatened him with castration. Other serial killers who conform to this pattern are Henry Lee **Lucas**, John Wayne **Gacy**, Edmund **Kemper**, and Jeffrey **Dahmer**—in short, some of the most monstrous criminals of our (or any other) time.

"It is probable that he first cut the throats of his victims, then ripped open the abdomen and groped among the intestines. In some instances he cut off the genitals and carried them away; in others he only tore them to pieces and left them behind. He does not seem to have had sexual intercourse with his victims, but very likely the murderous act and subsequent mutilation of the corpse were the equivalents for the sex act."

RICHARD VON KRAFFT-EBING,
discussing Jack the Ripper

"I always had a desire to inflict pain on others and to have others inflict pain on me. I always seemed to enjoy everything that hurt. The desire to inflict pain, that is all that is uppermost."

ALBERT FISH

SATANISM

If you believe everything you hear on *Geraldo*, you might well think that our country is overrun with satanic cultists who regularly indulge in human sacrifice and every other manner of unspeakable perversion. In fact, beyond the highly unreliable testimony of various religious nuts and sexual hysterics, there is little or no evidence that such devil-worshipping covens actually exist, at least not in the United States of America.

On the other hand, since serial killers are inexorably drawn to all that is dark and depraved, they often enjoy embellishing their crimes—and themselves—with a bit of satanic symbolism. Wayne Nance, a Montana truck driver who killed five people in the mid-1980s, used a white-hot coat hanger to brand the number of the Beast—"666"—onto his own flesh. Similarly, John Kogut—a young, Long Island landscaper who led a gang that raped and murdered three young women—burned an inverted cross onto his forearm.

Other self-styled devil devotees like to leave satanic markings at the crime scene. After breaking into the suburban home of an eighty-four-year-old Los Angeles woman and beating her to death, Richard the "Night Stalker" **Ramirez** drew pentagrams on her skin, then painted a few more on the walls before fleeing. At his trial, he kept the press corps entertained by shouting salutations to Satan and flashing a pentagram that he had inscribed on his palm. "You don't understand," he sneered at the judge. "You are not expected to. I am beyond good and evil. Legions of the night! Night breed!"

One of the most notorious of all Lucifer-related cases was the savage 1984 mutilation-slaying of Long Island teenager Gary Lauwers by the devil-besotted druggie, Rickie Kasso. "Say you love Satan!" Kasso commanded over and over again, while slashing Lauwers to pieces with a pocketknife. Horrific as it was, however, the murder was not—as originally reported—a ritualistic sacrifice but rather a vicious act of revenge over some bags of stolen angel dust.

The only documented case of satanic serial murder occurred in Matamoros, Mexico, where a devil-worshipping drug gang slaughtered fifteen sacrificial victims in a demonic rite designed to insure supernatural protection (see **Cults**).

SLIPPING THROUGH THE CRACKS

S erial killers tend to possess two characteristics typical of psychopaths. Lacking normal human emotions, they are able to stay absolutely calm under intensely stressful circumstances. They also have the ability to appear so utterly, blandly normal that it is virtually impossible for anyone to conceive of them as crazed, cold-blooded killers (see **"Mask of Sanity"**). Both of these traits have stood many serial killers in extremely good stead, allowing them to fool even highly trained investigators and elude arrest for years.

For several decades, Albert **Fish** roamed across the country, in search of young prey. During that time, he was frequently in and out of custody for charges ranging from petty theft to public indecency. At no time, however, did authorities suspect that he was capable of insanely violent crime. Only in 1934 did the appalling truth come to light: the gray-haired, grandfatherly old man, who looked so sweet and kindly that strangers would entrust their children to his care, had spent his lifetime torturing, mutilating, and ultimately cannibalizing little boys and girls.

In the mid-1970s, a string of young women were abducted and murdered in Seattle after meeting a man named "Ted." One of the many suspects in the case turned out to be a law student named Ted **Bundy.** When police checked into his background, however, they decided that the bright and ambitious young Republican couldn't possibly be the killer—leaving the sociopathic Bundy free to murder, rape, and mutilate young women for another four years.

One of the most notorious instances in which a serial killer slipped through the hands of police occurred on the night of May 27, 1991, when two Milwaukee cops, alerted by a 911 call, found a naked teenaged boy apparently attempting to flee from an older man. The man—a soft-spoken thirty-year-old named Jeffrey **Dahmer**—explained that he and the boy were gay lovers who had been engaged in nothing more serious than a "domestic dispute." Dahmer was so polite and persuasive that police let him take the teenager back to his apartment—where Dahmer proceeded to strangle him, have sex with the corpse, and dismember the body.

Police are not the only ones who have been known to let real-life monsters go free. In 1978, the world's most prolific serial killer, Pedro Lopez, was caught by a group of Peruvian Indians as he tried to kidnap one of the girls from their village. The outraged Indians were in the process of putting Lopez to a slow, agonizing death, when a female missionary happened onto the scene and persuaded them to desist. Lopez was turned over to the Peruvian police, who simply deported him to Ecuador. As a result of the missionary's misplaced compassion—and the gross negligence of the Peruvian police—the "Monster of the Andes" went on to rape and murder scores of Ecuadorian women.

It is one thing for a Christian missionary, whose faith demands forgiveness, to be fooled by sociopathic evil. It seems much less comprehensible when the sucker is a trained psychiatrist—supposedly an expert in the darker workings of the human mind. In September 1972, an entire panel of state-appointed psychiatrists interviewed Edmund **Kemper** to determine how well he had adjusted to life since his release from a mental hospital three years earlier. The doctors were unanimous in their judgment—Kemper was no longer a threat to society. Kemper drove away from the interview free from any further psychiatric supervision.

Inside the trunk of his car was the head of a fifteen-year-old girl he had decapitated the previous day.

SONGS

Though the crime-ridden lyrics of "gangsta" rap have come in for all kinds of flak, the truth is that people have always enjoyed songs about sex and violence. Moralists who long for the good old days before songs like "Murder Was the Case" ruled the airwaves might keep in mind that one of the biggest hits of the 1950s was the Kingston Trio's "Tom Dooley"—a mournful ditty about a guy who is about to be hanged for slaying his girlfriend ("Met her on the mountain, / There I took her life. / Met her on the mountain, / Stabbed her with my knife"). And indeed—though folk songs are generally thought of as cheery and uplifting—some of the oldest songs in folklore tradition are so-called murder ballads, many of which date back hundreds of years and describe violent crimes in horrifying detail. A popular ballad called "Expert Town," for example, contains lyrics like: "Little attention did I pay, / I beat her more and more; / I beat her till the blood run down— / Her hair was yellow as gold."

In America, songs about serial killers date at least as far back as the nineteenth century. In her book *American Murder Ballads,*

Olive Burt reprints a song about the notorious **Black Widow** killer Belle Gunness whose first few verses go like this:

> Belle Gunness was a lady fair,
> In Indiana State.
> She weighed about three hundred pounds,
> And that is quite some weight.
>
> That she was stronger than a man
> Her neighbors all did own;
> She butchered hogs right easily,
> And did it all alone.
>
> But hogs were just a sideline
> She indulged in now and then;
> Her favorite occupation
> Was a-butchering of men.

Contemporary songs about psychokillers, in short, are not just a modern-day aberration but a continuation of a genre that undoubtedly extends all the way back to the Middle Ages and probably further. In any case, the following is a list of ten memorable recordings dealing with serial murder and mayhem:

1. *Warren Zevon*, "Excitable Boy." From the sardonic singer/songwriter best known for his hit "Werewolves of London" comes this toe-tapping tune about an "excitable boy" who rapes and murders his high school prom date. After doing ten years in prison, he digs up her grave and "fills a cage with her bones."

2. *Talking Heads*, "Psycho-killer." A catchy musical foray into the mind of a homicidal creep, this is the song that put David Byrne and his band on the map. *Qu'est-ce que c'est?*

3. *Police*, "Murder by the Numbers." An ironic commentary on the culture of violence disguised as a paean to the art of murder. Sting's lyrics play a pivotal role in the plot of the 1995 serial-killer movie *Copycat*.

4. *The Beatles*, "Maxwell's Silver Hammer." Not everyone is a fan of this infectious little ditty penned by Paul McCartney about a homicidal maniac. Ian MacDonald, author of the definitive *Revolution in the Head: The Beatles Records and the Sixties*, calls it a "ghastly miscalculation that represents McCartney's worst lapse in taste."

5. *Slayer*, "Dead Skin Mask." A brain-pummeling tribute to Ed

"Psycho" **Gein** from a band that is one of the leading purveyors of "black metal" rock.

6. *Serial Killers*, "Heidnik's House of Horrors." A rarity. Released on the obscure "Suspiria" label and pressed on blood-red vinyl, this punk-rock tribute to killer Gary **Heidnik** features a melody that can best be described as "primitive." But how can you hate a song with lyrics like "He had a basement straight out of hell / Marquis de Sade would think it was swell"?

7. *Bruce Springsteen*, "Nebraska." The haunting title song of Springsteen's 1982 acoustic album is a first-person account of Charles Starkweather's infamous killing spree across the badlands of Nebraska (see **Killer Couples**).

8. *Alice Cooper*, "I Love the Dead." Not exactly a serial-killer song but—with lines like "I love the dead before they're cold / They're bluing flesh for me to hold"—it's certainly one that serial killers could relate to.

9. *Guns 'n' Roses*, "Look at Your Game, Girl." This song set off a firestorm of controversy when it appeared on G 'n' R's 1993 *The Spaghetti Incident?* album, even though it has nothing to do with serial killers. The reason? It was written by none other than Charles **Manson**, who—before he gained notoriety as the kill-crazed leader of a cult of homicidal hippies—was an aspiring songwriter. Manson's own version of "Look at Your Game, Girl"

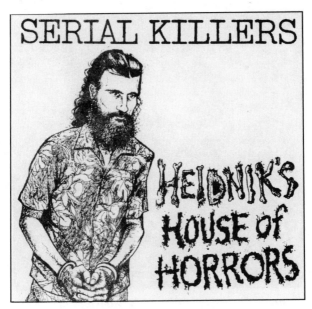

Record sleeve from "Heidnik's House of Horrors,"
art by Liz Pop *(Courtesy of Larry Kay and Paul Bearer)*

appears on his legendary LP *Lie,* along with such other immortal compositions as "People Say I'm No Good," "Garbage Dump," "Sick City," and "Don't Do Anything Illegal." The Manson discography also includes: *The Manson Family Sings, Charles Manson Live at San Quentin,* and a recent CD called *Commemoration,* which includes his tribute to Hank Williams Sr. and several heartfelt numbers about the environment.

10. *Joe Coleman's Internal Machine.* Unlike the previous titles in this list, this is an *entire album* of mayhem-related music assembled by the one-and-only Joe Coleman (see **Art**). Among its many treasures are Red River Dave's yodelling country-western number, "California Hippie Murders" and "Strangler in the Night," with lyrics by Albert "Boston Strangler" **DeSalvo!**

In the realm of serial-killer-related pop music, mention must also be made of the now-defunct punk group Ed Gein's Car; the 1991 album *Too Much Joy* by a group called Cereal Killers (get it?); and the limited edition single "Biter" by the Kansas City band Season to Risk, which features a jacket painting by John Wayne **Gacy.**

Album cover for *Joe Coleman's Infernal Machine*
(Courtesy of Joe Coleman

SOUVENIRS

See **Trophies.**

RICHARD SPECK

Richard Speck; from
52 Famous Murderers
trading cards *(Courtesy of Roger Worsham)*

Strictly speaking, Richard Speck was a **Mass Murderer,** not a serial killer, since the crimes that earned him everlasting infamy were all committed in a single night. Still, those crimes were so horrific that they place Speck squarely in the ranks of twentieth-century American monsters.

A hulking, acne-scarred thug addicted to booze and drugs, Speck had logged nearly forty arrests by the time he was twenty for offenses ranging from burglary to assault with a deadly weapon. Mass murderers are sometimes referred to as "human time bombs"—and the description certainly fits Speck, whose life had been one slow, inexorable buildup to a devastating explosion of violence.

That explosion occurred on the night of July 13, 1966. Speck—who worked as a merchant seaman—was in Chicago, waiting to ship out to

New Orleans. He spent the day guzzling booze, popping downers, and ogling the women as they sunbathed in the park behind Jeffey Manor, a town house for student nurses working at a local hospital. At around 11 P.M., Speck returned to the town house and knocked on the door. It was opened by a twenty-three-year-old student nurse named Corazon Amurao, who found herself face-to-face with a pockmarked stranger brandishing a knife and a gun. "I'm not going to hurt you," Speck said as he shoved his way inside. "I need your money to go to New Orleans."

Speck led her upstairs, where he found five more student nurses. Herding them all into one bedroom, he ordered them to lie on the floor. Then, ripping a bedsheet into strips, he proceeded to truss his terrified victims. Over the next hour, three more young women arrived at the town house. They, too, ended up bound and helpless on the bedroom floor.

Toying with his gun, Speck sat on the floor with his nine captives, as though debating what to do with them. Finally, he came to a ghastly decision. Untying twenty-year-old Pamela Wilkening, he led her into an adjoining bedroom, where he stabbed her in the breast and strangled her. Mary Ann Jordan and Suzanne Farris were next. Speck shoved them into another bedroom and savaged them with his knife.

Pausing to wash the blood from his hands, Speck returned to his grisly work. One by one the young women were led off into different bedrooms and brutally killed—some had their throats slashed, others were strangled. The last to die was twenty-two-year-old Gloria Davy. Speck took his time raping her twice before sodomizing her with a foreign object and strangling her to death.

Having dispatched every one of the young women—or so he thought—Speck shuffled off into the night. But during his rampage, he had lost count of his victims. One of the student nurses—Corazon Amurao—had managed to hide herself under a bed. Waiting until five in the morning, she wriggled out from under the mattress, made her way to the balcony, and began screaming, "They are all dead! My friends are all dead!"

From Amurao's description, along with other clues—primarily the fingerprints he had left all over the apartment and the telltale knots he had tied, which were characteristic of a seaman—police quickly identified Speck, who was arrested in Cook County Hospital after a failed suicide attempt. He was given the death sentence, but when the U.S. Supreme Court abolished the death penalty, he was resentenced to consecutive life terms amounting to four hundred years. He had served only nineteen of them when he died in prison of a heart attack.

THE SPECK TAPE

In May, 1995, the public got its first stunned look at a grainy VHS tape that gave new meaning to the term "pornographic video." Shot in Stateville prison in 1988—three years before his death—the tape shows Richard Speck snorting cocaine, engaging in oral sex with another inmate, and flaunting his monstrously repulsive body.

Looking unspeakably grotesque in a blonde, bobbed hairdo, Speck—lounging in a cell with his young African-American lover—jokes about his murders, talks about how much he loves to be anally penetrated by other men, and brags about the good life he has been enjoying in prison. "If they only knew how much fun I was having in here," he laughs, "they would turn me loose."

In what is perhaps the most revolting moment in this thoroughly odious tape, Speck—at the behest of his lover—strips off his clothes to reveal that he is sporting blue silk panties and a floppy set of hormonally-induced female breasts. He then proceeds to perform fellatio on the other man.

When this video was shown to Illinois lawmakers, it set off a storm of outrage. "This is the kind of thing that really shakes the public's confidence in the criminal justice system," remarked one state legislator. Indeed, this comment was a significant understatement. The tape was so abhorrent that—after portions of it were broadcast on news stations around the country—even some die-hard opponents of the death penalty found themselves regretting that Speck had escaped execution.

SPREE KILLERS

In its efforts to establish precise criminal classifications, the FBI distinguishes between serial killing and spree killing. According to the Bureau's definitions, a serial killer always experiences an emotional "cooling-off" period between his crimes—a hiatus lasting anywhere from days to years. By contrast, a spree killer is someone who murders a string of people in several different locations with no cooling-off period between homicides.

A classic case of spree killing occurred in 1949, when a crazed ex-GI named Howard Unruh strode through his Camden, New Jersey, neighborhood with a 9mm Luger in hand, gunning down everyone who crossed his path. In the space of just twelve minutes, he killed thirteen people and wounded three more. More recently, a twenty-seven-year-old Englishman named Michael Ryan decked himself out like Rambo—complete with an AK-47 and Kalashnikov assault rifle—and spent the morning of August 19, 1987, shooting thirty people around the British market town of Hungerford.

Other spree killers, however, commit their crimes over a much more extended period of time. This can make the FBI's distinction between spree killing and serial murder seem a little blurry. In 1984, for example, a homicidal maniac named Christopher Wilder went on a murder spree that left six women dead in a month's time. Perhaps the most famous of all American spree killers, Charles Starkweather, killed ten people during a twenty-six-day rampage through the badlands of Nebraska and Wyoming (see **A Couple of Crazy Kids**).

Perhaps a more useful distinction between spree killing and serial homicide has to do with underlying motives. Serial killing

Charles Starkweather; from *Murderers!* trading card set (*Courtesy of Roger Worsham*)

is, at bottom, a sexual crime. The serial killer spends a great deal of time (perhaps years) indulging in dark, obsessive fantasies about dominance, torture, and murder. Finally, driven by an overpowering hunger, he goes out in search of a very precise type of victim (women with long dark hair parted in the middle, for example, or Asian teenage boys). Once he has fulfilled his depraved desires, his blood lust subsides for a certain length of time, until it builds again to an irresistible need.

Spree killing, on the other hand, is really a form of mobile **Mass Murder.** While the mass murderer commits his crimes in a single location (for example, the disgruntled employee who suddenly goes berserk and blows away all his co-workers), the spree killer moves from place to place (throughout a neighborhood, around a town, or even across an entire county or state). But his rampage is essentially a single extended massacre (even when it lasts for several weeks).

In short, the spree killer is generally not a sexual psychopath but a deeply unbalanced individual who suddenly snaps and embarks on a murderous jaunt, leaving a trail of corpses in his wake. Spree killers share another trait with mass murderers: they are driven by profoundly self-destructive impulses. Typically, their rampages end with their own deaths, either by suicide or in a barrage of police gunfire. They are walking time bombs who detonate without warning, destroying everyone in sight—themselves included.

STATISTICS

If you live in California and you're the kind of person who worries obsessively about encountering a serial killer, you might consider moving to a different place—like Maine. Of all the states in the union, California has the single highest number of serial homicide cases in this century—fully 16 percent of the national total. Maine, on the other hand, has the lowest—none. Other states to avoid: New York, Texas, Illinois, and Florida. The safest places in America, at least in terms of serial murder, are Hawaii, Montana, North Dakota, Delaware, and Vermont, each of which has had only one case of serial murder since the start of the century.

For the statistically minded student of serial murder, here are a few other interesting facts and figures:

- The United States is the hands-down leading producer of serial killers, with 76 percent of the world's total. Europe comes in a distant second with a measly 17 percent.
- England has produced 28 percent of the European total. Germany is a very close second with 27 percent, and France is third with 13 percent.
- In terms of demographics, the vast majority of American serial killers—fully 84 percent—are Caucasian and a mere 16 percent black.
- In terms of gender, men constitute the overwhelming preponderance of serial killers—at least 90 percent. Indeed, depending on how the crime is defined, many experts believe that serial murder is an exclusively male activity. (See **Definition** and **Women.**)
- While women constitute, at most, an infinitesimal fraction of serial murderers, they make up the majority of victims—65 percent.
- It is very rare for a serial killer to prey on members of another race. Since most serial killers are white, so are the vast majority of victims—89 percent.
- Serial murder tends to be a young person's crime. Most serial killers—44 percent—embark on their deadly careers in their twenties, with 26 percent starting out in their teens and 24 percent in their thirties.
- If you're seeking a career that will keep you safe from serial killers, you'll want to avoid prostitution, since hookers are prime targets for sociopathic sex-slayers. The bad news is that there really isn't any profession that will necessarily protect you from a run-in with a serial killer. In almost 15 percent of serial-murder cases, the victims are chosen entirely at random.

SUICIDE

See **Death Wish.**

JANE TOPPAN

They call nurses "angels of mercy"—and to all appearances, Jane Toppan fit that description. Besides her obvious competence, she seemed to be a sensitive, sympathetic woman who had worked for some of Boston's best families. Of course, none of her employers knew anything about Jane's early years. They did not know about her mother's tragic death when Jane was just an infant—or about her father's subsequent insanity, which impelled him to stitch his eyelids together one day in his Boston tailor shop. They weren't aware of Jane's own suicide attempts after being jilted by her fiancé. Or the morbid obsessions she displayed during her student nursing years at a Cambridge hospital, where her bizarre fascination with autopsies became a source of dismay to her supervisors.

It wasn't until members of the Davis family began dropping like flies in the summer of 1901 that the terrible truth about the skilled, seemingly compassionate nurse finally came to light. Far from being an "angel of mercy," Jane Toppan turned out to be one of America's most bloodthirsty "angels of death."

Mrs. Mattie Davis was the first to go, presumably of heart failure. She died while visiting her old friend Jane Toppan. The elder Davis daughter, Mrs. Annie Gordon, was so grief-stricken that she turned to Nurse Toppan for relief. Toppan obliged by administering some injections. Shortly thereafter, Annie Gordon followed her mother to the grave. A few days later, the patriarch of the family, Captain Alden Davis, was felled, supposedly by a massive stroke. He, too, had been receiving medication from Nurse Toppan. That left just one surviving member of the family, another married daughter, Mrs. Mary Gibbs. Several days after her father's funeral—after placing herself under the care of kindly Nurse Toppan—Mary Gibbs dropped dead, too.

With his wife's entire family wiped out in less than six weeks, Mary Gibbs's husband demanded an autopsy. Toppan did her best to prevent it, but Gibbs—suspecting foul play—called in the Massachusetts State Police. The autopsy on Mary Gibbs's body confirmed her husband's darkest fears. His wife had been killed with a lethal injection of morphine and atropine, obviously administered by Jane Toppan.

By then, Toppan had fled Boston. She was finally arrested in Amherst, New Hampshire, on October 29, 1901—though not before she had knocked off her own foster sister.

At first, Toppan insisted on her innocence, though she admitted to the police that she "was frequently troubled with her head." As investigators dug into her past, they discovered a string of former patients who had suffered sudden, mysterious deaths. Questioned by psychiatrists (or "alienists" in the lingo of the day), Toppan finally confessed to poisoning not only the four members of the Davis family but also seven other people as well—eleven victims altogether. Later, she would tell her own attorney that the true total was thirty-one.

At her 1902 trial, doctors testified that Toppan had been "born with a weak and nervous mental condition" and suffered "from a lack of moral sense and defective self-control." There was reason to believe that her condition was hereditary: not only her father but her sister, too, had ended up in an insane asylum. Toppan's own testimony helped persuade the jury of her madness. "That is my ambition," she declared. "To have killed more people—more helpless people—than any man or woman who has ever lived." Declared insane, she was confined to a state asylum, where she died in 1938 at the age of eighty-four.

> *"That is my ambition, to have killed more people—more helpless people—than any man or woman who has ever lived."*
>
> JANE TOPPAN

TOURIST ATTRACTIONS

Ever since the summer of 1994, one of the most popular sight-seeing spots in Los Angeles has been the Brentwood condo where the late Mrs. O. J. Simpson and her waiter-friend, Ron Goldman, met their brutal ends. What are we to make of this phenomenon? Are the tourists who come to gape at this celebrated crime scene little more than morbid voyeurs satisfying their prurient fascination? Well . . . yes. And does such fascination reflect something alarming about the decline of moral values in our violence-obsessed society? Absolutely not. The fact is that for better or worse intense public fascination with sensational crimes has always been a feature of human society—and enterprising hucksters have always found ways to exploit it.

One hundred years ago, our nation was riveted by the case of the Chicago "multi-murderer" H. H. **Holmes,** who knocked off an indeterminate number of victims in the labyrinthine depths of his so-called Murder Castle. Much like today's O. J.-crazed public, Americans couldn't get enough of the Holmes story. Perceiving the commercial potential of this mania, an aspiring showman named A. M. Clark leased the "multi-murderer's" notorious residence and announced his plans to turn it into a "murder museum," complete with guided tours by a Chicago homicide detective. The Castle, however, was gutted by a mysterious blaze before Clark could cash in on its gruesome reputation.

Sixty years later, another suspicious fire razed the ramshackle farmhouse of the Wisconsin ghoul, Ed **Gein,** shortly before the property was scheduled to be auctioned. For months, the place had drawn hordes of curiosity seekers. The torching of the house (apparently by outraged townspeople) scotched any plans to turn it into a permanent tourist site. A sideshow exhibitor named Bunny Gibbons, however, came up with another way to capitalize on "Crazy Ed's" notoriety. Successfully bidding on Gein's beat-up Ford sedan, Gibbons equipped the car with a pair of wax dummies—one in the driver's seat, simulating Ed, the other representing a mutilated female corpse. Then he displayed "Ed Gein's Death Car" in county fairs all around the Midwest, charging gawkers two bits apiece for a peek at THE CAR THAT HAULED THE DEAD FROM THEIR GRAVES!

This ghoulish sideshow, however, paled before the carnival atmosphere that prevailed at the property of the infamous **Black Widow** killer Belle Gunness, in the weeks following the discovery of her crimes. Traveling by wagon, automobile, and special excursion train, thousands of midwesterners flocked to the farmstead where a dozen murder victims had been unearthed. Once there, they could gape at the open graves and peer at the decaying remains on display in the carriage house. After viewing the decomposed body parts, they could settle down for a family picnic, then treat themselves to candy and ice cream peddled by local hawkers. And for those desiring a souvenir of the occasion, there were handsome picture postcards of one of Gunness's dismembered victims.

As the local sheriff cheerfully proclaimed, "I never saw folks have a better time!"

TRANSVESTISM

Homicidal transvestites have been a feature of horror films ever since Normal Bates put on his mother's clothes and carved up Janet Leigh in the shower. In real life, of course, there is no correlation at all between cross-dressing and violence. On the contrary, guys who enjoy wearing angora sweaters and high heels tend to be perfect gentlemen. There *are* several cases, however, where transvestism has been a factor in the backgrounds of serial killers.

Early in their childhoods, both Charles **Manson** and Henry Lee **Lucas** were compelled to dress as girls. Manson, who endured the kind of brutalized upbringing that seems guaranteed to produce extreme psychopathology, was constantly being shuttled between relatives while his wayward mother was off whoring or doing jail time. At six, he was shipped off to Virginia to live with an aunt and uncle. The latter proved to be a sadistic bully who was constantly deriding his little charge as a "sissy." To drive home the point, he imposed a vicious punishment, forcing young Charlie to attend the first day of school in a dress.

Lucas was subjected to the identical cruelty, only this time the perpetrator was his own hard-bitten mother, an insanely vicious woman who—among her countless other forms of abuse—curled her little boy's stringy blond hair into ringlets and sent him off to school in girl's clothes.

Clearly, neither Manson nor Lucas enjoyed being a girl. One legendary serial killer who *did* was Edward **Gein,** but he was less a transvestite than a thwarted transsexual. In his deranged efforts to turn himself into a woman, Gein attempted to fashion a suit made of skin flayed from the torsos of disinterred female corpses. Arrayed in this ghastly costume—a "mammary vest" and human-skin leggings, with a vulva affixed to his crotch—he would caper around his decaying farmhouse, pretending to be his own mother. Gein, of course, served as the real-life model for the cross-dressing Norman Bates, as well as for Buffalo Bill, the malevolent female-wannabe of Thomas Harris's *The Silence of the Lambs.*

DRESSED TO KILL

Michael Caine plays a New York City psychiatrist who turns out to be (surprise!) nuttier than a twelve-ounce jar of Jif in this 1980 Hitchcockian homage, directed with typical flair by Brian de Palma. Its most memorable scene—in which Angie Dickinson gets sliced to shreds in an elevator car by a cross-dressing killer—carries a real wallop (though it doesn't match the brilliance of its source, the renowned shower scene in *Psycho*). All in all, *Dressed to Kill* is an outstanding cinematic example of the transvestite serial-killer genre.

TRIAD

Although it's impossible to predict if a young person will grow up to be a serial killer, there are three childhood symptoms that criminologists regard as major danger signals. They are:

1. *Enuresis* (more commonly known as bed-wetting). Lots of children wet their beds. But this behavior may be a sign of deeper pathology when it persists beyond the age of twelve. (More than 60 percent of serial killers were still wetting their beds as adolescents).

2. *Fire-starting.* Children like to play with matches because they are intrigued by the bright, colorful, flickering flames. But budding serial killers carry this interest to a frightening extreme. Their fascination with fire is an early manifestation of their fondness for spectacular destruction. Ottis Toole—the cretinous sidekick of Henry Lee **Lucas**—burned down a neighborhood house when he was six. Teenage thrill killer George Adorno was even younger when he first displayed his pyromaniac tendencies, setting fire to his own sister when he was only four. The incorrigible Carl **Panzram** was thrown into a reformatory when he was eleven. A few months later, he torched the place, causing damage to the tune of $100,000.

3. *Sadistic activity.* Before they are big enough to inflict harm on other human beings, future serial killers get their kicks from tormenting small creatures. See **Animal Torture.**

The word *triad* simply means any group of three. When criminologists use it in relation to serial killers, they are referring to this particular set of symptoms. Of course, even when a child exhibits all three—prolonged bed-wetting, fire-starting, and sadistic cruelty to animals—there is no guarantee that he will turn out to be a serial killer.

Still, it's a *really* bad sign.

TRIGGERS

A distinguishing characteristic of serial murder is the so-called **Cooling-off** period. Weeks, months, even years can lapse between a killer's crimes. All the while, however, his hunger for blood is building inside him, his fantasies of torture and death are growing more urgent by the day. Suddenly, something pushes him over the edge from morbid daydream to murderous action, driving him to fulfill his lethal fantasies on living victims. Criminologists call that "something" a *triggering factor.*

The problem of preventing serial murder might be easier if there were some way to identify the specific triggers that cause psychos to kill. Unfortunately, no such means exist. Almost anything can ignite a serial killer. Sometimes, it's the way a victim looks. Ed **Gein**'s homicidal mania was inspired by matronly women, while David **Berkowitz** vented his psychotic fury on pretty young women with long brown hair.

Cases like these make a certain amount of psychoanalytic sense, since the triggers can be seen as symbolic stand-ins for hated figures from the killer's past. (In Gein's case, it was his monstrous mama; in Berkowitz's, the various girls who had rejected him since childhood.) But—as is true of so many aspects of serial murder—the triggers that set these creatures off are sometimes beyond rational comprehension. One maniac butchered his victims after receiving instructions from UFO aliens, while German lust murderer Heinrich Pommerencke was inspired to commit serial slaughter by a scene in Cecil B. De Mille's *The Ten Commandments.*

The wholly unpredictable nature of these triggering factors is one of the scariest things about serial killers. One young woman may be murdered because she tries to run away. Another may be slain for the very opposite reason. By agreeing to perform whatever sex acts her abductor wants, she threatens his sense of control. Perceiving her desperate offer as an attempt to take charge of the situation, he grows enraged and kills her.

In short, there's just no way of telling what will send a serial killer into a sudden, homicidal rage. One evening in late December of 1981, a sociopath named David Bullock went to the apartment of an acquaintance named Herbert Morales. Morales was very proud of his Christmas tree, which he had taken great pains to decorate. While Bullock was there, Morales began adjusting some of the ornaments.

As Bullock later explained to police, Morales "started messing with the Christmas tree, telling me how nice the Christmas tree was. So I shot him."

> **"He started messing with the Christmas tree, telling me how nice the Christmas tree was. So I shot him."**
>
> DAVID BULLOCK, explaining why he murdered an acquaintance following a 1981 Christmas party

TROPHIES

For serious students of serial murder, a standard reference book is Michael Newton's encyclopedic *Hunting Humans*. The title of this work is meant to convey the predatory nature of serial killers—the way they stalk and slay their victims, as though other people were nothing more than game animals to be butchered for pleasure.

But Newton's title is apt for another reason, too. Like big-game hunters who commemorate their feats by bringing home a trophy of the kill—a set of antlers, a stuffed head, or a prize pelt—the serial killer often does the same thing, removing an item from his victim and preserving it as a precious keepsake.

Sometimes, these objects are completely mundane—a piece of costume jewelry, a cheap wristwatch, a family snapshot, or some other personal effect with little or no apparent value. But the object clearly has great value to the serial killer, or else he wouldn't run the risk of being caught with such an incriminating piece of evidence in his possession. Depending on what this value is, these items are classified by the FBI as either "souvenirs" or "trophies." "Souvenirs" are defined as items that are used to fuel the fantasies of a serial killer, whereas "trophies" are objects that are saved as proof of his skill.

For all intents and purposes, however, there really isn't much difference between the two. Ultimately, they both serve the same purpose for a serial killer, filling him with a sense of his own power and allowing him to relive his crimes in fantasy as he contemplates his morbid treasures. In short, these items are essentially *fetish objects* that provide intense, perverted pleasure to their collectors.

The proof of this perversity lies in the nature of many of these trophies. While some are commonplace, others are clearly sexual. A female victim's underwear is a particular favorite among lust murderers, with high heels and nylon stockings running a close second.

The most hideous trophies of all, of course, are human body parts. Serial killers have been known to collect everything from fingernail clippings to entire bodies. British sex-killer John Reginald Christie kept three complete corpses in his kitchen cupboard, while Jeffrey **Dahmer**'s extensive collection included painted skulls, refrigerated heads, and male genital organs stored in a lobster pot.

The most infamous of all collectors of human trophies was the Wisconsin ghoul, Ed **Gein**, who turned his ramshackle farmhouse into a kind of museum of unnatural history, full of carefully preserved human artifacts. Among his ghastly treasures were chair seats made of human flesh, soup bowls fashioned from skulls, a nipple belt, and a box full of preserved vulvas. Perhaps most shocking of all were the items found in his bedroom: a collection of female faces, skinned from their skulls, tanned, stuffed, and mounted on the wall—exactly like prize hunting trophies.

TYPES

The exact definition of serial murder remains a matter of debate in criminological circles. In the view of some experts, serial killing, in the strict sense of the term, is essentially synonymous with sadistic lust murder. Other authorities, however, take a broader view of the matter and believe that there are different types of serial killers. According to these specialists, serial killers can be divided into the following four categories:

1. *Visionary* killers. Most serial killers are psychopaths—i.e., intelligent but utterly amoral human beings characterized by a complete lack of conscience or empathy. "Visionary" killers, by contrast, are *psychotics*—people whose minds are gripped by bizarre delusions and hallucinations. David "Son of Sam" Berkowitz, for example, claimed that he was obeying a demon who transmitted his orders through a neighbor's pet dog. Herbert Mullin, who killed thirteen people in the early 1970s, was a paranoid schizophrenic who heard "telepathic voices" commanding him to kill in order to avert a natural disaster, a catastrophic earthquake that would destroy California.

2. *Mission-oriented* serial killers see themselves as avenging crusaders, ridding society of "undesirables"—harlots, homosexuals, "foreigners," etc. In the late 1970s, for example, a Hitler-worshipping thug named Joe Franklin embarked on a one-man war against interracial couples, killing thirteen people before he was stopped.

3. *Hedonistic* serial killers have no motive beyond their own pleasure. They kill because it feels good. Inflicting death is the ultimate high for them, a source of intense, even sexual, pleasure.

4. *Power seekers*. The primary motive of these killers is the urgent need to assert their supremacy over a helpless victim, to compensate for their own deep-seated feelings of worthlessness by completely dominating another human being.

The problem with these categories is that there is often so much overlap between the different "types" that the whole system breaks down. For example, a "missionary" killer who targets prostitutes may well be responding to "divine" voices commanding him to clean the streets of whores. And the pleasure that a "hedonistic" killer gets from binding and torturing a teenage girl might derive from the complete power he is exerting over his victim.

> *"Satan gets into people and makes them do things they don't want to."*
>
> HERBERT MULLIN, "Visionary" serial killer

UNSOLVED

Serial killers are the scariest of all criminals not simply because they do such appalling things. What also makes them really frightening is that—though capable of the most insanely violent acts—they are not raving lunatics. On the contrary, the typical serial killer is a man with an above-average IQ, exceptional cunning, and an uncanny ability to appear as boringly normal as the next guy. As a result, serial killers often go undetected for years. Indeed, some of them have been known to elude capture forever—leaving a trail of corpses in their wake but no real clues as to their own identities.

The classic example of this phenomenon, of course, is **Jack the Ripper.** More recently, the "Green River Killer"—so-called because he dumped some of his victims around Washington state's Green River—vanished without a trace after slaying dozens of people (perhaps as many as sixty-six). Other still-unidentified serial killers include the **Axeman of New Orleans** and **Zodiac.**

Why are some serial killers never caught? One possibility is that they simply decide to stop before they are arrested—in effect, to quit while they're ahead. But this seems unlikely. After all, homicidal maniacs are as addicted to death as alcoholics are to drink, and since there are no twelve-step recovery programs for lust murderers, it seems improbable that a compulsive killer would simply kick the habit on his own. A more plausible explanation is that some serial killers are *forced* to stop. They might find themselves locked up behind bars—either imprisoned for an unrelated crime or confined to a mental asylum. Or (like other mortals) they might die very suddenly, possibly at their own hands.

Suicide has been offered as a theory in the case of "Jack the Stripper"—a serial killer of prostitutes—who terrorized London in the mid-1960s. Though the case remains officially unsolved, many believe that the culprit was a security guard who took his own life just after the final murder (see **Rippers**). In the case of the mysterious "Toledo Slugger," another plausible explanation has been offered. In 1925 and 1926, a string of women were raped and bludgeoned to death by a shadowy assailant in Toledo, Ohio. In their zeal to find the culprit, the police rounded up every known "mental defective" they could get their hands on and shipped them off to state asylums. Since the Slugger's crimes came to an abrupt halt around this time, some people believe that the police managed to nab the killer in their city-wide sweep.

Other cases, however, continue to pose enduring—and tantalizing—puzzles. Another Ohio maniac—the so-called "Cleveland Torso Killer" (aka "The Mad Butcher of Kingsbury Run")—is a case in point. During a four-year span in the 1930s, this blood-thirsty maniac chopped up a dozen people, leaving body parts strewn around the city. Nevertheless, in spite of an all-out effort by law officials (led by no less an eminence than Eliot Ness, the former "Untouchable" who was serving as Cleveland's director of public safety), the "Mad Butcher" eluded arrest. In the spring of 1938, his atrocities came to a sudden, mysterious halt. To this day no one knows who he was. Suspects range from a mentally unbalanced premed student to a Bohemian immigrant to a psychopathic hobo. Perhaps the most unsettling theory of all was put forth by a Cleveland detective who believed that the torso slayings stopped because the culprit pulled up stakes and headed west to California—where he committed the infamous (and also unsolved) "Black Dahlia" murder.

UPBRINGING

It is common to describe an especially harsh, deprived childhood as "Dickensian"—but in the case of serial killers, that adjective is wildly inadequate. Compared to the boyhoods of most serial killers, Oliver Twist's early years in a Victorian poorhouse seem like an extended vacation at Disneyland.

Albert "Boston Strangler" **DeSalvo** was raised by a monstrous father who liked to bring whores home with him, screw them in front of the kids, then beat his wife savagely when she complained. One of DeSalvo's most vivid childhood memories was of watching his father knock out all of his mother's teeth, then break her fingers one by one as she lay sprawled beneath the kitchen sink. DeSalvo himself not only received regular, vicious thrashings with a lead pipe but, along with his two sisters, was sold into slavery. An acquaintance of the senior DeSalvo paid nine dollars for the three children, who were shipped off to Maine and forced to work as farm laborers.

Henry Lee **Lucas** was raised in unimaginable squalor by a brutal, alcoholic prostitute who compelled her paraplegic husband to watch her have sex with her tricks. Henry was forced to watch, too—generally while dressed up in the little girl's clothing his mother made him wear. She also beat him mercilessly with objects ranging from broomsticks to two-by-fours and took pleasure in killing his pets.

Little Charlie **Manson**'s mother was a bisexual alcoholic prostitute, who reportedly once traded her son for a pitcher of beer. After she was thrown into prison for armed robbery, Manson was taken in by a brutal uncle, who derided him as a sissy and sent him to school in a dress. In later years, he was placed in an institution where he was routinely beaten with a wooden paddle for bed-wetting.

Raised in a gothically grim orphanage, Albert **Fish** was schooled in sadism by a female teacher who disciplined disobedient boys and girls by stripping them naked and beating them in front of the other children. Sex-murderer Joseph Kallinger—whose victims included his own son—was raised by adoptive parents who kept him in line with a hammer, a cat-o'-nine-tails, and constant threats of castration. Serial killer Hugh Morse was brought up by an insanely tyrannical grandmother, who once punished him for sneaking out to the movies by butchering his pet mice.

According to FBI findings, 42 percent of serial killers have suffered severe physical abuse as children, 43 percent were sexually molested, and a full 74 percent were subjected to ongoing psychological torture.

Of course, there are those who sneer at the notion that an unhappy childhood is the main cause of serial killing, pointing out that countless people who grow up in seriously dysfunctional households do not turn out to be homicidal maniacs. These critics also refer to monsters like Jeffrey **Dahmer** and Ted **Bundy,** who appear to have come from more-or-less normal, middle-class backgrounds. And indeed, childhood snapshots of little Ted, dressed up in a cowboy suit or posing beside a snowman, would not look out of place in Ozzie and Harriet's family album.

It's undoubtedly true that other factors are involved in the making of serial killers (see **Causes**). Still, "negative parenting" (as the sociologists quaintly call it) is invariably present in their backgrounds. (There are indications that Dahmer and Bundy were both victims of sexual abuse by relatives.) Brutalized in childhood, the serial killer grows up full of a murderous rage that is turned against all of humanity. He can know pleasure only by administering pain. He can feel alive only when he is inflicting death.

> *"I hated all my life. I hated everybody. When I first grew up and can remember, I was dressed as a girl by mother. And I stayed that way for two or three years. And after that I was treated like what I call the dog of the family. I was beaten. I was made to do things that no human bein' would want to do."*
>
> **HENRY LEE LUCAS**

JOSEPH VACHER

One of the scariest things about serial killers is how normal they can seem. Ted **Bundy** looked like a frat boy, Jeffrey **Dahmer** like a computer nerd, and John Wayne **Gacy** like the president of the local Rotary Club. Frenchman Joseph Vacher (1869–1897) was different. In his case, appearances weren't deceiving at all. He had the kind of face that could give children nightmares. And his actions were consistent with his looks.

A repulsively seedy tramp with a palsied face and an eye that leaked a steady stream of pus, Vacher was born into a poor peasant family, the last of fifteen children. He committed his first known crime—the attempted rape of a young boy—when he was nineteen. Two years later, he was conscripted into the army, and he cut his own throat with a razor when he failed to win promotion to corporal. Several years later, he tried suicide again when a young woman he coveted spurned his advances. Vacher shot her three times with a pistol, then turned the gun on himself and fired point-blank into his own face.

The woman survived. So did Vacher, though half his face was now permanently paralyzed and his right eye was reduced to a raw, suppurating hole. After a year in an insane asylum, he was discharged as "cured." Equipping himself with a few basic necessities (maps, an umbrella, a cudgel, several butcher knives, and a cleaver), he tramped around the countryside for three and a half years. Stopping at a farmhouse whenever he grew hungry, he would pound on the door and demand food from the owner, who was usually happy to oblige just to get rid of the hideous tramp.

But Vacher was possessed by other, infinitely more loathsome appetites. During the course of his wanderings, he set upon and slaughtered eleven people of both sexes, assaulting them in a demonic frenzy—stabbing, strangling, mutilating, biting, disemboweling. Most of his victims, male as well as female, were raped after death.

The "French Ripper," as the shadowy killer began to be called, was finally apprehended in August 1897. At his trial, he argued that he was not mentally competent. His mind, he claimed, had been twisted as an eight-year-old boy when he was bitten by a mad dog. The court was not convinced. On New Year's Eve, 1898, the twenty-nine-year-old Vacher was sent to the guillotine.

VAMPIRES

There's both good and bad news about vampires. The good news is—they don't exist, at least not the kind found in old Bela Lugosi movies. There are plenty of things to worry about in life, but being attacked in your bedroom by a four-hundred-year-old Transylvanian demon isn't one of them.

The bad news about vampires is that some sexual psychopaths derive intense satisfaction from drinking human blood and will resort to serial murder to satisfy this monstrous craving. Deviants like these don't sleep in coffins or turn themselves into bats, but in one crucial respect, they are infinitely scarier than Bram Stoker's Dracula or the sexy bloodsuckers of Anne Rice's novels. These ravenous fiends are for real.

One of the most infamous real-life vampires was the Italian lust murderer Vincenz Verzeni. From an early age, Verzeni took exquisite delight in strangulation. At twelve, he discovered that he got tremendous pleasure from wringing the necks of chickens. By the time he reached late adolescence, he had progressed from poultry to women. At first, he simply throttled his victims until he achieved orgasm. Once he climaxed, he would let his victims live. In his early twenties, however, Verzeni's perversion took a horrific turn. In 1871, he pounced on a fourteen-year-old girl, dragged her to a field, and choked her to death. Then—in a sadistic frenzy—he chewed at her thigh and sucked her blood, ripped out her intestines, tore out her genitals, and removed a chunk of her calf, which he carried away with him, intending to roast and eat it. Eight months later, he savaged another young woman, garroting her with a leather thong, then biting open her neck and gorging on her blood. Verzeni was arrested after attacking his own nineteen-year-old cousin, who managed to fight him off, then immediately reported him to the police.

In the late 1940s, British serial slayer John George Haigh murdered half a dozen people to get his hands on their money, then dissolved their remains in his basement acid vat. At his 1949 trial, the notorious "Acid-Bath Murderer" insisted that before disposing of each body, he had tapped the victim's jugular, drawn off a glassful of blood, and quaffed it. Though Haigh's vampiric claims were viewed by many as a clumsy attempt to cop an insanity plea, it seems fairly certain that at the very least he was afflicted with a severe case of *hematomania*—a lifelong obsession with blood.

One of the weirdest cases of vampirism was that of Florencio Fernandez, a twenty-five-year-old Argentine stonemason who, in 1960, slipped through the windows of fifteen sleeping women and attacked them in their beds—pinioning their arms, biting into their throats, and drinking their blood. Like the Nicholas Cage character in the 1989 cult movie *Vampire's Kiss*, Fernandez apparently suffered from a serious vampiric delusion. He lived in a cave, prowled the night in a black Dracula-like cloak, and spent the daylight hours sunk in a comalike sleep.

Like Dracula's zoophagous servant, Renfield, young Richard Chase loved to drink the blood of animals—rabbits, cats, dogs. In 1978, however, he progressed to infinitely more monstrous crimes. During a four-day spree, he broke into several homes, killed and butchered the inhabitants (including a pregnant woman and a twenty-two-month-old infant), and wallowed in

10. RICHARD "VAMP. OF SACTO." CHASE

Richard Chase; from *Murderers!* trading card set (*Courtesy of Roger Worsham*)

299

their gore. After his arrest, he confessed to drinking the blood of his victims. Chase—who was dubbed the "Vampire of Sacramento"—served as the real-life model for the unspeakable killer in the 1992 movie *Rampage,* a thought-provoking (and occasionally harrowing) film directed by William Friedkin of *Exorcist* fame.

> *"I had an unspeakable delight in strangling women, experiencing during the act erections and real sexual pleasure. The feeling of pleasure while strangling them was much greater than that which I experienced while masturbating. . . . It never occurred to me to touch or look at the genitals. It satisfied me to seize the women by the neck and suck their blood."*
>
> VINCENZ VERZENI

THE VANISHING

Holland isn't exactly known for its epidemic of serial murder, so it's surprising that one of the most disturbing cinematic depictions of a psychopathic killer appears in the 1988 Dutch film *The Vanishing,* directed by George Sluizer.

The movie focuses on an obsessed young man named Rex Hofman, whose girlfriend disappears without a trace when they make a pit stop at a roadside rest station. Though Hofman eventually concedes that his girlfriend must have been abducted and killed, he can't live with the tormenting uncertainty and refuses to rest until he discovers what befell her.

The villain of the piece is one of the most unsettling psychos in movie history, a meek, soft-spoken family man with a taste for a particularly unspeakable form of torture. Portrayed with chilling perfection by an actor named Barnard Pierre Donnadieu, the killer ultimately offers to show the haunted young man what the vanished girl experienced. In a shattering (if somewhat implausible) conclusion, Hofman accepts the killer's proposition—leading to one of the most nightmarish endings ever put on film. This is one of those small, understated European fright films that has infinitely more impact than the typical Hollywood splatter fest.

Hollywood, in fact, produced a remake of *The Vanishing* in 1993, starring Kiefer Sutherland and Jeff Bridges. Though directed again by Sluizer, this second version falls completely flat. Stick to the original!

VICAP

See **FBI.**

WANNABES

According to outraged moralists, serial-killer trading cards encourage young children to regard blood-crazed sociopaths as role models. (See **Cards, Comics, and Collectibles**). While it's hard to conceive of any twelve-year-old boy tearing down his Michael Jordan posters and replacing them with pictures of Jeffrey **Dahmer,** there's no doubt that some homicidal maniacs have found their inspiration in the bloody deeds of infamous killers.

A classic example is Peter **Kürten,** the "Monster of Düsseldorf," who was fascinated by **Jack the Ripper** and spent hours poring over accounts of Saucy Jack's atrocities. (The fictional fiend of the 1995 movie *Copycat* is, like Kürten, a student of serial murder, who emulates America's most notorious killers, from the "Boston Strangler" to "Son of Sam.") Killers like this are the psychopathic equivalent of celebrity wannabes—the Elvis imitators of the criminal world.

Kürten is an example of another, related phenomenon—the megalomaniac killer who yearns for grotesque recognition. These psychos strive, not simply to imitate their homicidal heroes, but also to outdo them in evil—to go down in the history books as "the greatest criminal of all time" (in Kürten's words). The highly questionable confessions of Henry Lee **Lucas**—who admitted to over three hundred murders—were apparently motivated by such self-aggrandizing impulses. (Lucas's overwrought claims knew no bounds: at one point, he maintained that he was the man who delivered the poison to the Reverend Jim Jones just prior to the infamous Jonestown massacre.) Dr. H. H. **Holmes,** the nineteenth-century "multi-murderer" sometimes described as America's first serial killer, possessed the same bizarre ambition. Taking perverse pride in his status as the country's preeminent criminal (or "arch-fiend," as the newspapers liked to call him), Holmes eagerly confessed to the murder of several dozen victims—many of whom subsequently turned out to be alive and well.

Indeed, so hungry are some serial killers for celebrity status that they grow actively incensed when their crimes are underestimated. When German sex-killer Rudolph Pleil was charged with nine savage murders, he indignantly insisted that the actual number was twenty-eight. Only one thing mattered to the monstrous Pleil—that he be universally acknowledged as *"der beste Totmacher"*—the world's "best death-maker."

WARTIME

There's an old Chinese saying that goes "in crisis there is opportunity." This pearl of proverbial wisdom is epitomized by certain serial killers, who have turned the greatest crisis of them all—global warfare—into an opportunity for wholesale murder.

If World War I had never occurred, a small-time French sociopath named Henri Landru might have lived out his days as nothing more than a petty crook. When the conflict broke out, however, Landru suddenly perceived a unique opportunity to exploit his nation's woes for his own personal profit. With France's male population decimated, the country was suddenly full of young, well-off widows. Landru set about preying on these vulnerable women, luring them through seductive matrimonial ads, then wooing them, wedding them, and murdering them for their money (see **Bluebeards**).

Some twenty years later—during World War II—France's worst fears were realized when Hitler's troops occupied Paris, succeeding where the Kaiser's had failed. Parisian Jews desperately sought a way to escape the Nazi terror. Waiting to prey on them was another French psychopath, Dr. Marcel **Petiot**. Posing as a sympathetic Resistance agent who would help smuggle them out of the country, Petiot slowly killed the would-be refugees with lethal "vaccines," then looted their possessions.

At roughly the same time in London—as the German Luftwaffe bombarded the city night after night—an English airman named Gordon Cummins found a chance to unleash his long-simmering sadism. Taking advantage of the city's mandatory blackouts, he prowled the darkened streets and, in less than a week, savagely murdered four women (see **Rippers**).

The chaotic conditions of war allowed another notorious lust murderer—Bela Kiss of Hungary—not to commit his crimes but to escape punishment for them. Before the outbreak of World

War I, Kiss had succeeded in slaying no less than twenty-three women without arousing suspicion. By the time his crimes were uncovered, he had already enlisted in the army and been killed in action. Or so it appeared. Only later did authorities surmise that Kiss had actually switched dog tags with a dying soldier, assumed the latter's identity, and vanished without a trace (see **Whereabouts Unknown**).

WEAPONS

Cinematic serial killers are artists of death, constantly searching for imaginative new ways to create carnage. In their homicidal hands, everything from a scythe to a staple gun becomes an instrument of mayhem, wielded with the virtuosity of a maestro.

By contrast, real-life serial killers are much more conventional in their choice of weapons. What distinguishes them from ordinary killers is their preference for "manual" means of murder—stabbing, strangling, clubbing—over firearms. While the majority of American murders are committed with guns, serial killers favor the "hands-on" approach, which offers a more intense physical experience. When it comes to sick, sadistic pleasure, shooting people from a distance of twenty feet just can't compete with plunging a serrated hunting knife into their flesh.

Of course, there are notable exceptions. Ed **Gein** dispatched his victims with a bullet to the back of the skull. And before he began signing his letters "Son of Sam," David **Berkowitz**—the serial assassin who terrorized New York City in the late 1970s—was nicknamed after his favorite weapon: "The .44-Caliber Killer."

WHEREABOUTS UNKNOWN

The crimes perpetrated by serial killers are so appalling that—when one of these creatures is on the loose—it sometimes seems as if a supernatural monster has risen from the underworld. Newspaper reporters trip all over themselves to come up

Investigators display the saw Fish used to dismember Grace Budd's body

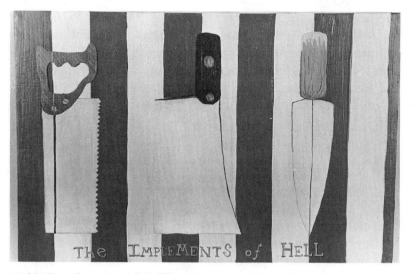

Fish's "Implements of Hell"; painting by Michael Rose

with lurid, horror-movie monikers—"The Mad Beast," "The Vampire-Killer," "The Werewolf Slayer." So it's easy to feel a jolt of surprise when the monster is finally caught. The supernatural demon turns out to be a nondescript loser who looks about as threatening as a computer geek. The demon is reduced to pathetically human dimensions.

Unfortunately, some serial killers are never captured. In cases like these, the killer often continues to live on in popular fantasy as a kind of phantom or specter. Myths and folktales grow up around them. This is certainly true of the most famous of all serial killers, **Jack the Ripper.** But there are other well-known serial killers who vanished without a trace and whose fate continues to tease the imagination of crime buffs. The anonymous axe murderer who butchered a string of derelicts in Cleveland during the mid-1930s is one of these cases. In spite of the concerted efforts of the Cleveland police—including the legendary Eliot Ness of "Untouchables" fame, who was running the department at the time—the so-called "Cleveland Torso Killer" was never apprehended.

Like the Ripper, the "Cleveland Torso Killer" is a fascinating figure because he remains a total enigma. No one knows who he was or what became of him. There are other cases, however, where a killer's identity is not in question. The mystery has to do with the maniac's ultimate whereabouts.

Sifting through the ruins of the incinerated farmhouse belonging to notorious **Black Widow** killer Belle Gunness, searchers came upon a charred female body and assumed it was Gunness's remains. There was only one problem. The corpse had no head—so making a positive ID was a little tricky. Eventually, investigators concluded that the corpse was a substitute—a woman that Gunness had murdered expressly for that purpose. In subsequent years, Gunness was allegedly sighted in different parts of the country, from New England to Los Angeles. But to this day, no one knows what really became of her.

A few years later, during World War I, officials in the Hungarian town of Czinkota discovered the bodies of twenty-three murdered women in and around the abandoned house of a retired tinsmith named Bela Kiss. Unfortunately, there seemed to be no way to punish the killer, since Kiss (who had enlisted in the army) had reportedly died in combat. Reports of his death, however, were greatly exaggerated. As it turned out, Kiss—while recuperating from his wounds in a military hospital—switched dog tags with a dying soldier and disappeared under the other man's name. From that point on, his trail vanished. Alleged sightings on both sides of the Atlantic—from Budapest to New York City—kept his legend alive.

Kiss's countryman Sylvestre Matuschka was one of the most bizarre serial killers of all time, a maniac who derived intense sexual pleasure from bombing railroad trains and listening to the dying shrieks of the passengers. Matuschka was actually convicted and imprisoned in the 1930s, but somehow he managed to get free during the turmoil of World War II. What happened to him next is anybody's guess. According to some crime historians, however, Matuschka was forced to join the Soviet army, which recognized his special talents and gave him a job for which he was unique qualified—explosives expert.

WOMEN

One of the most hotly debated questions among people who study violent crime is: "Is there such a thing as a female serial killer?" The simple answer is: "Yes . . . and no." It all depends on how you define serial murder.

If you follow the FBI's definition—three or more separate killings with an emotional cooling-off period between each homicide—then the answer is clearly affirmative. The annals of crime are full of fatal females who have knocked off large numbers of victims—**Black Widow** brides who dispatch a succession of hubbies; homicidal **Nurses** who administer death to dozens of patients; evil **Housekeepers** who dispose of entire families. Serial killer encyclopedist Michael Newton has compiled a volume called *Bad Girls Do It!* that profiles nearly two hundred women multiple murderers—an assemblage almost imposing enough to confirm Rudyard Kipling's famous line, "the female of the species is more deadly than the male."

Of course, many specialists—Newton included—believe that true serial murder always involves another element, specified in the definition put forth by the National Institute of Justice in 1988: the presence of "sadistic, sexual overtones." Even when you add this ingredient, there's a sizable number of women who fit the bill, from "Lonely Hearts Killer" Martha Beck, to the British sex-killer Rosemary West (accused of the grisly torture and murder of ten victims, including her own daughter), to Elizabeth Bathory, the notorious "Blood Countess" of sixteenth-century Romania, reputed to have slain as many as six hundred victims for her own erotic delectation.

The problem arises when you try to find a female criminal who matches the model of the modern-day serial killer epitomized by **Jack the Ripper**—the lone psychopathic lust murderer, coolly stalking and snaring his victims, then butchering and mutilating them in a sex-crazed frenzy. Here, the issue becomes much more tricky. Indeed, it is virtually impossible to find a single woman in the whole history of crime who fits this mold. (As culture critic Camille Paglia puts it with characteristic bluntness, "There is no female Jack the Ripper.") Beck and West, for example, were part of **Killer Couples.** And Bathory falls into the venerable—if thoroughly depraved—tradition of the evil **Aristocrat,** exemplified by monsters like Caligula and Gilles de Rais.

The single, if arguable, exception to this is Aileen **Wuornos,** the former Florida hooker who slew a string of male pickups between December 1989 and the following November. Not everyone regards Wuornos as a serial killer. Some see her as a brutalized woman who killed only when she was threatened by violence and rape. Among other things, they point out that she committed all her murders with a gun—rarely the case with serial killers, who prefer to do their killing by "manual" means, like strangulation and stabbing, which affords them a higher degree of perverse physical pleasure (see **Weapons**).

Others, however, perceive Wuornos as a classic serial murderer—a cold-blooded predator who killed for the sheer joy of it. If this is the case, then she may well represent the first of a frightening new breed.

"Wuornos isn't a trend, she's an isolated case," says Robert K. Ressler, the former FBI agent who coined the phrase "serial killer." "Males are definitely the killers among us. But I think the numbers of female murderers will increase during the 1990s, and the fact that women are getting involved at all is alarming.

Women have always provided a balance to male violence, and I'd hate to see them tip that balance."

AILEEN WUORNOS

Aileen Wuornos; from *Bloody Visions* trading cards *(© & ™ 1995 M. H. Price and Shel-Tone Publications. All rights reserved.)*

Some people regard her as "the first female serial killer in history"—a cold-blooded predator who stalked and murdered a string of victims over an extended period of time. Others (herself included) claim that she only killed in self-defense, when threatened with violence and rape. Whichever of these views is correct, one thing is certain. Between December 1989 and the following November, seven middle-aged male motorists, driving the highways of central Florida, stopped to pick up Aileen "Lee" Wuornos and ended up dead.

Virtually from the day of her birth in 1956, Wuornos's life was a non-stop nightmare of deprivation and violence, abandonment and abuse. She was the child of a teenage couple whose marriage had ended before she was born. Her father would eventually hang himself in jail after being arrested on child-molestation charges. One day when Aileen was only six months old, her mother left the infant girl and her brother with a baby-sitter, then telephoned to say she wouldn't be coming home. Aileen was taken in by her grandparents but kicked out of their house when she was thirteen after giving birth to an illigitimate child (the consequence, she claimed, of rape). By the time she was fourteen, she was living a desperately brutalized life—sleeping in an abandoned car, hustling for drinks, drugs, and an occasional meal. At twenty, she married a seventy-year-old man, but their union lasted only a month (according to her account, she abandoned him because he beat her with a cane; according to his, he sued for divorce after she beat him up to get his car keys). Two years later, she attempted suicide by shooting herself in the stomach. After recuperating, she robbed a convenience store at gunpoint, was promptly arrested, and spent thirteen months in prison. Other arrests—for check forgery and auto theft—followed.

In 1986, Wuornos met the love of her life—a lesbian named Tyria Moore—at a Daytona gay bar. Even after their sexual passion cooled, the two remained inseparable for the next four years. During that time, Wuornos's rage and resentment toward men grew increasingly violent. She continued to hustle. Now, however, she carried a .22-caliber gun in her handbag when she worked the truck stops and roadhouses.

On November 30, 1989, Wuornos took a ride with a fifty-one-year-old electronics repair shop owner named Richard Mallory. The next day, his abandoned car was found in a stretch of secluded woods, along with his wallet, a half-empty vodka bottle, and a torn package of condoms. Twelve days later, Mallory's bullet-riddled corpse was uncovered in a junkyard. Six more nearly identical killings followed.

After Wuornos and Moore were spotted driving one of the victim's cars, Florida police were able to pick up their trail. Wuornos was arrested in a seedy biker bar called The Last Resort. Once in custody, she confessed to all seven killings, though she claimed she was acting in self-defense. Tried for the murder of Richard Mallory, she insisted that she had shot him after he choked and tortured her, raped her anally, and threatened to kill her. The jury was unpersuaded. Wuornos was convicted and sentenced to death. "I'm innocent," she shouted when the verdict was read. "I hope you get raped! Scumbags of America!"

Wuornos (whose former lover, Tyria Moore, had turned state's evidence and testified against her at her trial) is the subject of a fascinating, highly acclaimed documentary, *Aileen Wuornos: The Selling of a Serial Killer*, which was shown as part of the 1993 New York Film Festival.

THE WRONG MAN

There's only one thing worse than being arrested, convicted, and imprisoned for a crime you didn't commit: being executed for it. And when the crime in question is serial murder, the outrage is compounded. Not only is an innocent man put to death, but the real culprit remains at large and continues to get away with murder.

Unfortunately, cases like this have occurred from time to time. One of the most egregious was that of Timothy Evans, a dim-witted English truck driver convicted of the brutal murder of his wife and baby daughter in 1950. The chief prosecution witness against Evans was his downstairs neighbor—a quiet, eminently respectable gentleman named John Reginald Christie. Three years after Evans was hanged at London's Pentonville Prison, Christie vacated his flat at 10 Rillington Place. The tenants who replaced him immediately noticed a foul odor emanating from somewhere in the kitchen. Tracing its source to a hollow section of wall, they tore off the wallpaper, peered inside, and discovered the decomposed remains of three women shoved into a concealed cupboard. Another body—that of Christie's wife—was found under the floorboards, and two more female corpses were unearthed in the backyard. Altogether, the quiet little man had committed eight murders—four of them following Evans's execution. Christie himself was hanged in July 1953. Another thirteen years would pass before the British government finally admitted it had made an error in Evans's case and granted him a posthumous pardon.

Fatal mistakes of this kind can happen anywhere, of course. But they are particularly common in totalitarian nations, where "justice" is meted out with alarming speed. During the 1930s and early 1940s, Nazi authorities periodically picked up and executed suspected deviants for a series of lust murders taking place in the town of Kupenick, just east of Berlin. The real culprit, however—a sociopath named Bruno Ludke—wasn't identified until 1943, by which time he had, according to his own admission, committed an astonishing eighty-five murders.

A similar story took place in the former USSR. In 1978, the savaged corpse of a teenage girl was found in a forest outside the industrial city Rostov-on-Don. The Soviet police quickly arrested and executed a known sex offender. Unfortunately, they shot the wrong man. By the time they identified the right one—Andrei **Chikatilo,** the "Mad Beast of Rostov"—he had butchered over fifty women and children.

THE MILQUETOAST MURDERER

The story of John Reginald Christie and his fall-guy neighbor, Timothy Evans—one of the most sensational cases in the annals of modern British crime—is told with understated power in Richard Fleischer's absorbing 1970 film, *10 Rillington Place.* Shot on location at the actual murder house (which was torn down the following year to make way for a parking garage), the movie achieves its genuinely creepy power by presenting the sensational facts of the case in a subdued, low-key manner, consistent with the apparent drabness of the killer himself.

Richard Attenborough—who went on to achieve fame as the Oscar-winning director of *Gandhi* and other high-prestige pictures—turns in a striking performance as the homicidal Milquetoast who raped and murdered eight women over a thirteen-year span, storing their corpses in and around his flat at the infamous address. Equally good are John Hurt as the pathetically dim-witted Evans and Judy Geeson as his wife, Beryl. Highly recommended for those who enjoy subdued, tasteful psychofilms. If you're looking for hard-core gore—forget about it.

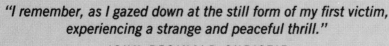

> *"I remember, as I gazed down at the still form of my first victim, experiencing a strange and peaceful thrill."*
> JOHN REGINALD CHRISTIE

X CHROMOSOME

During the 1960s, some scientists tried to establish a link between violence and excessive masculinity. According to their research, the presence of an extra Y (or male) chromosome made a man more prone to violent crime (see **Y Chromosome**).

Nowadays, this theory isn't given much credence. Interestingly, however, there *has* been a documented case of a serial killer suffering from the opposite defect. Bobby Joe Long, who murdered ten women in the 1970s, had an extra X—or female—chromosome in each cell of his body. As a result, his glands produced an inordinate amount of the female hormone estrogen, causing him to grow breasts during puberty.

His humiliation over this condition may well have contributed to his mental imbalance—though it was certainly not his only problem. Wildly accident prone, Long suffered a string of grievous **Head Injuries** throughout his life. And like so many serial killers, he was also subjected to what sociologists like to call "negative parenting." Among other things, his mother slept in bed with him until he was thirteen.

THE X-FILES

Sometimes described as the *Twilight Zone* of the 1990s, Fox Television's creepily atmospheric series *The X-Files* has developed a devoted cult following since it first aired in September 1993. According to the premise of the show, the FBI is regularly called in to consult on cases involving various bizarre phenomena. Investigating each case is the handsome, brooding hero, Fox "Spooky" Muldaur, a specialist in the strange who has been obsessed with all things paranormal ever since his kid sister was abducted by aliens. His loyal, if slightly more skeptical, partner is the lovely and frighteningly competent Dana Sculley, an auburn-haired knockout who is much less likely to assume that every unexplained crime is the work of poltergeists, genetic mutations, or extraterrestrials (though she's invariably wrong).

Full of dark humor, unsettling horror, and some of the grisliest effects on TV, *The X-Files* is a cornucopia of quirky entertainment. And its various monsters have included some of the most grotesque serial killers in the history of pop culture. One of the most memorable of these was the ineffably creepy Eugene Tooms, a bloodthirsty mutant with Silly Putty–like powers of distension who emerged from a thirty-year hibernation to go on a murder spree. Equally unnerving was a leechlike killer known as the "Flukeman," another genetic mutation who inhabited sewers and had a nasty habit of slithering through the seat holes of rest area latrines.

In their ongoing war against the world's weirdest adversaries, Muldaur and Scully have also confronted vampire serial killers, telepathic serial killers, reincarnated serial killers, and a serial killer with a nutritional deficiency that required him to dissolve the flesh of his victims and suck up their fat.

X-RATED

According to the experts from the FBI's Behavioral Science Unit, perhaps as many as 80 percent of serial killers display a fondness for hard-core pornography, particularly movies and books featuring violent, sadomasochistic sex. Of course, this isn't exactly the world's most startling finding. Indeed, it would be far more surprising to learn that *Horton Hears a Who* was Henry Lee **Lucas**'s favorite book or that Jeffrey **Dahmer** was a big fan of the Nancy Drew series.

Still, various moral crusaders have used this statistic to help bolster their argument that pornography—along with other types of transgressive entertainment (like "slasher" movies and "death metal" rock)—is a leading cause of sexual homicide. Social scientists remain divided on this issue. For every psychologist who insists that there is a direct, causal link between X-rated entertainment and violent crime, there are others who argue the opposite—that material which depicts graphic sex and violence may actually help defuse aggressive impulses.

In short, the relationship between media violence and real-life crime remains extremely murky. It is worth noting, however, that—for as long as there has been such a thing as popular culture—it has been blamed for everything from juvenile delinquency to multiple murder.

A hundred years before porn videos and splatter movies, the favorite target of social reformers was the genre known as "dime novels"—cheap little paperbacks relating the lurid adventures of bloodthirsty bad men, cutthroat pirates, and two-fisted detectives. Writing in the late 1800s, Dr. Elizabeth Blackwell—America's first female physician—warned that "the dangers arising from such vicious literature cannot be overestimated by parents." The appalling case of the Boston child-fiend, Jesse Pomeroy, seemed to bear out Blackwell's claim. The grotesque-looking Pomeroy began torturing younger children when he was eleven. He graduated to murder at fourteen, savaging a ten-year-old girl and a four-year-old boy. After his arrest, outraged moralists blamed his crimes on the corrupting influence of dime novels like *Desperate Dan, the Dastard* and *The Pirates of the Pecos*. Unfortunately, their argument was somewhat undermined by the fact that Pomeroy had apparently never read a book in his life.

In our own century, other forms of pop entertainment have been attacked for their presumably pernicious influence. In the 1950s, horror comics were condemned as a major cause of juvenile delinquency. More recently, America's rising crime rate has been blamed on everything from *Friday the 13th* movies to gangsta rap.

In truth, it is very hard to establish a straightforward link between media images and human behavior, particularly when it comes to serial killers, whose minds work in such bizarre ways. The notorious 1930s cannibal-killer, Albert **Fish,** found certain passages in the Bible wildly arousing. Charles **Manson**'s murderous fantasies were inspired by one of the most benign works of popular art ever created—the Beatles' *White Album*.

The case of German sex-murderer Heinrich Pommerencke—known as the "Beast of the Black Forest"—is another case in point. One night in February 1959, Pommerencke went to the movies, and after seeing a bunch of women cavorting on screen, he became convinced that all females deserved to die. Shortly afterward, he committed the first of four savage rape-murders.

The film that inspired this rampage? Cecil B. De Mille's *The Ten Commandments*.

PORNOGRAPHY MADE ME DO IT

The night before his execution, Ted **Bundy** gave his final interview to evangelist James Dobson. With death just hours away. Bundy—the slayer of anywhere from thirty to fifty young women—had a message for America: beware of pornography. Bundy confessed that at an early age, he had become addicted to images of sexual violence and claimed that his exposure to brutal pornography had turned him into a sex-killer.

Antiporn crusaders embraced Bundy's statement. Here, they argued, was conclusive proof of everything they'd been claiming—pornography leads to ultimate evil.

There were a couple of problems with Bundy's statement, however. For one thing, he was born in 1946, which means that he grew up during the 1950s—an era when it was considerably harder to come by sadomasochistic porn than it is today. Back in the Eisenhower era, you couldn't just stroll into your neighborhood video shop and rent *Teenage Bondage Sluts* from the "Adults Only" section. If Bundy was really getting off on violent pornography back then, there must already have been something dark and twisted inside him that was driving him to go out and hunt for these images.

There is another serious problem with Bundy's admission, conveniently ignored by antiporn activists: Bundy was a psychopathic liar. For ten years, he had done everything possible to deny his guilt. Even when the jig was finally up, he found a way to shrug off responsibility for his atrocities by putting the blame on outside influences.

He wasn't responsible for his crimes. Pornography made him do it.

X RAYS

n the view of many crime buffs, the single most perverted killer in American history was the cannibalistic pedophile Albert **Fish.** Perhaps the most compelling evidence in support of this opinion were a series of X rays taken shortly after Fish's arrest for the kidnapping and murder of twelve-year-old Grace Budd.

Interviewed in his jail cell by two state-appointed psychiatrists who were trying to evaluate his sanity, Fish revealed that—as an act of contrition for killing the girl—he had purchased a pack of sewing needles and, using a thimble, had shoved five of them up behind his testicles so deeply that they had remained permanently embedded inside his body.

Though this story seemed too outrageous to believe, Fish was a degenerate of such extravagant proportions that the authorities decided to check it out. The old man was taken from prison to a nearby hospital, where his pelvic region was X-rayed by the hospital's chief roentgenologist.

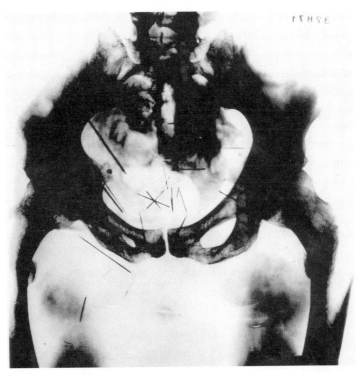

One of the X rays of Albert Fish's pelvic region, showing more than two dozen needles shoved into his lower body
(*New York Daily News*)

323

As it turned out, Fish's incredible claim was actually an under-statement. The X rays clearly revealed a number of sharp, thin objects scattered throughout the area of the old man's groin and lower abdomen. These objects—which resembled long, black splinters floating in the bright tissue around and between the hip bones—were unmistakably needles. Their location—around the rectum and bladder, just below the tip of the spine, and in the muscles of the groin—made it clear that they had been in-serted into Fish's body from below, evidently through his peri-neum, the flesh between his anus and scrotum.

Unbelievable as it seemed, the old man had been telling the truth—or at least part of it. He had told the psychiatrists that he had punished himself by pushing five needles into his body. But when the physician counted the objects in the X rays, he came up with a significantly different figure. Lodged inside Fish's body were no less than twenty-seven needles! Among his dizzy-ing array of masochistic pleasures, the wildly perverted old man had been sticking sewing needles into his own groin for years (see **Paraphilia**).

"These X rays are unique in the history of medical science."
DR. FREDERIC WERTHAM, commenting on the X rays
of Albert Fish's pelvic region

Y CHROMOSOME

S erial murder is such an overwhelmingly evil act that it's natural for people to wonder "Why? Why would a human being commit such a monstrous crime?" There's a desperate need to find an explanation that would make sense of this incomprehensible horror. For at least a hundred years, scientists have been searching for a single, identifiable cause for criminal violence. In 1968, they finally came up with one. The answer to the question *why?* turned out to be . . . *Y*.

More precisely, it turned out to be a *Y chromosome*. As everyone who's taken high school biology knows, there are two sex chromosomes, X (female) and Y (male). Every cell in the average man contains one of each. A few men, however, have an extra Y, or male, chromosome—a condition known as the XYY Syndrome. Once they made this discovery, scientists began theorizing that this extra dash of maleness made its possessor even more masculine—i.e., crude, aggressive, and violent—than normal.

Their theory seemed to be borne out by the case of Richard **Speck,** the notorious multiple murderer who, in 1966, slaughtered eight student nurses in their Chicago apartment. Speck, who was diagnosed as an XYY type, fit the image of a supercharged male brute to perfection. He was big, dumb, and savage, with a face ravaged by acne scars and a "Born to Raise Hell" tattoo proudly displayed on one arm. At his trial, his attorney argued that Speck wasn't responsible for his crimes because he was suffering from XYY Syndrome. In effect, Speck's tattoo was telling the truth—his extra male chromosome had made him bad from birth.

There was only one problem with this defense. Speck, it turned out, had been misdiagnosed. He was normal—at least from a chromosomal point of view.

Undaunted, proponents of the theory pointed out that there is an unusually high proportion of XYY types in the prison population. But these findings were shown to be skewed. The vast majority of men born with XYY Syndrome display no abnormally violent tendencies. By now, the theory has been largely discredited. As of this writing, serial murder remains what it has always been—an unfathomable evil. Or as the Bible puts it, a "mystery of iniquity."

THE "YORKSHIRE RIPPER"

32. PETER SUTCLIFFE
"The Yorkshire Ripper"

Peter Sutcliffe; from *Bloody Visions* trading cards. *(© & ™ 1995 M. H. Price and Shel-Tone Publications. All rights reserved.)*

The five-year search for the homicidal maniac known as the "Yorkshire Ripper" was the biggest manhunt in British history. The police interviewed more than 200,000 people, took more than 30,000 statements, searched over 20,000 homes. In the course of this mammoth investigation, a young truck driver named Peter Sutcliffe was called in for questioning no less than nine times—so often that his co-workers jokingly nicknamed him "Jack the Ripper." Each time, however, his interrogators swallowed Sutcliffe's alibi and let him go free.

On January 2, 1981, police discovered—almost accidentally—that Sutcliffe was, in fact, the killer. By then, thirteen women, ranging in age from sixteen to forty-seven, had been savagely murdered—bludgeoned, stabbed, and mutilated.

Sutcliffe led the kind of schizoid life so characteristic of serial killers. On the one hand, he was a reliable worker and devoted husband. On the other, he was a woman-hating sociopath whose crimes were motivated by intense sexual loathing. Sutcliffe himself claimed that his vendetta against prostitutes began after a hooker cheated him of money. But the roots of his pathology clearly ran much deeper. As a teenager, he took a job as a mortuary attendant and enjoyed manipulating corpses as though they were ventriloquist dummies. He also spent hours at a local wax museum, transfixed by a display that showed the devastating effects of VD on the human body.

Sutcliffe began by assaulting prostitutes with homemade bludgeons—socks weighted with gravel or bricks. His first few victims survived these attacks. A twenty-eight-year-old hooker named Wilma McCann wasn't as lucky. On October 30, 1975, Sutcliffe smashed the back of her skull with a ball peen hammer, then stabbed her fourteen times. Three months later, he killed again. Following this second homicide, Sutcliffe's murderous impulses seemed to subside. A year later, however, they erupted with a vengeance. In the fifteen months between February 1977 and May 1978, he killed seven more women, bludgeoning them first with his hammer, then savaging them with his knife. In some cases, he mutilated the genitalia. Most of these victims were streetwalkers, though one was a sixteen-year-old shop assistant who had been on her way home from a disco.

With all of northern England in a panic, police mounted an all-out hunt for the killer. They were sidetracked, however, by a tape recording they received in June 1979, which purported to be from the Ripper. While police pursued this lead (which turned out to be a hoax), Sutcliffe continued to kill. By then, he was no longer restricting himself to prostitutes. Sutcliffe's final four victims were female college students and young working women.

His arrest came in January 1981 when a police officer on stakeout—Sergeant Robert Ring—spotted Sutcliffe in a car with a prostitute. A check of Sutcliffe's plates revealed that the car was stolen. Before being hauled down to the stationhouse, Sutcliffe asked for permission to go behind some shrubbery and "pee." Sergeant Ring obliged.

The next morning, while Sutcliffe was still being questioned, a lightbulb went off in Ring's head. Rushing back to the spot where he'd arrested Sutcliffe, he searched behind the shrubbery and discovered a ball peen hammer and knife. Confronted with this evidence, Sutcliffe quickly confessed. He attempted to plead insanity, claiming that God's voice, emanating from a grave, had ordered him to kill. The court was not impressed. The "Yorkshire Ripper" was sentence to life in prison.

ZEALOTS

There are plenty of people around who blame our country's social ills—including our epidemic of violent crime—on the loss of old-fashioned religious values, as if the murder rate would miraculously decline if Americans spent fewer hours in front of the TV and more time studying the Bible. Unfortunately, there is a slight problem with this theory. Some of the most monstrous killers in American history were religious fanatics who could recite Scripture from memory and—when they weren't busy torturing children or mutilating corpses—loved to do nothing better than read the Good Book.

Albert **Fish,** the cannibalistic monster who spent a lifetime preying on little children, is a terrifying case in point. From his earliest years, Fish was fascinated by the Bible and at one point actually dreamed of becoming a minister. As he grew older, his religious interests blossomed into a full-fledged mania. Obsessed with the story of Abraham and Isaac, he became convinced that he, too, should sacrifice a young child—an atrocity he actually carried out on more than one occasion. From time to time, he heard strange, archaic-sounding words—*correcteth, delighteth, chastiseth*—that he interpreted as divine commandments to torment and kill. He would organize these words into quasi-Biblical messages: "Blessed is the man who correcteth his son in whom he delighteth with stripes"; "Happy is he that taketh Thy little ones and dasheth their heads against the stones." Fish not only tortured and killed children in response to these delusions but subjected himself to a variety of masochistic torments in atonement for his sins. One of his favorite forms of self-mortification was to shove sewing needles so deeply into his own groin that they remained embedded around his bladder. For the hopelessly demented Fish, his ultimate crime—the murder, dismemberment, and cannibalization of a twelve-year-old girl—also had religious overtones. As he told the psychiatrist who examined him in prison, he associated the eating of the child's flesh and the drinking of her blood with the "idea of Holy Communion."

Fish's near-contemporary Earle Leonard **Nelson** was another religious fanatic, who spent countless hours poring over passages from the Book of Revelation: "And the woman was arrayed in purple and scarlet color . . . having a golden cup in her hand full of abominations and filthiness of her fornication: and upon her forehead was a name written, MYSTERY, BABYLON THE GREAT, THE MOTHER OF HARLOTS AND ABOMINATIONS OF THE EARTH." Nelson's familiarity with the Bible was one of his most disarming features, allowing him to win the confidence of his landlady-victims, who never guessed that such a well-read and obviously devout young man was actually the infamous "Gorilla Murderer," the shadowy serial strangler responsible for nearly two dozen savage killings from coast to coast.

There have been plenty of other psychos who have committed their crimes in the name of religion, from self-ordained street preacher Benjamin Miller, who murdered a string of black prostitutes in the late 1960s as punishment for their sinful ways, to the homicidal hippie couple James and Susan Carson, who believed they were complying with the biblical injunction—"Thou shalt not suffer a witch to live" (Exodus 22:18)—when they murdered their victims.

Homicidal religious fanatics have been the subject of two memorable movies: the splendid 1955 thriller *Night of the Hunter* (in which Robert Mitchum does a terrifying turn as a sin-obsessed preacher) and the gruesomely baroque 1995 hit, *Seven*, about a serial killer who arranges his victims in grotesque tableaux inspired by the seven deadly sins: gluttony, lust, sloth, pride, anger, envy, and greed.

> *"And I will cause them to eat the flesh of their sons and the flesh of their daughters, and they shall eat every one the flesh of his friend in the siege and straitness, wherewith their enemies, and they that seek their lives, shall straiten them."*
>
> Jeremiah, 19:9 (Albert Fish's favorite passage of Scripture)

ZEITGEIST

Anyone who makes a serious study of criminal history quickly discovers an intriguing, if depressing, fact—every period has produced many more cases of appalling murder than most people realize. To cite just one of countless examples: in 1895, a clean-cut medical student named Theo Durrant murdered and raped two young women in San Francisco and stashed their mutilated corpses in his neighborhood church. The Durrant case was a nationwide sensation—but who besides the most ardent crime buff has heard of it today?

This raises an interesting question: why do some heinous killers fade into instant obscurity, while others achieve an almost mythic status? Part of the answer certainly lies in the singularly horrific deeds of the latter. The legendary serial killers (**Ed Gein**, Albert **Fish**, Jeffrey **Dahmer**, etc.) have a larger-than-life quality. Their crimes seem less pathological than supernatural—the doings of demons and ghouls. But there is another factor, too. Certain criminals exert a powerful fascination because they seem to embody the darkest impulses and obsessions of their day—all that is most reprehensible about any given age. As much as any hero or celebrity, they personify the spirit of the time—what the Germans call the zeitgeist.

The nineteenth-century "multi-murderer" Dr. H. H. **Holmes** is a classic example. A debonair ladies' man with a deadly allure, Holmes seemed like the living incarnation of the fairy tale monster Bluebeard, killing and dismembering a string of nubile young women in the murky depths of his "Horror Castle." At the same time, he was the terrifying epitome of all the excesses of the Gilded Age, a money-mad psychopath whose murders were motivated as much by greed as by blood lust.

In the 1930s—the era when the Lindbergh baby was kidnapped—Albert **Fish** represented every parent's worst nightmare, a fiendishly cunning child snatcher in the guise of a kindly old man. While the case of Edward **Gein** had the timeless horror of a "Hansel and Gretel"-type fairy tale (the seemingly innocuous, out-of-the-way dwelling that turns out to be the abode of an ogre), his crimes also reflected the prevailing cultural pathology of postwar America, a time and place marked by extreme sexual hypocrisy, when the realities of erotic behavior were masked by an official culture of prudery.

Charles Starkweather—the sociopathic James Dean–wannabe who slaughtered eleven people during a three-week killing spree—embodied another quintessentially 1950s phenomenon: the wildly antisocial "juvenile delinquent" with a grudge against grown-up society. During the 1960s, Charles **Manson**—the sex-and-drug crazed demon-hippie—was the nightmare realization of "straight" society's darkest fears, while Ted **Bundy** seemed to embody all that was most perilous about the 1970s me-generation, swinging-singles scene: the danger of finding yourself with the wrong pickup and ending up in a very nasty one-night stand.

THE A-Z ENCYCLOPEDIA OF SERIAL KILLERS

Bret Easton Ellis's much-reviled book *American Psycho* actually plays very cleverly with the notion of the serial killer as symbol of the zeitgeist. Its sociopathic yuppie protagonist, Patrick Bateson, is meant to be a metaphor for the greediness of the 1980s Reagan era. His only concern is the fulfillment of his own appetites, and he regards other people as nothing more than highly disposable commodities to be used for his own pleasure.

> *"To parallel such a career one must go back to past ages and to the time of the Borgias or the Brinvilliers, and even these were not such human monsters as Holmes seems to have been. He is a prodigy of wickedness, a human demon, a being so unthinkable that no novelist would dare to invent such a character. The story, too, tends to illustrate the end of the century."*
>
> From an 1896 newspaper article on H. H. Holmes

ZINES

Whether you are a mud-wrestling fan, conspiracy buff, or corset collector, a popular way to indulge your obsession nowadays is to publish your own "zine" on the subject. All you need is a word processor and/or mimeo machine, a functioning stapler, and a handful of fellow enthusiasts willing to fork over a few bucks for your publication. Given today's audience for sensationalistic horror, it's no surprise that a number of these alternative magazines deal with sex, gore, and violence. Like other zines, the ones described below vary widely in terms of production values. Some look as though they were assembled in somebody's basement (probably because they *were*). Others are surprisingly slick and professional.

Murder Can Be Fun. John Marr, P.O. Box 640111, San Francisco, CA 94164. Features sharp, well-researched articles on a range of outré topics, from "Karen Carpenter, Queen of Anorexia" to mass murder and serial killing.

Answer Me! Jim and Debbie Goad, Goad to Hell Enterprises, P.O. Box 31009, Portland, OR 97231. Hailed by some as one of "the greatest zines on the planet," denounced by others as ex-

Murder Can Be Fun (Courtesy of John Marr)

ploitative porn, *Answer Me!* combines (in the words of its creators) "a *National Lampoon*-style sensibility with a snuff-film esthetic." Dedicated to the unflinching exploration of "the darkest side of humanity: the killers, the perverts, the freaks, the religious wackos, the gangs, the Nazis, and the overtly schizophrenic," *Answer Me!* became the focus of a fierce controversy in the fall of 1995 when a magazine shop proprietor in Bellingham, Washington, was arrested on obscenity charges for selling issue no. 4, which dealt in shockingly graphic ways with the subject of rape and included an interview with Richard "Night Stalker" **Ramirez.**

Cold Pee. Douglas Thompson, 1633 N. Damen Avenue, 2nd Floor, Chicago, IL 60647. Wild and weird assemblages of jarring images, some seriously unnerving. A typical issue might combine a sampling of John Wayne **Gacy**'s art with photos of decapitated heads and graphic pictures from medical textbooks.

Fatal Visions. P.O. Box 133, Northcote, Victoria, Australia 3070. A semi-slick Australian publication dedicated to all that is violent in the media. Several issues have included contributions by G. J. Schaefer, the Florida ex-policeman convicted of two mutilation slayings and connected to thirty-four dead and missing women.

Ben Is Dead. P.O. Box 3166, Hollywood, CA 90028. This hip, hefty zine covers every aspect of American trash culture. As the contents page says: "Warning! May Contain Murderers! Psychos! Sex! Death! Voyeurs! Victims!"

ZODIAC

Zodiac; from *Murderers!* trading card set *(Courtesy of Roger Worsham)*

California in the late 1960s was a hotbed of hippiedom—the site of the Summer of Love, the birthplace of the "be-in," the land where visitors were advised to wear flowers in their hair. At the same time, it was home to some of the most notorious psychos of the late twentieth century. Charles Manson and his blood-crazed "family" slaughtered seven people in Los Angeles in 1969. A year later, a hippie named John Linley Frazier wiped out a household of five in the Northern California town of Santa Cruz. Perhaps even more unnerving was the night-prowling gunman known only as "Zodiac," who terrorized San Francisco during a nine-month spree that began in December 1968. Before he was finished, five people were dead and two more desperately wounded.

His motive? "I like killing people because it's so much fun," he explained in an anonymous letter.

The first to die was a teenage couple, shot dead in a lovers' lane. Six months later, he gunned down another young couple, killing the young woman with nine blasts from a 9mm pistol (the young man, shot four times, survived). Forty minutes later—in what would be the first in a series of chilling communications from the killer—the police received an anonymous phone call from a gruff-voiced man: "If you will go one mile east on Columbus Parkway to a public park, you will find the kids in a brown car. They have been shot with a 9mm Luger. I also killed those kids last year. Good-bye."

While panic spread through the area, the killer began sending **Letters** to local newspapers, signed with the astrological symbol of the zodiac. Each letter contained a line of cipher. Decoded by a local high school teacher, the cryptic lines formed a single message that explained the killer's motivations: "I will be reborn in Paradise, and then all that I have killed will become my slaves. I will not give you my name because you will try to slow or stop my collecting of slaves for my afterlife."

Two months later, Zodiac (as he was know called) set out to collect some more slaves. Wearing a black hood with eye slits and the zodiac symbol painted on it in white, the killer accosted a young couple at gunpoint, bound them with rope, then attacked them with a hunting knife. The young man survived with five wounds in the back, but the girl—stabbed fourteen times—died.

His last known victim was a San Francisco cabdriver who was shot once in the back of the head. Before fleeing the crime scene, the killer tore off parts of the victim's shirt. Shortly afterward, the editor of the *San Francisco Chronicle* received an envelope. Inside was a swatch of the cabdriver's shirt and a letter from Zodiac in which he promised to "wipe out a school bus some morning." Fortunately he never made good on this threat. Nor—as far as anyone knows—did Zodiac ever kill again.

The classic Clint Eastwood movie *Dirty Harry* (1971) is a gripping, fictionalized account of the hunt for the Zodiac killer, with Andy Robinson turning in an unforgettable performance as the unspeakable psycho-creep. Needless to say, the movie has a much more satisfying ending—

with Clint blasting the psycho into well-deserved oblivion—than real life supplied. In actuality, Zodiac simply vanished, and though theories abound, his identity remains one of the great **Unsolved** mysteries of modern crime.

ZOMBIES

J oyce Carol Oates's harrowing 1995 novel *Zombie* deals with a psychopath named Quentin P———, who is obsessed with the idea of creating a zombie who will become his personal slave. To that end, he performs a series of makeshift lobotomies on various half-drugged victims by sticking an ice pick under their eyelids and up into their brains. All he succeeds in doing, however, is killing them—though a few of them manage to survive for a brief period (see **Recommended Reading**).

Reviewing Oates's novel in the *New York Times Book Review*, one prominent critic interpreted this story as an "allegory" about "what American society itself is capable of." The character's "efforts to create zombies," this critic wrote, "is derived from the irreversible psychosurgical procedures performed during the 1940s and 1950s on thousands of unfortunate Americans judged to be psychotic, dangerous or incompetent."

While this is an ingenious theory, it ignores a crucial fact: Quentin P———'s zombie obsession derives not from the psychosurgical practices of the 1940s but from the far more recent atrocities of Jeffrey **Dahmer**, the obvious inspiration for Oates's novel. In addition to his many other unspeakable acts, Dahmer

> *"A true ZOMBIE would be mine forever. He would obey every command & whim. Saying 'Yes, Master' & 'No, Master.' He would kneel before me lifting his eyes to me saying, 'I love you, Master. There is no one but you, Master."*
>
> From *Zombie* by Joyce Carol Oates

performed a number of do-it-yourself lobotomies in an effort to turn his victims into passive sex slaves whom he could violate at will.

Unlike Oates's fictional monster, Dahmer did not rely on an ice pick. Instead, after drugging his victim, he would drill a hole in the young man's head and inject muriatic acid into the brain with a hypodermic syringe. Most of the victims died instantly, though one actually remained alive and ambulatory for two days after being injected.